STATELESS

STATELESS

THE POLITICS OF THE ARMENIAN
LANGUAGE IN EXILE

TALAR CHAHINIAN

For Colette,
with love,

Syracuse University Press

Copyright © 2023 by Syracuse University Press
Syracuse, New York 13244-5290

All Rights Reserved

First Edition 2023

23   24   25   26   27   28   6   5   4   3   2   1

∞ The paper used in this publication meets the minimum requirements
of the American National Standard for Information Sciences—Permanence
of Paper for Printed Library Materials, ANSI Z39.48-1992.

For a listing of books published and distributed by Syracuse University Press,
visit https://press.syr.edu.

ISBN: 978-0-8156-3802-5 (hardcover)
978-0-8156-3795-0 (paperback)
978-0-8156-5580-0 (e-book)

Library of Congress Cataloging-in-Publication Data
Names: Chahinian, Talar, author.
Title: Stateless : the politics of the Armenian language in exile / Talar Chahinian.
Description: First edition. | Syracuse : Syracuse University Press, 2023. |
Includes bibliographical references and index.
Identifiers: LCCN 2022038623 (print) | LCCN 2022038624 (ebook) |
ISBN 9780815638025 (hardcover ; alk. paper) | ISBN 9780815637950 (paperback ; alk. paper) |
ISBN 9780815655800 (ebook)
Subjects: LCSH: Armenian literature—20th century—History and criticism. |
Literature and transnationalism. | Armenian diaspora. | West Armenian dialect—
Political aspects. | LCGFT: Literary criticism.
Classification: LCC PK8516 .C44 2023 (print) | LCC PK8516 (ebook) |
DDC 491/.992—dc23/eng/20221027
LC record available at https://lccn.loc.gov/2022038623
LC ebook record available at https://lccn.loc.gov/2022038624

Manufactured in the United States of America

supported by grant

Figure Foundation

drifting to reunion

To the memory of my grandmothers,
Mayreni and Gulistan

Contents

Acknowledgments

The story of this book's becoming is long and spans over two decades. Those who have helped me, guided me, and supported me throughout this journey are many, and my deep gratitude for them is unbounded.

I am grateful to my editor Deborah M. Manion and the wonderful team at Syracuse University Press for their guidance in bringing this book to light. I thank Allison Van Deventer and Annette Wenda for their keen editorial help during the revising and copyediting process of the manuscript.

This book is about the possibility of continued creation, expression, and representation in a language forcefully cut off from its historic place of belonging. Its focus on two spaces of exilic production, Paris and Beirut, forms the two parts of the book, which carry within them two distinct intervals of my scholarship.

My discussions of Armenian literature in post–World War I Paris are based on research I conducted as a graduate student at the University of California at Los Angeles (UCLA). My early readings and analysis were shaped by enriching discussions I had with my former advisers S. Peter Cowe, Gil Hochberg, Françoise Lionnet, and Kathy Komar, as well as from my friend and mentor Hagop Gulludjian. For their close engagement with my work and their continued support of its development, I remain forever grateful. My gratitude also extends to the late Gia Aivazian (UCLA Library), Raymond Kévorkian (former director of Bibliothèque Nubar of Paris), the Mekhitarist Congregation of Vienna, and the Zoryan Institute for their help with the initial phase of my research.

My graduate years also gave me an incredibly beautiful and empowering community of friends, who have provided so much moral support, intellectual stimulation, and comic relief throughout the years. I could not have navigated my academic path, with all its instabilities, and arrived at a position to write this book without the unwavering encouragement and friendship of Carole Viers-Andronico, Neetu Khanna, Myrna Douzjian, Shushan Karapetian, Lilit Keshishyan, Tamar Boyadjian, Arpi Siyahian, Rosie Aroush, Marian Gabra, Jeannine Murray-Roman, Lisa Felipe, Guilan Siassi, and Melissa Gonzalez.

The expansion of my research to post–World War II Beirut was initiated by my participation in the conference "Armenia and Its Diaspora: Institutional Linkages and Cross-Border Movements," held at the University of Michigan at Dearborn. I am indebted to the conference organizer, Ara Sanjian, for bringing to my attention the debate around the 1946 Congress of Soviet Armenian Writers and his subsequent feedback on my presentation. My copanelists at the conference Khachig Tölölyan and Vartan Matiossian were instrumental to my process of developing the initial paper's scope to encompass an emphasis on the Syrian and Lebanese literary scene of that period. I continue to learn from them.

I thank Krikor Moskofian (Centre for Western Armenian Studies), Hagop Panossian (ARPA Institute), Kevork Bardakjian (the former Marie Manoogian Chair in Armenian Language and Literature at the University of Michigan at Ann Arbor), Gerard Libaridian (the former Alex Manoogian Chair in Modern Armenian History, also at the University of Michigan at Ann Arbor), Stephan Astourian (Armenian Studies Program, UC Berkeley), S. Peter Cowe (Narekatsi Chair in Armenian Studies, UCLA), and the late Vazken Madenlian (GARS Academy) for inviting me to workshop parts of my writing, which later turned into chapters in this book. As my in-text engagement with their critical works attest, I owe much of my intellectual formation to Marc Nichanian and Kirkor Beledian. I am grateful for all that they have shared with me through countless workshops and for the work they have done in expanding the limits of Armenian literary studies.

Throughout its marathon journey, this book has benefited greatly from the intellectual community offered by dear friends and colleagues. Through collaborations on various editorial boards, workshops, and projects, they have added invaluable insight to my theoretical wanderings. Sossie Kasbarian, Tsolin Nalbantian, Bedross Der Matossian, Sebouh Aslanian, Leila Pazargadi, Anny Bakalian, Vahe Sahakyan, Murat Yildiz, Boris Adjemian, Stéphanie Prévost, Vazken Davidian, Lerna Ekmekcioglu, Maral Aktokmakyan, Hovann Simonian, Jennifer Manoukian, Sima Aprahamian, Dzovinar Derderian, Katherine McLoone, Khachig Mouradian, Vahram Danielyan, Hayk Hambardzumyan, Helen Makhdoumian, Salpi Ghazarian, Arno Yeretsian, Hrayr Eulmessekian, Aram Kouyoumdjian, Hovig Tchalian, and Sonia Kiledjian, our conversations have no doubt left their imprint on my discussions in this book.

While bringing this book to its finish line, I have been lucky to be at the University of California at Irvine (UCI), where I have the opportunity to closely align my teaching and research interests. I am grateful to Nasrin Rahimieh and Jane Newman for welcoming me to the Department of Comparative Literature family there and for allowing me to call it a home. My profound thanks to Houri Berberian for her support and friendship and for her commitment to include language and literature in her vision for Armenian studies at UCI. Finally, my deep gratitude to my students, who renew my faith in the relevance of scholarship to the development of critical thought.

To my dear friends Aleen and Aram Andonian, Lori and Angelo Ghialian, Lisa and Shahan Kaprielian, Tara Daylami, Margie Rivera, Natalie Monegro, Justin Hughes, Mary Maghaguian, Alaettin Carikci, Suzie Abajian, Yerado Abrahamian, Annie Darakjian, Annette Berberian, Lisa Tokmajian, Alice Basteguian, Nellie Avakian, Vinka Bedrosian, Melissa Marukian, Andres Agudelo, Ramesh Srinavasan, Taleen Tertzakian, and Nancy Guiragossian: thank you for supporting me unconditionally and for allowing my intellectual queries to have meaning outside of academia.

To my cousins, aunts, and uncles from Los Angeles to Boston, to Montreal, to Paris, to London, to Beirut, thank you for the care you pour into family and familial memory in dispersion. Sarine Ashjian, thank you for always holding space for reflection within our very loud family. To my aunts Maral Der Hagopian and Loucine Ashjian, thank you for always helping me carry the load and for championing me throughout. My dear parents, Krikor and Nazeli Chahinian; my brother, Sako Shahinian; my adopted siblings, Elizabeth Shahinian, Annie Garabedian, and Vatche Garabedian; and my parents-in-law, Jean and Seissil Mahroukian, thank you for being the support net I can always fall on.

Alas, none of this would be possible without the tireless encouragement and partnership of my husband, Anto Mahroukian, and the limitless love my children, Aram and Arene, shower me with. I hope to make you proud.

I dedicate this book to the memory of my grandmothers, who insisted on making me a witness to their stories from a young age. This work is an attempt to reconcile my world with their past.

Note on Transliteration and Translation

All translations are my own, unless otherwise specified. Direct quotations from original Armenian source material are presented in my own English translations. In the case of some key terms, I present the Armenian word in transliteration and follow with a translation. I present quotations from French sources in the original language and follow them by my English translation.

All Armenian titles are transliterated using the Library of Congress romanization chart, adopted by the *International Journal of Middle East Studies* and the *Journal of the Society for Armenian Studies*.

Armenian proper names follow a phonetic romanization pattern, avoiding the diacritic system mentioned earlier.

STATELESS

Introduction

Western Armenian at the Intersection of Trauma and Transnationalism

The possibility of an impending expiration date haunted Western Armenian literary criticism of the twentieth century. In the background of most discussions about diasporic cultural production loomed the fear of language extinction, as the potential grand finale to the genocidal enterprise that took the lives of more than a million western Armenians and drove hundreds of thousands of them out from their native lands in the final days of the Ottoman Empire.[1] Many warned that in dispersion, with neither an attachment to territory nor the institutional support of a nation-state, Western Armenian would eventually lose its speakers and cease to maintain its vitality as a language. As a result, most initiatives that aim at building a language community in dispersion have a resisting impetus at their core: they construct themselves against this pending threat. In many ways, this imagined end to a stateless language's projected trajectory makes the story of Western Armenian a tale foretold.

In contrast, the transnationally organized communities that emerged in the postgenocide decades from Cairo to Beirut, Aleppo, Paris, and Boston, each equipped with networks of literary and linguistic production, gestured toward the diasporic possibility of regeneration. For a brief period, the diaspora was indeed a successful project in terms of establishing structures for standardizing the language, cultivating literacy, and preparing new generations of readers and writers of Western Armenian in exile. Within each of the communities mentioned above, educational and cultural institutions were formed to oversee the practice of Armenian

1

language through schooling, through the publication of books and peri-odicals, and through the preparation of future writers and educators. So, how do we reconcile the successful construction of a Western Armenian literacy apparatus in the diaspora with the idea of extinction's immi-nence? How do we approach the question of "How did we get here?" that was raised by many of the remaining Western Armenian speakers when UNESCO designated the language as endangered in 2010?[2] In the con-cluding remarks of an edited volume devoted to the debate of language revitalization, Vartan Matiossian reflects on the moment UNESCO's clas-sification was announced and what he describes as the "pandemonium" that broke out in diaspora communities because of it. He writes, "Institu-tions and individuals throughout the Diaspora seemed to have been wait-ing for an outside signal that validated the existence of a language crisis, something that everyone knew for decades, but had not been given neces-sary scholarly attention."[3] Matiossian's critique about the need for external validation points to stateless linguistic communities' perpetual struggle for legitimacy. Indeed, many Armenian writers had warned of the lan-guage's imminent demise long before the revered international organiza-tion sounded the alarm.

In the 1990s, as Armenia declared its independence from the Soviet Union, some diaspora writers predicted that Western Armenian would be adversely affected by the institution of an independent state that fur-ther legitimized its twin linguistic form, Eastern Armenian. Moreover, as the classic postgenocide diaspora communities of North America and Europe were transformed by new waves of migration in the 1970s and '80s, caused by historical circumstances like the collapsing Soviet Empire, the Lebanese Civil War (1975–90), and the Iranian Revolution of 1979, many diaspora intellectuals pondered the linguistic consequences of the new congregation of Armenian immigrant groups in places like Los Angeles. In such places, speakers of the two linguistic forms (and of many dialects within them) mingled to an unprecedented extent. Taking inde-pendence as a moment of transition in the Armenian world, many West-ern Armenian thinkers began to theorize the evolution of language over the previous decades and pointed to the current moment as a crossroads. In 1991, the Beirut-born, New Jersey–based diaspora writer Vehanush

Tekian wrote, "In the first decades of diaspora, language was our longing. Then it turned into our shield, and ultimately into our self-consciousness. But now, all of that is obscured, and instead, a strange solution is put forth: spirit. Without the pulsing body of language and culture, what is spirit if not a mere specter?"[4] For Tekian, Western Armenian is already in crisis at the time of her writing, something she attributes to a shift in the way the diaspora's educational institutions had begun to approach language in the last few decades of the twentieth century. She argues that their adoption of a framework that celebrates the Armenian spirit created a diluted understanding of culture and caused the abandonment of the rigorous language curriculum of the early years of the diaspora. She posits the materiality of language as a marker of identity against the more nebulous sense of Armenianness that "spirit" encompasses. Spirit, she suggests, cannot meet the demand for diasporic cultural continuity.

Around the same time, the Beirut-born, Los Angeles–based writer and translator Ishkhan Jinbashian sounded a similar warning. "It's astonishing that Armenians of the diaspora, in possession of an immense cultural treasury, have for a few decades now completely abandoned the Armenian language, their most salient instrument of expression," he wrote. Jinbashian's critique parallels Tekian's concern about diaspora organizations' move away from language and toward spirit. In his article, though, Jinbashian specifically situates the shift toward the celebration of an ambiguous sense of the Armenian spirit within the diaspora's nationalist narrative, especially its myth of return to the lost lands of western Armenia. Jinbashian argues that the perpetuation of the myth of return suspends the Armenian language in time, endowing it with a false sense of safety and preventing its cultivation. What remains, he suggests, is a recycled form of the language that cannot keep up with the communicative demands of the present. The language's body, he writes, "has turned so void that what is expressed is simply a pile of references, which can describe lofty abstractions, but say nothing."[5]

Both writers forewarn of Western Armenian's vitality crisis by stressing the corporeality of language. They understand the corporeal properties of a language as its material presence in the world of print and suggest that language maintenance requires the development of not only a literacy apparatus (educational system) but also a *literary* apparatus, something they see as being neglected in the diaspora toward the end of the twentieth century. In this book, which analyzes the postgenocide development of Western Armenian literature, I confirm that the question of linguistic vitality cannot be separated from the realm of the literary—in other words, from the processes of literary production, circulation, criticism, translation, and canon making, which I refer to as a literary apparatus. Focusing on two key moments and places in Western Armenian literary history, post–World War I Paris and post–World War II Beirut, *Stateless: The Politics of the Armenian Language in Exile* examines how a stateless language sustained itself in a diasporic setting. I argue that the shift from one literary center to another, from Paris to Beirut, was detrimental to Western Armenian, contrary to what is generally believed. Although the post-Mandate Middle East offered better prospects for language maintenance than the assimilationist West, as attested by the success of Syria's and Lebanon's Armenian school systems at their height in the 1950s, the shift of the literary center from Paris to Beirut produced a strict narrative of the diaspora that put an expiration date on the language. In other words, efforts to imagine the dispersed communities as a homogenous diasporic unit were ultimately counterproductive, for they mandated that literature be produced within a centered "national" category rather than a decentered "transnational" one. By the end of the twentieth century, as Soviet Armenia claimed its independence and as the Armenian world experienced a major reorganization of its globally dispersed population, the postgenocide diaspora communities evolved from their exclusive Western Armenian character to incorporate culturally diverse Armenian migrants. These shifts weakened the "national" model of Western Armenian literary production that was practiced in the diaspora and centralized in the Middle East. The "national" model, which held the integrity of Western Armenian identity at its core and positioned itself vehemently against the Soviet project, needed rebranding in the face of an independent Armenia and increasingly heterogenous diaspora communities. As a result, Western Armenian's linguistic development stalled.

In *Stateless*, after situating Western Armenian as an endangered, stateless language, I work backward to provide a historical context for the development of its literary tradition following the genocide of 1915. During the interwar period, while New York, Boston, Cairo, and Aleppo hosted the newspapers, schools, and publishing houses necessary for the establishment of language communities, Paris took center stage as the cultural stronghold of Armenians in dispersion. It was there that avant-garde groups emerged and made concerted attempts to develop a transnational literary theory. In the first part of the book, I focus on a group of orphaned Armenian writers who, having survived the genocide, regrouped in Paris in the 1920s and launched a short-lived transnational literary movement called Menk, meaning "we" in Armenian. In examining the Menk generation's public debates, critical writings, and prose fiction, I ask: What does literary belonging mean for a literature written in an exilic and endangered language? How did the politically violent origins of dispersion inform the aesthetic development of a new literature? Moreover, how did the absence of state institutions that could have pursued international recognition and reparations limit the scope of the new literature's representative authority?

In the second part of the book, I discuss a rare moment of transition, reflection, and organized planning that writers of the diaspora undertook as their intellectual stronghold shifted from Paris to the Middle East during the war years. Whereas the post–World War I writers in Paris, predominantly those gathered in Menk, attempted to carve out a new literature outside tradition and embraced their exilic condition, the post–World War II writers in Lebanon and Syria sought to establish continuity in time and centralization in cultural space. In doing so, they connected their literary output to the pre-1915 tradition and developed a national literature in Western Armenian against the backdrop of an imagined, unified homeland. In examining the activity and publications of the Writers' Association of Syria and Lebanon (WASL), I ask: In the absence of state institutions, how was the diaspora's literature nationalized? In other words, what were the mechanisms of language standardization, literary production, and canon formation?

I show that when Beirut took over as the nucleus of the diaspora's political, intellectual, and literary activity and intellectuals began to construct a unified and coherent narrative of the diaspora, the city came to be positioned as the thread that connected the current activities to the pre-1915 literary tradition, and the Menk generation was excluded from the modern Armenian literary canon owing to its writers' attempts to understand diasporic experience as interrupted time. Ultimately, I argue that post–World War II diaspora intellectuals' lack of engagement with Menk's proposition for a new literary orientation, which called for a redefinition of the concept of "national," limited the scope of Western Armenian's creative possibilities, potentially damaging its sustained development.

In examining the politics of language in transnationally produced Western Armenian literature, *Stateless* argues that the post–World War II adoption of the category of the "national" as the organizing logic of literary production in a diaspora setting proved detrimental to the long-term survival of this stateless language, for it ignored the multifarious composition of diaspora communities. Within a nationalized model of measuring literary legitimacy, the Western Armenian language was unable to transcend the shifting political realities of the Armenian world following the 1991 independence of the Armenian Republic. The new centrality that Armenia gained as an independent, concrete homeland destabilized the notion of a symbolic homeland integral to the diaspora's narrative, to which the Western Armenian language was tied. Furthermore, because this independence was officiated through Eastern Armenian, it inevitably called into question the identity of the Western Armenian diaspora. While this book does not focus on the diaspora's recent transitional years, it is informed by Western Armenian's vitality crisis, as developed in the past few decades. In grounding its retrospective gaze within the postindependence Armenian world, *Stateless* looks back at the diaspora's formation years to suggest alternative modes of imagining linguistic vitality and literary production outside of a state-centric paradigm.

Standard Western Armenian: Becoming a Literary Language

Armenian did not always consist of two different linguistic forms. The Western and Eastern variants, as distinct literary standards, emerged through a process of language modernization that began in the eighteenth century and came to fruition in the nineteenth century. Prior to this movement toward modernization, the Armenian literary canon consisted of works written in Classical Armenian (*krapar*), cultivated since the development of the Armenian alphabet around AD 405. Certainly, dialectal differences existed in the spoken vernaculars across Armenia. The East-West demarcation, as a mode of grouping regional dialects, emerged as Armenia lost the last of its kingdoms in the fourteenth century and its lands fell under the control of neighboring powers and differing cultural influences. By the sixteenth century, the western Armenian lands were under the Ottoman Empire's rule, whereas eastern Armenia was ruled by the Safavid shahs of Persia[6] until most of it was annexed by the Russians in 1828.[7] By the beginning of the twentieth century, Armenians lived across three empires: Ottoman, Russian, and Iranian. As Houri Berberian notes, the largest populations of Armenians resided in "the six Ottoman provinces of Van, Bitlis, Erzurum, Diyarbekir, Van, and Harput, with a smaller, commercially and intellectually developed minority in the urban hubs of Istanbul/Constantinople and Izmir/Smyrna."[8] In other words, before the 1915 genocide, speakers of Western Armenian dialects were a majority in the Armenian world.

Some scholars have put the number of Armenian dialects spoken at the turn of the twentieth century close to 120. According to linguist Hrachia Ajarian, these dialects can be divided into two main groups, roughly corresponding to the eastern and western portions of the Armenian linguistic area (defined essentially by their positions relative to the Armenian-Turkish border), the presence of a locative case (eastern dialects), and present-tense formations employing forms of the particle *gě* (western dialects).[9] Within the parallel movements to develop literary standards on each side of the border, the Ararat plain dialect served as the basis for the Eastern Armenian Standard, while the Western Armenian Standard was modeled after the dialect of Constantinople. By the nineteenth century, Constantinople, as the Ottoman Empire's capital, had become what poet and literary critic Vahé Oshagan has referred to as "the spiritual and social center of the Armenians."[10] It was in a cosmopolitan city outside historically Armenian lands, therefore, that a movement arose to standardize the Western Armenian language and modernize its literature.

Western Armenian's standardization movement was both cosmopolitan in practice and guided by the growing demands of an emergent

Armenian national consciousness. In the early part of the nineteenth century, as Armenians from the provinces gathered in Constantinople, the city's Armenian population reached 125,000,[11] accentuating the need to forge a common language that could accommodate the dialectical diversity of the city's community and, by extension, of western Armenians within the empire. Even though the efforts to develop a literary language were concentrated in Constantinople, the movement's key players lived in numerous urban centers outside of Armenian populated lands. Central among them were Mekhitarist[12] scholars from Venice and Vienna as well as Armenian elites, mainly of the merchant class, from Madras and Calcutta. These Armenians who had moved to the west and east of the empire were responsible for translating books into Armenian, commissioning and developing grammar books and dictionaries, opening printing houses, and establishing schools and newspapers. In contrast, the young intellectuals who wrote in the newspapers, taught in the schools, and engaged in public debates about standardization were locals, though many of them had studied at European universities. They sought to modernize the Armenian literary language, distancing it from the classical iteration that was accessible only to clergy and elites and embracing the spoken vernacular of the masses. They believed that shaping a new literary *ashkharhapar* (vernacular) would serve as a means of enlightening the Armenian masses of the Ottoman Empire and in time lead to freedom from oppression.

What Vahé Oshagan terms "Revival"[13] and what literary scholar Kevork Bardakjian refers to as "Renaissance"[14] is the period in western Armenian cultural history known in Armenian as *zart'onk'* (awakening). In this process of awakening the Armenian masses to their shared literary and cultural heritage, the Ottoman Armenian intellectual class assigned language the role of not only bringing enlightenment but also signaling inclusion within the imagined national community they sought to forge within the empire. According to this new designation of national identity, Armenianness was understood less as a Christian minority experience within an Islamic empire than as a cultural and linguistic presence on native lands.[15] A national literary language was needed to communicate with the population at large, but intellectuals disagreed on whether Classical or

Modern Armenian should be the national standard. This dispute unfolded between the 1840s and 1880s, with the Armenian Church, the Mekhitarists, and conservative elements of Ottoman Armenian society on the side of Classical Armenian and what Bardakjian refers to as "youthful liberals" on the side of Modern Armenian. He writes that the conservatives saw *krapar*, or Classical Armenian, as "the scriptural tongue of the ancestors, which to them was a fully developed uniform vehicle of expression and, possibly, a unifying body for the Armenians dispersed far and wide," while they viewed *ashkharhapar*, or the vernacular, as "a rudimentary and vulgar language, contaminated with numerous loan words from Turkish, Persian, and Arabic."[16] In fact, while *ashkharhapar* emerged victorious in this debate and a literary Western Armenian based on the Constantinople variant of the vernacular took shape, the process consisted of efforts to purify the language by adding thousands of new words that could replace foreign borrowings. By the 1870s, a modern Western Armenian Standard was available to be used for various purposes from the press to education and across discourses from literature to the sciences.[17]

In the decades that followed, with the help of a literary network of newly founded presses and schools, Western Armenian produced a new wave of poetry and prose that is celebrated to this day as the height of national literature in that standard. Writers like Krikor Zohrab, Srpuhi Dusap, Hagop Baronian, Misak Medzarents, and Mateos Zarifian came to prominence through publications inspired by European literary movements and explored both the constraints and the indulgences of these traveling literary genres within the limits of their own newly adopted literary standard of Western Armenian. Their output has been classified by later literary historians through designations like symbolist and realist, which correspond to European literary and artistic schools. Vahé Oshagan has even suggested that the term "westernization" is more apt than "modernization" in Western Armenian literature, arguing that in the eighteenth and nineteenth centuries, "in spite of the bitter animosity aroused among Armenians by the aggressive missionary movements in the Ottoman Empire, in India and in Eastern Europe, westernization became synonymous with progress and enlightenment, and conferred a much needed sense of dignity on an enslaved people, to say nothing of security."[18] Here,

Oshagan signals the European colonial project by alluding to the Catholic and evangelical missionaries in Ottoman Armenian communities whose presence incited fierce opposition from the Armenian Apostolic Church, which saw itself as a marker of national identity. Oshagan argues that in the context of literature, Armenian intellectuals of the nineteenth century sidestepped their critique of the West as a threat to Armenian identity and replaced it with reverence for the West's linguistic and literary innovations. Having studied the role of printing in European nationalist and revolutionary movements, they believed that the printed word could similarly be used to emancipate the Armenians living under oppression in the Ottoman Empire. Western Armenian's attachment to European literary traditions is precisely what was attacked by the postgenocide generation of writers that emerged in Paris in the 1920s. These writers blamed their literary predecessors for having missed the opportunity to cultivate a strong national literature that could in turn cultivate an autonomous collective consciousness.

The role of language and literature in the national awakening of Armenians in the Ottoman Empire, as well as in the Armenian revolutionary movements[19] that followed, has been debated extensively by each surviving generation of western Armenians. Some have even suggested that the revolutionary uprisings may have incited the genocide of 1915, further amplifying the influence of language in social and political dynamics.[20] While the drive to find an explanation for the perpetrator's genocidal will and to rationalize genocides is common in survivor responses to mass violence and catastrophe, from the perspective of literary scholarship in general, and this book's inquiry specifically, the question that matters is not how language modernization or linguistic autonomy could have provoked genocide but rather how the genocide impacted language and literature. Indeed, the literary trajectory of the burgeoning Western Armenian Standard was radically interrupted, if not completely halted, by the systematic extermination of the empire's Armenians, making it impossible for surviving writers to overlook the connection between violence and literature. While the genocide's central mode of extermination consisted of mass killings and deportations in the Armenian provinces, in its initial phase, it was the intellectuals of Constantinople who were targeted. On April

23–24, 1915, Turkish authorities arrested 235 public intellectuals, writers, editors, and educators in the capital. After an initial holding at the central police station, they were exiled to camps in Ayash and Chankiri in central Anatolia. Most of the arrested were later killed, along with another 600 public figures and 5,000 working-class Armenians rounded up from the capital during the coming months.[21] This targeted attack on the Western Armenian literati which also included the elites in the cities of the interior, as an attempt to terminate the community's leadership, had profound effects on the surviving population's capacity for intellectual continuity during the postgenocide dispersion. In literary histories of the period, a decadelong break often precedes the beginning of the next phase, in which orphaned writers began their activity in Paris and other diasporic centers.

While the genocide's impact on literary production amounted to a nearly complete rupture, some writers survived, including Aram Andonian, Hagop Oshagan, Vahan Tekian, Zabel Yesayan, and Yervant Odian. After a period of hiding and exile, they emerged in cities like Cairo, Boston, and Paris and congregated around established Armenian printing presses or established new ones. Referred to as surviving writers, these few remaining figures of a once booming literary tradition became the voices against which the upcoming dispersed generation of writers, like the Menk generation, constructed its literature as new. In contrast to the surviving writers, the orphaned writers, as the new voices in dispersion were called, believed that the writings they produced could not be conceived as the continuation of the Constantinople tradition.[22] Their literature, cultivated in exile, would forever be different, for it had to account for the new, identity-transforming dual realities of the western Armenian experience: genocide and dispersion.

From Catastrophe to Genocide

In 1929, when the Parisian Armenian newspaper *Harach* advertised a commemoration event organized by various community groups in memory of the genocide's victims, the word "genocide" did not yet exist, nor did its Armenian translation, *ts'eghasbanut'iwn*. The title of the announcement reads "April 11/24 Mourning Event"[23] and uses the Armenian compound word *skadōn*, literally meaning "mourning holiday." April 24 (or April 11, its iteration in the Julian calendar) marks the date of the arrests of Constantinople's Armenian intellectuals and the launch of the subsequent massacres and deportations. In the *Harach* announcement, the date is used as a naming device for the genocide itself. Indeed, in the decades immediately following the genocide, the events of 1915 are referred to in the Armenian-language press with an array of descriptive terms, such as "massacre" (*chart*), "heinous crime" (*eghern*), "crime" (*ojir*), "deportation" (*deghahanut'iwn*), and "catastrophe" (*aghēd*).[24] Often the qualifier "great" is added to the term to distinguish the events of 1915 from the more localized instances of massacre that Ottoman Armenians had undergone in 1895–96 and in 1909. The term "genocide" became available only later, toward the end of World War II. In the wake of the Holocaust and using the Armenian case as an example, a legal scholar by the name of Raphael Lemkin coined the term "genocide" (a compound of Greek and Latin words meaning "race" and "killing") and campaigned for the acceptance of international laws forbidding the act. In 1948, the United Nations adopted a definition of and laws against genocide at the Convention on the Prevention and Punishment of the Crime of Genocide.

The Armenian communities were quick to claim Lemkin's formulation "genocide" as the term that best described their recent experience as an ethnic group systematically targeted for extermination. In the few decades that had elapsed since the events, the globally dispersed Armenian masses had been slow to reflect, theorize, or historicize the gravity of being victims of an annihilation attempt. Their energies were spent instead on survival and resettlement. During the events of 1915, many Armenian-populated areas of the empire had undergone indiscriminate massacre. In a number of provinces, however, only the Armenian male population was singled out for immediate massacre, while the women and children were deported and sent on what has become known as "death marches" through the Syrian desert. Living as refugees in camps and orphanages, in abject poverty, Armenian survivors emerged in various cities of Syria and Lebanon, and many moved on to Jordan, Palestine, Egypt, Cyprus, Greece, France, or the Americas. As they reconnected with surviving members of their families and established new homes and communities in host states, their general approach to the past was marked by mourning, on both the personal and the communal levels. Therefore, in the late 1940s, the designation of the events of 1915 with the new legally delineated term "genocide" immediately politicized the experience in the collective memory of the surviving generations. The past would soon become a matter of politics rather than a matter of mourning.

The major shift in the collective memorialization of the genocide occurred in April 1965, in what political scientist Razmik Panossian has described as "a turning point." As many historians argue, the fiftieth anniversary of the genocide marked a major shift in the way the past was remembered by Armenians worldwide: mourning was replaced by a justice framework that called for recognition and the return of lost lands. For Panossian, the major catalyst for the 1965 shift was the start of Soviet Armenia's nationalization process: for the first time, Moscow had allowed Armenians to commemorate the genocide. Following World War I, many survivors of the genocide had ended up on the Russian side of the border, in eastern Armenia, which became part of the Soviet Union in 1920. In addition, encouraged by Soviet authorities' need to bolster population numbers for their own purposes, one hundred thousand Armenians from diasporic communities had emigrated to Soviet Armenia between 1946 and 1948. In other words, while there was a large presence of western Armenian descendants of the genocide within Soviet Armenia, the remembrance of the catastrophic events was deemed too nationalistic and thereby forbidden until 1965. Panossian argues that the surprisingly fervent demonstrations that accompanied the formal commemoration ceremony in Yerevan had significant reverberations throughout diaspora communities. He writes, "After 1965 the commemorations were *reformulated*. Explicitly politicised in the diaspora, and implicitly in Armenia, the Genocide became the core of what it meant to be Armenian in the political domain (it was already central in the cultural, religious and psychological domains)."[25] From 1965 onward, Armenians in the diaspora changed the tone of their collective commemorations: once mournful, the tone was now demanding.

The key Ottoman orchestrators and executioners of the massacres and deportations had never been held accountable by the Turkish state that

came to power in the years following the empire's collapse or by the international community. The planning and administration of the genocidal
orders were carried out by the Young Turk regime and their main political party, known as the Committee for Union and Progress. At the end of
World War I, the interim Turkish government created a special tribunal
to try the leading members of the regime for war crimes. Though the key
players of the regime had fled Turkey by then, they were sentenced to death
in absentia, right before the trials were permanently suspended owing to
the growing nationalist movement led by Mustafa Kemal, the founder of
the Republic of Turkey in 1923.[26] During this period of transition from
1918 to 1923, the international community, which was by then referring to
the genocide as "crimes against humanity," participated in brokering an
agreement between the Ottoman Empire and its expelled and displaced
minority groups. The Treaty of Sèvres, signed between the Allied powers
and the Ottoman Empire in 1920, promised to partition the Anatolian
lands between the Armenians, Greeks, and Kurds.[27] These terms, unfor-
tunately, were overturned by the Treaty of Lausanne in 1923 that ensured
Turkish sovereignty over the empire's former territorial expanse.[28] As
the new Turkish Republic tried to distance itself from its Ottoman past,
schoolbooks and curricula were written to efface the fate of the empire's
non-Muslim minorities, turning the topic of the Armenian genocide into
what Taner Akçam has referred to as a "taboo."[29]

After 1965, Armenians worldwide began campaigning for recognition, calling on their host states and on Turkey to classify the atrocities
committed against Ottoman Armenians as genocide. These initiatives,
while political in nature, also placed pressure on artists. Organizations,
political parties, and individual consumers of culture wanted the diaspora's literary and artistic apparatus to serve what had been termed the
Armenian Cause. This new mandate for artists to place their production
in service of the genocide-recognition campaign had a negative impact
on literature in the long run: it limited the topics considered suitable for
literary exploration, restricted the literary canon that was taught in diaspora school curricula, and decreased the literary capital of the Western
Armenian language. Under these conditions, writing in the host country's

dominant language proved more effective than writing in Western Armenian; the goal was to reach an outside audience and educate them about the forgotten genocide of the Armenians.

The political mandate for Armenian literature to tell the story of the genocide raises questions about aesthetic representation within the context of trauma. Trauma studies scholarship, the multidisciplinary subfield that burgeoned in the 1990s and continues to evolve, attempts to theorize trauma's representation in language and more broadly its impact on literature. Using a psychoanalytical approach based on Freud's theories of trauma's dissociative effects, the first wave of trauma studies scholarship focused on trauma's unrepresentability. Taking as their departure point Freud's understanding that traumatic experiences cause dissociation in the psyche, first-wave scholars like Cathy Caruth and Shoshana Felman examined psychoanalytical theories of catastrophe and Holocaust testimonies to argue that trauma's inability to be assimilated within consciousness in the time of its original occurrence produces pathological effects in the survivor, making the experience painful through the act of remembering, and therefore traumatic only belatedly. For Caruth, this dynamic produces a paradoxical experience wherein "trauma describes an overwhelming experience of sudden or catastrophic events in which the response to the event occurs in the often delayed, uncontrolled repetitive appearance of hallucinations and other intrusive phenomena."[30] In other words, trauma describes the presence of an occurrence that is experienced repeatedly through absence. As a result, she argues that any attempt to represent the traumatic experience in language, a system of meaning making, will leave the survivor at an impasse. Shoshana Felman and Dori Laub similarly understand trauma as an unassimilated event. They argue that the Holocaust was an event without a witness because bystanders failed to respond, and those inside the event, because of the inherent nature of the event, could not "step outside of the coercively totalitarian and dehumanizing frame of reference in which the event was taking place, and provide an independent frame of reference through which the event could be observed."[31] In other words, the Holocaust's traumatic and catastrophic nature can be partially attributed to the fact that it is an event that makes witnessing, and by extension testimony, impossible for the survivor. Adhering to the definition of the Holocaust as an event without an inside witness, Italian political philosopher Giorgio Agamben also examines the question of how survivors can bear witness to something that makes witnessing impossible. According to Agamben, testimony always contains a lacuna, or gap: those individuals who really witness the genocidal intent to kill do not survive, meaning that the complete witness is the dead victim.[32] Subsequently, he concludes that survivors are only pseudowitnesses who can bear witness to nothing but a missing testimony.[33]

In the context of the Armenian genocide, questions of naming and representation have best been theorized by French Armenian philosopher Marc Nichanian, who has argued for the use of "Catastrophe" over "Genocide" as the proper name for the experience of 1915. In one of his earlier discussions of this term, Nichanian resurrects *aghēd*, the Armenian word for "catastrophe," from the writings of Hagop Oshagan, a writer of the surviving generation and author of a ten-volume work titled *Hamabadger Arewmdahay Kraganut'ean* (Panorama of Western Armenian Literature), written in Jerusalem between 1938 and 1944. In it, Oshagan makes a case for developing the theme of catastrophe in literature by claiming, "While the Catastrophe is style and temperament for our historians, it is only a theme, subject to literary developments, for our modern writers."[34] In reference to the distinction between style and theme, Nichanian contests Oshagan's proposition for the stylization of catastrophe, which he argues would entail the integration of the violence into language. Instead, he makes a case for a literary confrontation of the Catastrophe that accounts for the limits of language and thereby the impossibility of representation. He expands on the distinction between style and theme in *Writers of Disaster* (2002) to address the question of representation by contrasting the categories of fact and event, Genocide and Catastrophe, and history and literature. Nichanian expresses his preference for the latter term in each of these pairings as appropriate for discussing the events of 1915 and states, "It is a question of liberating the Catastrophe of everything that transforms it into an object, an instance, or a fact, that gives a delusory meaning to it."[35] Nichanian's understanding of the genocide as an event that defies meaning and is thereby called Catastrophe is elaborated in a conversation with literary scholar David Kazanjian. Commenting on Nichanian's proposition, Kazanjian writes, "The Catastrophe of which we are speaking, then, is a loss of the law of mourning and a denial of that loss. Not just targeted mass murder, but also the withdrawal of sense from those subjected to that mass murder, the inability to name or imagine or apprehend the series of events that surround and make up that targeted mass murder. Not just the denial of those events and that Event, but also the denial of that inability to name or image or apprehend."[36] In this summary, expanding on the contention that the Catastrophe is an event impossible to define and impossible to represent, Nichanian presents it as an event that is impossible to mourn.[37]

This conception of catastrophe as an interdiction of mourning, owing to both the impossibility of witnessing and the unavailability of sense-making mechanisms for survivors, and the Caruthian understanding of trauma as a belated occurrence and thereby experienced through absence are fundamental to the theory of indexical representation that I propose when reading the Menk generation's literature. By indexical, I wish to draw our attention to the context both of and in the literary works. I argue that Menk's literature contains traces of the genocide's trauma without explicitly narrating the past events. I regard the Menk writers' work as a literary confrontation with the catastrophe, despite or even because of the absence of explicit genocide memory. I approach the representation of the genocide through the lens of Caruthian trauma theory, in which an event is traumatic insofar as it is not understood by the survivor in the midst of the experience and is relived belatedly. I argue that the Menk generation's prose fiction, written by and about orphans of 1915 and set in France in the aftermath years, represents the trauma precisely by narrating its belated reification and its inherent defiance of meaning. In other words, instead of looking back to the past, the Menk writers look to their present in France as the site of the genocide's trauma and, thereby, as the setting for their fiction. While never explicitly narrated as a coherent series of events from the past, the trauma of the Armenian characters is everywhere in the Menk authors' stories. It is the *context* of belatedness and the historical specificity of the writers that allow for certain things in the text to be read indexically. In other words, my reading of Menk's work as testimonial is dependent on the postcatastrophe milieu in which the action of their novels (as well as the authors' writing and publishing circumstance) takes place. This theoretical framework of what I refer to as "indexical representation" forms the basis of my approach to analyzing the explicit absence of the genocide in the narratives published by the Menk generation during the interwar period.

Ultimately, what I add to the discussion of trauma's limits in representation is a distinction between historical explanation and narrative understanding. Throughout this book, I make the case that the mimetic approach to representing the genocide, while offering a historical explanation of the event, does not represent the trauma. A narrative understanding of trauma is possible only through a work's confrontation with the trauma's unspeakability. In my readings, while I use the word "genocide" to refer to the atrocities of 1915, historically understood, I rely on the word "catastrophe" when discussing trauma's representation in literature, for it maintains the integrity of the traumatic experience as something that defies meaning. I posit that in the postgenocide Armenian diaspora, the post–World War II intellectuals favored literature that gave a straightforward, coherent representation of the past, and consequently they dismissed the young Menk writers, who refused to portray the genocide in explicit terms. By the late 1960s and the 1970s in diaspora communities, the fixity of the name "genocide" and the politically sealed meaning it gave to the catastrophic events had created a shift in public perception regarding the literary arts' narrative potential. As literary works came to be valued for their ability to return the reader to the past by narrating either life prior to the 1915 rupture or the violence of genocide, artistic production that located the catastrophe within the genocide's aftermath was pushed to the sidelines. A couple of decades earlier, when intellectuals in Beirut began to centralize the diaspora's discourse through curriculum building and language standardization in the Middle East, the new canon already exemplified what Robin Cohen has called a "victim diaspora."[38] Literature, in other words, became a space where banishment from native lands, victimhood, exile, and loss were narrativized as identity markers for diaspora Armenians.

From Dispersion to Diaspora

Stateless examines the development of the Western Armenian language in relation to literary production. My discussion in both parts of the book is driven by two questions: What happens to a language when its people are exiled from their historic lands and dispersed across other nations in the world? What does it mean to represent a diasporic cultural experience in an infinitely exilic linguistic form? As the two-part organization of the book suggests, Paris's Menk generation and Beirut's intellectuals who were affiliated with the WASL approached these questions differently. Whereas in the years following World War I, the Parisian writers imagined the new Western Armenian literary world as consisting of a pluralistic, transnational network of communities, the post–World War II writers based in the Middle East adopted a relatively homogenous, national model of literary production, centralized in Beirut. Their contrasting discursive approaches are reflected in community-wide processes of naming both the genocide and the diaspora. Similar to the process of solidification that the genocide underwent, "diaspora" became a fixed term used to describe the communities in dispersion only after World War II.

The compound word *sp'iwrashkharh* (diaspora world) appeared in the French Armenian press as early as 1926.[39] While there were a few appearances of *sp'iwrk'* (diaspora), neither it nor its compound formation gained currency and circulation in Armenian periodicals until after World War II. Instead, between the wars, the Armenian press of Boston, Paris, and the Middle East referred to the dispersed masses through a range of descriptive terms, including *ts'ruadzut'iwn* (dispersion), *t'rk'ahayut'iwn* (Turkish Armenians), *kaghut'ahayut'iwn*[40] (exiled community of Armenians), *kaght'ahayut'iwn* (migrant Armenians), and *ardasahmni hayut'iwn* (Armenians abroad). As a collection, these terms reflected the intersections of ethnic belonging and displacement that shaped the postgenocide experience for Armenians. Through them, the Armenian identity was characterized by a multiplicity of references hinting at Ottoman Turkish subjugation, the migrant experience, efforts at community building in exile, and the lost homeland. The terms collectively suggested diversity and lack of uniformity in the experience of dispersion, marked by the varied circumstances of the host states where Armenians eventually settled.

By the mid-1940s, however, around the same time the word *ts'eghasba-nut'iwn* (genocide) started circulating, *sp'iwrk'* (diaspora) gained traction as the word of choice to describe the dispersed community of Armenians, slowly pushing the alternative phrases out of use. The classical definition of diaspora, taking the Jewish example as its archetype, holds the idea of forced expulsion from native lands at its core. William Safran's now-famous definition of diaspora attempts to broaden the concept to other communities, such as the Armenians, and highlights the following as the first key feature: "They, or their ancestors, have been dispersed from a specific original 'center' to two or more 'peripheral,' or foreign, regions."[41] In other words, emphasis is placed on the catastrophic origins of a diaspora's creation as the qualifying marker. The concept, of course, has radically expanded in meaning, especially since the establishment of the multidisciplinary field of diaspora studies in the early 1990s. Roger Brubaker categorizes the term's evolution from implying dispersion in space, as in the case of the Jewish, Greek, and Armenian diasporas, to referring to population categories that are *not* dispersed in space, such as the queer diaspora. Eventually, the term spread to disciplines like black studies, women's studies, and cinema, dance, and pop culture studies, and its meaning broadened to imply at once a condition (diasporicity/-ism), a process (diasporization), a field of inquiry (diasporology/-istics), and an attribute (diasporic/diasporan).[42]

We must understand "diaspora" both as a contested term and as a theoretical concept if we are to explore its relationship to stateless power in this examination of Western Armenian literature. Khachig Tölölyan, for instance, discusses academics' transformation of dispersions into diasporas. In discussing the use of the term "diaspora" in the latter half of the twentieth century, he traces an expansion of the Jewish-centered definition of the word to include a wider semantic domain that includes exile, migrant, ethnic, and refugee communities alike. He argues that the process of renaming dispersions as diasporas, while it signals the era of transnationalism, "entails the inadvertent complicity between some diasporists and trans-nationalists in the attack on the nation-state; the displacement of the collective diasporic subject; and the occultation of the stateless power of the diaspora as a possible model for the nation-state rather than as only an adversary of it."[43] He warns us against idealizing diasporas as incubators of flexible, multiple identities by reminding us that stateless power can be just as prohibitive as it can be productive, since institutions and their institutionalizing constraints persist in diasporas as well. It is precisely this tension between flexibility and prohibitive power occasioned by a turn from "dispersion" to "diaspora" that I explore in Western Armenian literary production.

My reference to Western Armenian language as a stateless language acknowledges the tension between its users' evolving identification as communities in dispersion and their identification as diaspora communities, a tension that is characteristic of stateless power. Tölölyan has argued that the stateless power of diasporas "lies in their heightened awareness of both the perils and rewards of multiple belonging, and in their sometimes exemplary grappling with the paradoxes of such belonging, which is increasingly the condition that non-diasporan nationals also face in the transnational era."[44] In the case of Western Armenian, I show that there is an inherent crisis of belonging in the way the language has developed in the postgenocide years. The opposing transnational and national imaginings of literature, in the post–World War I and post–World War II years, respectively, created a clash between the language's natural development in relation to each host state's linguistic culture and policies and the Armenian diaspora's insistence on orienting the language toward a homeland, whether mythically or territorially bound.

What I mean by the idea of orienting the Armenian language toward a homeland is the cultivation of a direct link between language maintenance and a narrative of return. Within the national model of literary belonging developed by the Beirut intellectuals following World War II, language was viewed as the facilitator of that return. Language thus came to be regarded as symbolic territory that provided Armenians with a sense of home in exile that could be sustained until the Armenian people's eventual return to the homeland. Just as the politicization of the genocide through its naming called for the return of lost lands, the adoption of "diaspora" as the umbrella term with which to refer to Armenians in dispersion called forth a myth of homeland. The "return" implied by the myth of homeland was inevitably a return to an imagined, unified Armenia that consisted of not only the historically Armenian lands lost to Turkey, but also the eastern Armenian lands that were under Soviet rule at the time.[45] In this way, return became accepted as a deferred ideal, forcing the creation of an organized, centralized diaspora that functioned as a nation in exile, in what Tölölyan has termed "the Armenian transnation."[46] Within the transnational borders of this interim nation centered in the Middle East, the Western Armenian language underwent a second wave of standardization, consisting of the establishment of schools and printing presses and the preparation of school curricula, generating a new literary canon. In contrast to the nineteenth-century standardization process of Western Armenian that aimed to modernize the language, this process sought to nationalize the language and safeguard it for an eventual return to Armenian territories.

The notion of return has always been a complicated one for western Armenians expelled from their native lands. "Homeland" has referred to a multiplicity of referents, ranging from historically Armenian lands in eastern Turkey to Soviet Armenia (and later the Armenian Republic) and to a combination of the two in the vision of an integral Armenia that would unite its western and eastern territories. In the early years of dispersion, Levon Chormisian, who would later write a comprehensive history of the French Armenian community, lamented the western Armenian exilic condition, writing, "To have a homeland but not a home, to be patriotic yet an exile, herein lies the torment of the soul that each one of us suffers from."[47] Chormisian here comments on the difficulty with which exiled western Armenians are forced to reconcile their dispersed refugee status with the existence of a Soviet Armenian republic. Though it signaled a linguistically and culturally different space, and one that was within the broader Soviet imperial project, the idea of a plot of historical land still bound to the Armenian people was too enticing not to attract the generations that had survived the genocide. Aside from those individuals who repatriated to Soviet Armenia in the 1940s, many in the diaspora held Soviet Armenia to be the unequivocal homeland, believing that the Soviet path was the only option that could ensure a future for Armenia. In more recent years, this mode of adopting eastern Armenia as a replacement for the lost western Armenian homeland has been theorized by Sossie Kasbarian, who refers to the Armenian state as a "step-homeland" in the new narrative of return that emerged after Soviet Armenia's independence. She writes, "Owing to the absence of a direct link to an ancestral homeland, the Republic of Armenia (Hayastan), with whom the western diaspora has no historical physical connection, serves as a substitute for a 'homeland.' Diasporans therefore have to negotiate the gap between a mythical homeland and an actual 'step-homeland' in the shape of the Armenian State."[48] While highlighting the connotations of unfamiliarity and adjustment that the concept of "step-ness" evokes, Kasbarian's coinage also underscores the persistent power of the nation-state as the validating medium of ethnic belonging, especially in contrast to statelessness.

Beyond the dynamics of contended and multiple belonging in Western Armenian's literary output, I define it as a stateless language on the very basic premise that it is not the official language of any nation-state.[49] In cultivating it as a stateless language, intellectuals and writers in the Middle East positioned Western Armenian against Soviet Armenia, claiming that the Soviet Union's imperial aims threatened the Armenian national identity and language. As they developed a national rubric for language and literature in exile, Western Armenian writers and educators thus believed themselves to be preserving the Armenian language's integrity against the Soviet Empire's colonizing force with the aim of an eventual return to the historic, unified homeland. This national rubric, practiced as a form of diasporic transnationalism, became known as *hayets'i*, which loosely translates to "Armenian-oriented." It measured the literariness of works through its evocation of the Armenian spirit, whether through a narrativization of the past, a lamentation of victimhood, or a celebration of resistance. Its restrictive demands on Western Armenian literature helped solidify the dispersed communities as a single unit, known as the Armenian diaspora. Its homogenizing drive, while creating a vital Armenian literary apparatus in the Middle East, ultimately overpowered the pluralistic drive of statelessness and proved counterproductive to Western Armenian's survival in the face of the diaspora's changing circumstances.

In reading Western Armenian's postgenocide linguistic and literary development as relational and in comparing its two literary centers, I hope to expand our understanding of Western Armenian as a diasporic language by offering the paradigm of statelessness.[50] The framework of statelessness allows me to clarify the transnational and diasporic literary orientations of the post–World War I Paris and post–World War II Beirut groups, respectively, and to make a case for the former as a more viable alternative to long-term language vitality in exile. The framework of statelessness also makes it possible to trace Western Armenian's diverse paths of development and current modes of usage within communities like Istanbul, Yerevan, and Los Angeles that defy the postgenocide diaspora's imagined literary network.

My discussion of a stateless language's flexible and prohibitive production of transnational and national literature in exile intersects with current debates about world literature, which is often defined as the study of internationally canonized literature.[51] In mapping constellations of literary works, scholars of world literature like David Damrosch, Pascale Casanova, Franco Moretti, and Emily Apter focus on the tension between the local and the global as they inform the content and the form of works in the process of publication, translation, and circulation. They attempt to understand the world literature model as a classificatory system that moves beyond "national" categories to show intersections between literatures with connected histories that are unmediated by the concept of a "center." Within this model, critics like Casanova equate linguistic capital with literary autonomy, arguing that a literary language must be decoupled from the nation, or made "autonomous," before it can enter the international literary space. In my examination of Western Armenian literary history, I will show that the world literature paradigm has failed to expand literary historiography to account for stateless literatures that elude international canonization. I therefore opt instead to use the term "transnational literature," which encompasses the study of literatures rooted outside a single nation, notwithstanding the politics of translation.

My placement of the Menk generation's proposition for a transnational Western Armenian literature in opposition to the Beirut-based writers' conception of Western Armenian literature as symbolic national territory also challenges world literature's drive to enforce borders as a precondition for the mobility or circulation of texts. Along these lines, Amir Mufti and Gayatri Spivak have interrogated the disciplinary claims of world literature and comparative literature, respectively, and emphasized the border-making mechanism (or "regime," as Mufti calls it) of these ontological categories that seek to understand literary production on a global scale.[52] Mufti, who is interested in how the hegemony of English affects non-European languages, and Spivak, who is interested in the vitality of languages that were historically prevented from having a constituted readership, both argue that the autonomy of nonimperial languages lies in literary specificity that interrupts the impetus for mapping and border making. Mufti, for instance, claims, "A politics of language, literature, and culture affiliated with the struggle for survival and autonomy of postcolonial societies must therefore configure differently the relationship of the cosmopolitan and the vernacular, the universal and the particular, in order to facilitate ways of thinking about culture and society that do not simply replicate the extant antinomies of power on a world scale."[53]

With this project that examines a stateless language across many borders, I hope to make room for discussions about literatures that fall outside the West's discursive dynamics of the global literary scene. By juxtaposing the Menk generation's attempt to create a transnational literary space with the WASL's efforts to nationalize literature in exile, I present a theory of language vitality for stateless languages that is inextricably tied to a literary orientation grounded in dispersion rather than diaspora. While both camps' exclusion of the drive toward global circulation and international canonization leaves them out of discussions of world literary studies, they help us understand the critical inquiries into the intersection of trauma, transnationalism, aesthetics, and politics that Western Armenian literature makes possible.

Organization

Stateless: The Politics of the Armenian Language in Exile is divided into two parts, each of which examines the development of Western Armenian literary identity in a key historical moment and space: post–World War I

Paris and post–World War II Beirut. Chapter 1 introduces the intellectual and literary activity that took place around the world in the decade following the genocide. Focusing on the ways print culture helped to center communities of dispersion, I discuss emergent transnational spaces and describe Paris as a primary stronghold of Western Armenian literature. I introduce the journal *Menk'* and its members, situate them in the Parisian milieu, and discuss the limitations of their transnational project. In doing so, I highlight their attempts at articulating a transnational belonging through an analysis of their literary orientation and the orientations of some of their contemporaries. While their project can be interpreted as a form of community building, I argue that they envisioned a new literature on a decentered model, in which Western Armenian literature would be produced in conversation with horizontal networks linking spaces of exile or dispersion.

Chapter 2 examines the strategic value that the Menk generation attributed to the novel as a genre, which was thought to provide the largest platform for developing their understanding of diasporic time as interrupted. I focus on two novels, Zareh Vorpuni's *P'ortsě* (The Attempt) (1929) and Hrach Zartarian's *Mer Geank'ě* (Our Life) (1934), to argue that Menk writers implicitly represented the genocide as a loss of patriarchy. These autobiographical novels present the lives of male protagonists who face the impossible task of replacing their lost fathers within the surviving family structure. Just as the characters' attempts are always frustrated, the narratives struggle between the need to claim the father as dead (and therefore lost) and the inability to situate that loss in language (creating a hauntingly absent figure). Through the figure of the failed witness, these novels address the paradox of representation inherent to the experience of catastrophe. Menk's literary archive is often overlooked as a viable response to the genocide because the Menk members did not seek to historicize the story of genocide and dispersion in a coherent, chronological fashion. The group is often criticized for refusing to comply with the mandate to record their eyewitness accounts. This chapter makes a case for the value of their alternative approach, arguing that the aesthetic representation of genocide's trauma must be informed by notions of impossible testimony and interrupted time.

Within the gendered articulation of the catastrophe as the loss of patriarchy and an incongruent demand to reinstate it in dispersion, another
trope emerges: that of incest. Chapter 3 explores this literary trope by
examining works like Zareh Vorpuni's "Vartsu Seneag" (Room for Rent)
(1934), Nigoghos Sarafian's *Ishkhanuhin* (The Princess) (1934), and Shahan Shahnur's "'Buynuzlě'nerě" (The Cuckolds) (1932), which illustrate the
collapse of social and familial order following the genocide from a male
perspective. These works suggest that in dispersion, the young Armenian
men's gravitation toward the Same (represented through the figure of the
sister) is always incestuous and detrimental to the continuation of family,
and their gravitation toward the Other (represented through the figure of
the Frenchwoman) inevitably results in acculturation. In the literature of
Menk, the narratives of incest, told from the perspective of the brother,
unquestioningly imply the brother's position of authority in the postpatriarchy setting. The reconstitution of patriarchy presents itself as an imperative mandated by the absence of the father, yet also as something that is
impossible to achieve because of incest.

The idea of an undisrupted past-present-future became essential to
the later cultural narrative of diaspora, which attempted to historicize the
genocide and its dispersion in order to reconstruct the damaged notion of
continuity. Turning to Beirut, chapter 4 traces the critical response and
emblematic status given to Menk member Shahan Shahnur's 1929 novel,
Nahanchě Aṙants' Erki (The Retreat without Song), in the many decades
following its publication. By examining the misreading and mistranslation that made this acclaim possible, this chapter interrogates the role of
nationalism in the post–World War I diaspora's effort to preserve cultural
and literary traditions. I propose that the Menk writers are overlooked
because of their attempt to redefine the concept of national literature, as
the extraordinary treatment of this novel demonstrates. Furthermore, I
argue that the refusal of the diaspora's post–World War II intellectuals to
engage with Menk's proposition for a new, transnational literary orientation limited the possibilities for Armenian-language literature produced
outside the boundaries of "nation." After Menk, what remained particularly at stake was the production of literature in the Western Armenian
literary form.

In the years following World War II, those persons once referred to as Turkish Armenians, dispersion, the exiled community of Armenians, migrant Armenians, or Armenians abroad came to be known collectively as the diaspora, which imagined itself as a transnationally organized homogenous entity. Chapter 5 focuses on this period of transition to examine the making of the diaspora's grand narrative, founded on the notion of national cultural production in exile. I argue that the articulation of the diaspora's narrative was occasioned by two rival conferences: the Second Congress of the Soviet Armenian Writers' Union, held in Yerevan in 1946 with the participation of a select group of diaspora writers, and a reactive conference organized by the Writers' Association of Syria and Lebanon, held in Shtora, Lebanon, in 1948. These rival conferences caused diaspora intellectuals to recognize the threat facing Western Armenian language in exile and, incidentally, to position Beirut, and more broadly the Middle East, as the hub for the centralization and standardization of Western Armenian language and literature.

In the early 1950s, educational and publishing institutions became potent markers of "centering" as they joined the larger apparatus of language standardization, and thereby became a means of constructing the diaspora through narrative. Chapter 6 examines the process of canon formation within the context of a larger effort to develop a standardized curriculum for the schools and a turn toward poetry in the emergent *hayets'i* mode of literary production. It argues that in the decades following World War II, art in the diaspora gained a new framing as a national literature in exile rather than a transnational literature in dispersion. Writers like Mushegh Ishkhan, Garo Sasuni, Minas Teoleolian, and Antranig Dzarugian, many of whom were educators in the burgeoning Armenian day-school scene of Beirut, celebrated the Armenian language as a symbolic territory. Their work therefore perpetuated the myth of a unified homeland and the myth of return and formed the canon of Western Armenian literature that educated generations of diaspora Armenians for decades to come.

These efforts to nationalize diaspora culture, initially launched at the 1948 conference, were successful in forging a critical mass of "producers" and "consumers," to borrow Hagop Gulludjian's terms,[54] in the

Western Armenian language. In general, attempts to fashion the diaspora as a homogenous entity contributed to the flourishing of intellectual and cultural activity in Middle Eastern communities, but did not allow for pluralism. Consequently, they produced problematic forms of cultural essentialism that proved detrimental to literary expression and production, especially following Armenia's 1991 independence. As new diasporas have formed following the westward migration of Armenians from the Middle East and the mass exodus from the former Soviet Armenia, and subsequently from the Republic of Armenia, the current institutions and the hermetically sealed narratives of the traditional diaspora have proved insufficient to support the dynamic, pluralistic version of a diverse diaspora. In my concluding section, I make a case for Menk's model of a new literature informed by multilocal transnational belonging.

PART ONE

Decentering Western Armenian in Post–World War I Paris

1

Generative Orphanhood

Transnational Literature in Dispersion

Recalling the early experiences of his literary career in a 1979 interview, Zareh Vorpuni vaguely remarks on the dissolution of the Paris-based group Menk, of which he was a member. He states, "To put it frankly, a name is all that it left behind, not any work. Its outburst, though, is enough for there to have been something."[1] Vorpuni's ambivalent remarks express the unique position the journal holds in the Armenian literary imaginary. On the one hand, the author's dismissal of the literary group's significance echoes diaspora communities' neglect of the group's contribution to the development of Western Armenian intellectual thought and raises questions about the reason for Vorpuni's attitude. Did the author, at the end of his life and after many years of disregard from Armenian institutions, find the concept of an Armenian literary tradition futile? Was he pushed to a position of indifference? Had he hardened toward discussions of literary history in the diaspora? On the other hand, his framing of the group's endeavor as an "outburst" engages the language of eruption or interruption and acknowledges the groundbreaking effect of the group's legacy of potential.

Indeed, an air of mystery surrounds the story of Menk, owing both to uncertainties about the group's formation and breakup and to the decades of silence that buried its very existence. It wasn't until the 1980s, through the work of philosopher Marc Nichanian, critic Haroutiun Kurkjian, and writer Krikor Beledian, that Menk as a group and its individual writers were treated as topics of scholarly inquiry. Recognizing the group's immense contribution to Armenian literary thought, Beledian claimed,

"*Menk* is a history-making opus, not a basic product of history,"[2] and he later devoted a chapter of his encyclopedic volume *Cinquante ans de littérature arménienne en France* to the group. But by the time this new wave of criticism arrived, a new diaspora had emerged, overwriting the Paris scene and directly linking the post–World War II Beirut scene to the pregenocide literary tradition of Constantinople. Within this formulation, Paris was seen as playing only a marginal role in the development of modern Armenian's linguistic and literary tradition.

What we today consider modern Armenian literature dates back to the mid-nineteenth century with the initiation of the literary movement toward the standardization of the spoken vernacular, in both the Western and the Eastern forms of the language. In the second half of the nineteenth century, Armenian literature experienced a period of revival and witnessed the emergence of an active intellectual class. The Armenian national liberation movement in the Ottoman and Russian Empires coupled with the incoming waves of European artistic and literary movements, such as Romanticism and realism, produced an abundance of journals, poetry, and prose publications. Intellectual communities sprang up in cities such as Constantinople and Tbilisi. The catastrophic years of 1915–23 put a halt to Western Armenian intellectual life and literature. Most Armenian writers living in Constantinople were arrested on the evening of April 24, 1915. They were imprisoned and later killed. After a few years of complete rupture in the Western Armenian literary tradition, the surviving intellectuals, such as Hagop Oshagan, Teotig, Vahan Tekeyan, and Zabel Yesayan, returned to Constantinople or reemerged elsewhere to become the surviving "elders" of Armenian literature and language to the orphaned generation of future writers, including those of Menk.[3] Although many of the surviving writers were dispersed in the Middle East, the majority of them regrouped in France, mainly in Paris.

For the small number of surviving writers, the task of transference from the old to the new proved difficult. The physical relocation of the intellectual center from the East to the West did not allow for many of the former literary traditions to transfer smoothly into the post–World War I European intellectual world. Meanwhile, new writers were beginning to emerge within the next generation, which had been orphaned by the

genocide. In their efforts to gather as a collective the most prominent writers of the time, some young writers of the new generation formed a group
in Paris called Menk. Their aim was to found an emergent transnational
literature in the Western Armenian language. After they arrived in Paris
in the mid-1920s, the future members of Menk had lived in overcrowded
apartment buildings in Belleville, audited university courses, and thrown
themselves into the newly forming Armenian intellectual community of
the city. Having learned the Armenian language either in the day schools
of Constantinople or in orphanages in Greece or the Middle East, these
young men contributed articles to the existing literary and political periodicals, attended and organized public lectures, and began to hold frequent meetings in the cafés and restaurants of the Latin Quarter.[4] In 1931,
these informal gatherings translated into an organized effort with the
publication of the first volume of the journal *Menkʻ*, recognizing a number
of young writers as part of a collective. The publication was introduced by
a one-page announcement[5] signed by fifteen writers that highlighted the
aims of the group and the reasons for their solidarity.

Menk's group identity was formed around a series of deliberate nega-
tions that sought to jolt conventions and to present a new kind of literature
that would embody the writers' exilic condition. They gathered to make
a collective contribution to Western Armenian literature yet called for a
break with that same literary tradition. They denounced the earlier generation of writers, they proclaimed a change in the transmission of literary
customs, they announced a separation from the past, and they embraced
the newness of their experience as a people scattered around the world
and living in the shadow of a traumatic loss. This idea of "newness," which
arose from the group's commitment to narrating its present conditions—
however repressive, marginalized, and unpleasant—formed the foundation of the first wave of Armenian literature in dispersion.

In the years following the genocide, Armenians in the dispersion,
especially the ones in the urban centers of the West, inhabited a liminal
space that seemed momentarily suspended in time, awaiting the establishment of a new relationship with the past. To assert themselves as writers of
Armenian literature, the "Paris boys,"[6] as they were later called, attempted
to name this relationship between present and past or, to borrow from

Homi Bhabha, to "refigure" the past according to their present reality of living in an in-between space.[7] In other words, in submitting the pre-1915 years to evaluation from their new, marginalized position in the West, they called for an end to the nationalist and Westward-looking literature of the earlier generation. Accordingly, they proposed a literary theory that heralded the end of the Western Armenian literary tradition and the birth of a "new" literature that had yet to be defined. After an abrupt dislocation, finding themselves in the middle of the Parisian metropolis yet operating on the margins of the majority culture, they were forced to negotiate the terms and conditions of their scattered existence. Given that the language they were writing in was no longer connected to its place of origin, they concluded that their contribution could not be understood within the framework of national literature. At the same time, while they believed in the potential of transnational literature, they could not yet organize its global launch. Their works, therefore, were deeply rooted in the local, that is, in the French neighborhoods where they lived. They resolutely committed themselves to writing in Western Armenian and narrating their present in France. Their body of works, therefore, constitutes a repository of their experience in exile.

Regardless of their production of contemporary and testimonial works, and notwithstanding the efforts of a few critics, the Menk generation[8] remains outside the modern Armenian literary canon because of its attempts to disrupt the understanding of continuous time. The idea of an undisrupted past-present-future became essential to the later cultural narrative of the diaspora, which attempts to historicize the genocide and its dispersion in order to reconstruct the damaged notion of continuity. Yet for the orphaned Armenian youth of the 1920s, the postgenocide years represented an in-between space that was removed from the continuum of time. In their attempt to simultaneously distance themselves from and draw near their fellow Armenian survivors and their French host society, the Menk writers adopted a hostile relationship to the past and set themselves up for skepticism from Armenian readers and critics. The nonexplicit, indexical representation of the traumatic events of the past and the insistence on providing a testimony of their present, both salient characteristics of their fiction, could not fit comfortably into the nationalist cultural narrative of the genocide that emerged in the years following World War II. As the diasporan Armenian intellectual center moved to Beirut, Lebanon, in the late 1940s, Armenian poetry celebrating the language and the church or perpetuating the myth of a unified homeland and the myth of return formed the canon of Western Armenian literature, burying the short-lived literary production of Paris between the world wars.

Unlike the canonized literature that emerged from the Middle East, the novels and short stories of the Menk generation wrote the experience of the catastrophe by avoiding representation of the past. With this project, their authors sought to cultivate a transnational readership of the Western Armenian language rather than to gain validation from a global audience. In doing so, they initiated a movement, however short-lived, of possibility for Western Armenian literature in dispersion. Given Western Armenian's current endangered status, revisiting the Menk archives could offer diaspora institutions directives for framing language-revitalization projects within discussions of literary production and, more broadly, for pursuing the intersections of literature and language vitality.

This chapter introduces the dispersed Western Armenian intellectual and literary scene in the decade following the genocide. In focusing on print culture's role in centering communities of dispersion, I position Paris as a primary stronghold among other emergent "centers." Within this framework, I tell the story of the literary group Menk, composed of writers orphaned by the genocide. By examining the circumstances of the group's formation and breakup and the literary platform the writers developed in their journal and other periodicals of the time, I situate their story within transnational networks of forgetting. In other words, I show that against the backdrop of postgenocide community-building efforts, the transnationally formed fabric of groups, organizations, and publications initially emerged as a competitive space in which participating entities fought to shape literary discourse. While the newness of the dispersion experience allowed for an outburst of diverse voices, the various groups' shared desire for centralization ultimately excluded many initiatives, like that of Menk, and contributed to the institution of diasporic power structures that erased the heterogeneity of dispersion.

More specifically, this chapter argues that Menk's call for new literature proposed a decentered model in which Western Armenian literature
would be produced within lateral, nonhierarchical networks of spaces of
dispersion. I also suggest that Menk's later exclusion from the Western
Armenian literary canon was a result of its decentered literary orientation
and attempts to disrupt the understanding of continuous time. For the
Menk writers, the postgenocide years represented an in-between space in
which Armenian youth were removed from the continuum of time. This
temporarily suspended sense of time, coupled with their geographical
displacement, generated the idea of newness that permeates their literature. Specifically, their literary platform translated into their works as an
insistence on writing in Western Armenian, narrating the present, and
adopting prose as their preferred genre. This chapter revisits some of the
periodical publications of the Menk generation in the hope of examining
the forgotten intersections of literature and language vitality that developed during the early years of dispersion.

Paris between the Wars and the Changing Face
of Its Armenian Intellectual Life

The 1920s saw a great transfiguration of the small but active pregenocide
Armenian community in place within France, concentrated in Paris.
Within the impassioned, reactionary cultural atmosphere that reigned in
the city following the devastating war, survivors of the Armenian genocide arrived in Paris and transformed the city's prewar Armenian collective of elites into a community of refugees. With this transformation, the
newcomers also cultivated a new intellectual tradition borne out of the
conditions of their expulsion, their loss, and their current statelessness.
To situate the vision for a new transnational Armenian culture that many
emergent groups propagated within their publications, I would like to take
a quick glance at the larger Parisian cultural milieu that hosted the activities of the young Armenian survivors who began to voice themselves in
Western Armenian and created a linguistic sphere that transcended well
beyond the metropolis.

In reference to the avant-garde movements of Paris at the turn of the century, Jeremy Stubbs claims, "If nineteenth-century Paris was the capital of art, 1920s Paris was the capital of anti-art."[9] Indeed, although it was not the largest city in the world, nineteenth-century Paris is often seen as representative of its age, in the sense that it embodied the spirit of and became the site of the major social and economic struggles of the era.[10] During the early decades of the twentieth century, and especially following World War I, the city served as a stage for artistic movements born at the juncture of the celebratory atmosphere of victory parades and the shock of human loss and mass destruction. Avant-garde movements like futurism, Dadaism, and surrealism celebrated progress by dismantling the structures that claimed to produce it. Thus, they called forth new models for moving society forward in tandem with technological and scientific advances. Their radical objective was to revolutionize human experience, in the personal, social, and political senses, by freeing people from false reasoning and restrictive customs and institutions. It was within this cultural atmosphere that survivors of the Armenian genocide arrived in Paris and transformed the city's prewar diaspora of elites into a community of refugees. They were not alone in cultivating a new immigrant identity and a language community on the margins of white French culture.

Since France had changed its immigration laws to compensate for shortages in the labor force, the war years had seen an influx of migration from other European countries, Indochina, and North Africa. Furthermore, many of the 135,000 soldiers from French West Africa who fought as part of the black African troops during the war returned to France and were greeted with relative welcome.[11] In contrast with the racist attitudes with which white Americans received their returning black troops, France's more favorable treatment of blacks garnered attention among the black international community and made Paris a place of congregation for blacks from America, Africa, and the Caribbean. During this period, Paris maintained an attractive pull for artists coming from the United States and students from France's colonial territories. Within the heightened fervor of artistic movements, black students also found intellectual and political ferment there and began organizing groups that cultivated

Pan-African consciousness and challenged Europe's imperialism. In looking at the publications of these groups, Brent Hayes Edwards traces the linkages between the young black intellectuals of Paris and intellectuals in the United States or the French colonies. Without denying the centrality of Paris, Edwards maps out the practices that sustained these transnational alliances, which can be perceived as a form of decentered diaspora, in many ways akin to the vision of the Menk generation that I will discuss later. For Edwards, it is through the practice of reciprocity, performed in print culture through translation, that an imagined community represents itself as diaspora. Engaging with the links Benedict Anderson draws between print capitalism and the emergence of the nation and focusing specifically on his notion of simultaneity cultivated through the medium of the newspaper,[12] Edwards reflects on how a community can be imagined when instead of a single-language newspaper within the confines of a single nation, it is imagined across different languages and across different nations, as was the case of periodical articles that circulated through translation. He argues that a transnational community of "race," like the one that black internationalism calls for, "is above all practiced in the multilayered and convoluted exchanges between periodicals such as *Opportunity* and *Les Continents*, in their sometimes uneasy and sometimes misdirected attempts to carry blackness beyond the boundaries of nation and language, to read the race problem as a world problem. In this sense, diasporic reciprocity is above all a call to translate."[13] Edwards defines "racial" diasporic formation as practice, structured by a form of disarticulation that he calls *décalage*: an untranslatable term borrowed from Léopold Senghor, referring to gaps, discrepancies, and misunderstandings inherent in diasporic belonging, which simultaneously calls attention to transnational sameness yet demands a different discursive understanding of a person's position vis-à-vis a nation or a language based on historical context.

Black transnationalism refers to the struggle for black liberation that extends beyond the borders of white nation-states. Scholars trace its early iterations within the discourse produced by African American thinker W. E. B. Du Bois, whose speeches and writings drew attention to the problem of race and called for a new *emancipatory* social scientific study of race. While Du Bois's ideas most directly influenced movements that led to the Harlem Renaissance in the American context, their echoes can be found in the Negritude movement that grew out of the Paris scene, where the Senegalese poet and politician Léopold Senghor, Martinican poet Aimé Cesaire, and writer Léon Damas from French Guinea were gathered. In drawing a connection between the Harlem Renaissance and the Negritude movement, Lilyan Kesteloot claims that the acknowledgment of Africa was a central characteristic of both movements, because of which black writers "resolutely turned their backs on the preceding generation."[14] In other words, in growing increasingly aware of Africa and its indigenous cultures and values, black intellectuals began to question the assimilationist attitudes of the previous generations, who upheld the centrality of Europe in epistemological, literary, and cultural productions.

Senghor has defined "Negritude," a provocative term of resistance derived from overturning the derogatory French word *nègre* as "the cultural patrimony, the values and above all the spirit of Negro African civilization."[15] Here, the marked focus on the "Negro African civilization" has been understood as a comprehensive expression encompassing both African and international designations. In *The Negritude Movement*, Reiland Rabaka asks us to think about Negritude not exclusively as a continental African or a diasporan African movement, but rather as a political project that was Pan-African in nature. "Negritude is just as much a form of radical politics as it is a form of radical poetics," he writes, claiming that rather than focusing on the movement's attraction toward European aesthetic movements like surrealism or its affinity toward European anticapitalist thinkers such as Kant, Hegel, and Marx, Negritude should be understood within the African intellectual tradition.[16] According to Rabaka, if seen as emerging out of the writings of W. E. B. Du Bois, the New Negro Movement, and the Harlem Renaissance, all of which propagated the idea of black internationalism, the Negritude movement's focused criticism of racism and colonialism can be seen as a universal and international struggle. Moreover, the movement's literary objectives of deconstructing issues such as assimilation, creolization, and racialization through an anticolonial lens can be seen as means, methods, or modes that ultimately aim to destabilize French imperialism.

While Negritude and its iteration as such became more of a recognized movement following World War II, its foundational ideas of black liberation through black internationalism were already in circulation in the years contemporaneous to Menk's activities. While the issues of *Menk'* do not reveal a direct link between the black student groups of Paris and the Armenian ones, many of their pronouncements share similarly revolutionary gestures and underscore their shared proximity in the city's intellectual and artistic scene. The Parisian student newspaper *L'Etudiant Noir*, for instance, founded in 1934, called for the "end to the tribalization and clan feeling that were strong in the Latin Quarter" and, rather than seeing each other as students from Martinique, Guadeloupe, or Guinea, called for seeing each other as part of the same black race.[17] This internationalist drive to identify around race also gave precedence to culture as an area of cultivation necessary to precede any political revolution. The cultivation of a shared culture demanded black students ultimately reject Western imperialist values and look backward to the African heritage of their roots. Similarly, for the Menk generation, the need to gather as a dispersed, transnational collective required a realist outlook on their situation, which exposed the injustices of France's imperial project. Likewise believing in the priority of culture, and in their case the Western Armenian language, the Menk generation criticized the Eurocentric values of previous generations that they saw as a sign of assimilation within the Ottoman imperial project and its cultural alignment with France. Menk sought to rally dispersed Armenians together around a cultural identity built on the circumstances of their current situation consisting of expulsion, survival, and statelessness rather than the tribal divisions of their lost homeland. Furthermore, in prioritizing culture, they focused on developing a new literary voice, which could cultivate a sense of transnational identity for Western Armenian readers, ensured by the international circulation of the print medium.

From Elite Exiles to an Exiled Community

Before World War I, Paris was home, both permanent and temporary, to a small number of Armenians who had arrived there under privileged circumstances. The Parisian Armenian community consisted mostly of a wealthy merchant class and visiting students from Constantinople, most of whom returned home after completing their university studies. Among those Armenians who could not bear to leave France was Arshag Chobanian, a Francophile from Constantinople, who eventually settled in Paris in 1895. Chobanian soon established close contacts with leading French and European intellectuals and, in 1898, launched his celebrated periodical, *Anahid*, which (despite multiple publication breaks) lasted until 1949. As a result of his periodical's success and his social network, Chobanian came to be known as the father of the French Armenian intellectual community. During a 1938 event celebrating Chobanian's work, the lauded French author Georges Duhamel publicly announced, "M. Archag Tchobanian est depuis longtemps collaborateur au *Mercure de France*. C'est un grand lettré et il représente parmi nous l'un des plus illustres témoins de cette civilisation arménienne qui a souffert glorieusement et ne consent pas à périr" (Mr. Arshag Chobanian has been a longtime collaborator of *Mercure de France*. He is a man of letters and among us, he represents one of the most illustrious proofs of this Armenian civilization, which has suffered gloriously and refuses to perish).[18] To the prewar French intellectual community, Chobanian was the representative voice of a foreign culture from the East. While an Armenian-language chair at the *École spéciale des langues orientales* had been established in 1810 under Napoleon's rule,[19] Armenian history and literature did not gain interest among the French literati until the end of the nineteenth century, partly as a result of Chobanian's networking efforts. Chobanian, along with another writer originally from Constantinople named Minas Cheraz, concentrated his initial efforts on internationalizing the Armenian Question[20] by engaging French politicians to defend the rights of Armenians living in the Ottoman Empire and to pressure the Ottoman sultanate to enact reforms for the Armenian population living in the empire's eastern provinces. Alongside efforts such as the publication of Cheraz's French-language periodical, *L'Arménie*, to raise political awareness of the Armenians' plight, both writers organized initiatives to introduce Armenian culture and literature to their French contemporaries, with the main aim of showcasing Armenians as proprietors of an ancient civilization.

Even though these efforts were unsuccessful in securing international intervention in the Ottoman Empire, they contributed to an Armenophile movement in France. In 1916, pro-Armenian activists established a propaganda organization known as the Société France-Arménie, which was a section of the Amitiés Franco-Etrangères.[21] The members of the organization sought to cultivate a sympathetic perception of the Armenian people and to condemn the Turks and their allies for their crimes against the empire's minorities. In a tribute to the French participants in this endeavor, Chobanian profiled some of the prominent faces of the Armenophile movement in the 1927 *Annuaire Franco-Armenien*, in a piece titled "Friends of the Armenian Nation." He referred to the list of pro-Armenian European activists, which included Anatole France, Georges Clémenceau, Jean Jaurès, and Bertrand Bareilles, as "the noble children of civilized nations" and thanked them for their service to humanity.[22]

The Orientalist undertones of Chobanian's high regard for the French did not go unnoticed by the orphaned generation of writers, who arrived in Paris under very different conditions than had Chobanian. For these emergent authors, France's reputation as a great pillar of civilization carried no currency. Because they were refugees, their experience of the state's integrationist policies and discriminatory labor laws constantly affirmed their otherness and forestalled any sentiment of veneration or gratitude toward France. Although Chobanian's periodical, *Anahid*, offered space for the young postwar writers to make their literary debut, his Francophilia eventually became a target of the Menk generation's antagonistic stance against the writers of the previous generation, for whom French literature was celebrated as universal.

Nevertheless, Chobanian was integral to the formation of the new Armenian intellectual scene in Paris. His efforts had established a small community of Armenian intellectuals that received the post–World War I influx of exiled writers, editors, teachers, and other such public figures. Although the incoming group of intellectuals contained some former political leaders who had previously resided in the Balkans, the majority of the newcomers were from Constantinople, having arrived in France by way of Greece along with the orphans. By 1925, the Parisian Armenian community, which until then had not developed any particular national, political, or cultural agenda, was now composed of individuals who were eager to reorganize and reinstitute former political and cultural structures. They divided themselves along the traditional political party lines of the Social Democrat Hnchagian Party, the Armenian Revolutionary Federation (ARF), and the more recently formed Ramgavar Party, and built allegiances accordingly. Two of the diaspora parties, the Hnchagian and the Ramgavar, supported Soviet Armenia. While the Hnchagian Party, which adhered to Marxist socialism, supported the Soviet project for ideological reasons, the Ramgavar Party, a conservative party composed mostly of the bourgeois elite, believed in the Soviet project as a means of survival: a way of safeguarding the integrity of the homeland. In contrast, the ARF, a left-leaning socialist party, vehemently rejected the Sovietization of Armenia. Having been the dominant party of the short-lived republic, it opposed the idea that outside rule could serve Armenian interests. Exiled from Armenia by the Soviets in 1920, the party now tried to organize Armenians in dispersion by focusing its energies on community building. The reinstitution of the party system in France contributed to both the creation of a vibrant community life and an exceedingly polarized dynamic among community members. In addition to the political parties, Armenian exiles in France also founded new organizations such as the Union for Adult Orphans and multiple unions for compatriots, grouped around the various Armenian provinces of the former empire. In time, these social and political organizations began to produce newspapers and journals that represented their groups' interests and thus created a new realm of Armenian-language publications that situated Paris as a cultural, literary, and intellectual center.

In the postdispersion years, print culture played a central role in fashioning urban spaces into intellectual centers and facilitating the making of a transnational consciousness. In France, the newly formed organizations soon founded newspapers and journals, such as the weekly *Abakay* of the Ramgavar Party, the weekly *Nor Ergir* of the Hnchagian Party, the daily *Harach* of the ARF, and the journal *Ergunkʻ*,[23] the publication of the Union for Adult Orphans. Among these periodicals, *Harach* is the most significant representative source of the French Armenian community. In addition to having the widest distribution, the newspaper covered a broad range of topics. Apart from reporting daily news from Turkey, France, Soviet Armenia, and Armenian communities worldwide, *Haŕach* printed analytical articles on many of the pressing questions that occupied the minds of the exiled intellectuals and provided space for the serial publication of the short stories and novels of the new generation of writers.[24]

During the first decade of its publication, *Haŕach*, as Beledian states, "collect[ed] the entire history of the community" and provided a collage of information about that community it sought to represent.[25] From 1925 to about 1930, *Haŕach* filled a real void within the new refugee community of France by serving as a community center. In its pages, the newspaper's editorial office was often cited as a center for communication about matters ranging far beyond the paper's content. Readers were encouraged to contribute writing that documented descriptive information about the towns they had left behind and the customs of their particular regions. In each issue, they were offered the space of a column to search for lost relatives. They were also asked to respond to surveys that collected information about the demographics of the Armenian refugees in France. In such ways, *Haŕach* moved beyond the basic reporting function of a newspaper and acted as an interactive information source whose editors and contributors were well aware of their role in developing an archive of the dispersion of Armenians.

As a diverse media platform, *Haŕach* helped shape Paris into the literary center for dispersed Armenians. In France, the newspaper became the first public site of exchange among local writers, writers from other small intellectual centers of the diaspora, and Soviet Armenian writers in Yerevan, some of whom submitted articles under pseudonyms. Quickly building an international audience and modes of disseminating its papers globally, *Haŕach* offered exiled voices the semblance of institutional backing and validation of their public discourse. Compatriotic organizations, informal groupings of emergent writers, and organizations like the Union for Adult Orphans, Society of Armenian Writers, and Union of Bibliophile Armenians all sought to raise their voices in the print world. After *Haŕach*, specialized publications followed suit, and as their editorials suggest, they similarly envisioned a transnationally networked audience of Armenian readers.

The New Literati: Reclaiming Orphanhood
in Language and Literature

During these early years of social and political reorganization, as communities became increasingly aware of dispersion's expanse, intellectuals called for the scattered communities to form a united front around various issues concerning Armenians. As a result, the term "unity" began to gain currency in the press of the times. A 1921 *Abakay* editorial titled "Unity" bluntly asks, "To unite. But how? And around what?"[26] Here, the questions are politically framed: they refer to the Armenian Question and probe the implications of showcasing unity for the outside gaze of the international community. But more broadly speaking, the lure of unity was deceivingly promising for Armenians scattered around the world. The concept of unity gestured toward assembly, while at the same time it built an ambiguous expectation of shared interests. Dislocated Armenians from various Ottoman provinces were placed in a new proximity with one another and were asked, for the first time, to consider themselves as part of a singular unit. More dangerously, the calls for unity began to build a false assumption of homogeneity that reflected neither the cultural diversity of the survivors nor the incongruities among the host nations' integration policies. The objective of a united front, practically speaking, was unattainable for the remerging institutions that represented a heterogeneous population. Nevertheless, it remained the guiding ideology of collective survival in the aftermath of the genocide.

On the literary front, the notion of unity found resonance in the concerted efforts to forge new literati. In Paris, multiple groups emerged to gather writers around Armenian literature and the arts. Within this realm, unity was understood as an antidote to the problem of generation. The inaugural editorial of a literary journal published in 1924 states, "Tragic events, like strikes of an ax, cut up the years following the war. A generation was to reveal itself during this time. The dispersion is a second death, a moral and intellectual affliction. It is not an untimely alarm that we're sounding when we say that the new generation is living through a period that has an uncertain, dare we say mournful, end."[27] Published in Marseille by emerging writers Bedros Zaroyan and Zareh Vorpuni, who were acquaintances from their school years in Constantinople, the short-lived journal *Nor Hawadkʻ* (New Faith) framed its initiative with an alarmist attitude that recognized the impossibility of regeneration and continuity. Similarly, *Hay Kir* (Armenian Letters) commented on the problem of generation by claiming, "Our new generation is experiencing a terrible famine of national consciousness. It is neither a lie nor an exaggeration to say that whatever color we give this famine, it is more tragic than the massacre of the blade. It is the masterpiece of the dreadful crime that our history already once witnessed."[28] The comments above equate the physical loss of the parent generation to the loss of collective memory, resulting in the lack of national consciousness. Ultimately, the editorial defines dispersion as the masterpiece of the massacres—in other words, as a cultural genocide. Nevertheless, both journals ground a faint sense of optimism in the possibility of unification. Their editorials promise to give voice to the new generation by providing a space for the cultivation of their ideas and perspectives. In doing so, they underscore the task of gathering young writers around their journals as the primary function of their publications.

The problem of generation and the parallel drawn between the massacres and their later revivification in the form of cultural genocide call into question the very idea of youth. Indeed, for a period of about ten years, from 1914 to 1924, Armenian youth were nonexistent as a visible category. The geographic changes in demographics, the loss of human life and social infrastructure, and the shifting political paradigms that consecutively split and gathered the Armenian collective drastically disturbed any sense of continuity and history. The links that could join events together in a succession or allow for the transmission of traditions were broken, leaving black holes within what would later be narrativized as the story of a people. During this time, the idea of youth seemed to be temporarily lost. The concept of youth, which is charged with promise and potential, could not be integrated into the postgenocide experience of dispersed Armenians. In the physical sense, the surviving youth lived mostly in orphanages, refugee camps, or overcrowded apartment buildings in the Middle East, Europe, and the United States. Yet they did not play an active role in the consciousness of dispersed survivors. Since the majority of survivors were women and children, the absence of fathers and elders threatened the notion of generation itself. The survivors were not only geographically dispersed, but also internally dispersed as a collective, without a sense of inner order, age groupings, or continuity.

Not surprisingly, the literary clubs and journals borne out of these years of uncertainty present themselves as projects that seek to reclaim orphanhood, both as a state of being and as a national allegory. In other words, the journals appropriate orphanhood as a marker of unity and rebrand it as a position full of potential rather than of loss. "Long live the new generation! Especially the multitude we call orphans!"[29] exclaims a 1929 editorial of *Ergunk'* (Birthing), the publication of the Association of Adult Orphans, cofounded by Shavarsh Nartuni. By the late 1920s in Paris, emerging writers who had survived the genocide as young adults began to hold regular meetings and to forge a new literary community that branded itself a community of "orphaned writers."[30] Hart'kogh (Band of Light), a society for art and literature, and the Armenian Literary Club held weekly meetings every Thursday and Saturday night, respectively, to discuss works produced by both contemporary French Armenian writers and artists and those of the prewar generation. In these circles, certain figures rose to prominence as representative voices and eventually became the key actors of Menk. Notable among them were Nshan Beshigtash-lian, born in 1898 in Constantinople; Kevork Kegharkuni, born in 1900 in Constantinople; Nigoghos Sarafian, born in 1902 en route from Constantinople to Bulgaria; Puzant Topalian, born in 1902 in Aintab; Paylag Mikaelian, born in 1905 in Erzenka; Zareh Vorpuni, born in 1902 in Ordu; Shahan Shahnur, born in 1903 in Constantinople; Vazken Shushanian, born in Rodosto in 1903; and Shavarsh Nartuni, born in 1898 in Armash, near Constantinople. Having taken many different paths to survival, their lives converged when they launched a movement that sought refuge in language and literature.

Hrant Palouyan's *Zuart'nots'*, first published on January 1, 1929, was a product of the Hart'kogh meetings and was the first journal devoted to showcasing the literary works of the orphaned generation.[31] The journal's opening editorial concludes by saying, "And now, within this chaotic state, *Zuart'nots'* serves as a phase that will allow us to collect, to gather, and to organize."[32] The bimonthly journal, which provided a forum for discussions of all facets of cultural production, including art, architecture, music, literature, theory, and criticism, served only as a "phase," as its editorial indicates.[33] Less than three years after its launch, the journal came to a halt just after it announced the publication of the first issue of *Menkʻ*. Many of its contributors, including Sarafian, Beshigtashlian, Frenkian, Nartuni, and Vorpuni, migrated to *Menkʻ*, and thus *Zuartʻnotsʻ* served as a stepping-stone for a larger movement.

The Menk Movement

The October 1931 issue of *Zuartʻnotsʻ* ends with a review article introducing a new literary movement called Menk. The reviewer, A. Hagopian, a writer from the surviving generation, applauds the efforts at collaboration among young writers but likens the group to a jazz band, saying that each individual within it produces a different sound.[34] While the analogy suggests the promising potential of diversity, Hagopian uses it to emphasize the group's lack of a clear doctrine or platform. Using Menk's proposal for a "new literature"[35] as a point of departure, Hagopian stresses the impossibility of such an avant-garde endeavor for Armenians in the dispersion, both because of the lack of a territory or a nation-state and because of the initiating group's lack of cohesion. This latter assertion about the group's internal disunity masks a greater pessimism about the possibility of literature after the genocide, which stemmed from anxieties about the survival of the Armenian language in exile. In truth, Hagopian's generation was less concerned about the absence of solidarity among the young writers than about their insufficient training in and knowledge of the Armenian language. Furthermore, for Hagopian, Menk's attempt to situate itself within the greater literary traditions of the East and West was futile, since it involved a certain literary politics reserved only for territorially based national literatures.

Rejecting the skepticism of Hagopian's generation, the Menk writers embraced the concept of a linguistically bound and borderless literature. Following multiple informal meetings in the cafés of Châtelet, they published the first issue of *Menkʻ* on April 20, 1931, via the Arax printing house in Paris.[36] The sixty-four-page issue, which displays a variety of articles, poetry, short stories, journal entries, satirical pieces, and literature reviews, strives to carve out the parameters of a transnationally linked body of works produced in the Western Armenian language. Over the course of the next year, the group published four more issues, the latter two as a joint volume. Altogether, the collection amounted to 280 pages. While the first issue displays diversity of genre, there is a steady decline in poetry in subsequent publications. The final two issues contain no poetry at all, reinforcing the group's commitment to prose, a position that Menk members publicly advocated during the group's active years.

The inaugural issue opens with a manifesto-like announcement signed by the following fifteen writers: Nshan Beshigtashlian, Ghevont Meloyan, Hrach Sarkisian, Rafael Zartarian, Harutiwn Frenkian, Ostanig, Kevork Kegharkuni, Nigoghos Sarafian, Puzant Topalian, Paylag Mikaelian, Arsham Daderian, Zareh Vorpuni, Shahan Shahnur, Vazken Shushanian, and Shavarsh Nartuni.[37] Using the first-person pronoun "we," the announcement highlights the group's immediate and distant goals and claims, "By our very solidarity and cooperation, which will never infringe on the development of each of our individuality, to form a cohesion among young writers spread to all corners of the world, and by such, to facilitate the free development and flourishing of a new Armenian literature."[38] The emphasis on solidarity and cohesion echoes the mandate for unity expressed by the previous publications launched by the young, orphaned generation of writers. Yet here an equally substantial claim accompanies the expressions of gathering. The efforts of Menk privilege the individuality of each writer, rather than subordinating these individualities to a specific group ideology.

In fact, immediately following the announcement, the first article of the journal contains an editorial note at the bottom of the page that once again reinforces the individual writer's superiority. The note claims, "The thoughts expressed in this article are the sole responsibility of the author. This is also true for all other articles. The addition of this note did not seem unnecessary to us, since due to its position as the first article in the publication, it could have made way for a number of assumptions."[39] While this disclaimer seems a bit jarring following the call for solidarity that precedes it, the two claims are not entirely contradictory. The pluralistic notion of a collective was precisely the basis of Menk's transnational project. Rather than assuming uniformity in cultural production, Menk sought to gather young writers from around the world around the Western Armenian language to forge a new literary tradition that celebrated difference borne out of dispersion. In other words, the insistence on immediate group solidarity marked a requisite for Menk's long-term goals: the formation of a transnational community of writers and the establishment of a new Armenian literature. Even though many of the signatories were already published authors prior to the journal's publication, they thenceforth became bound to the group's legacy and were read through the framework of Menk's "new" literature.[40] The next sections highlight the group's theoretical platform for Western Armenian literature: a platform they cultivated by resolutely positioning themselves against the historical past and the previous generation and, thereby, around the idea of the new.

Between Explicit and Indexical Representation

For the Menk writers, the proposition for newness in literature required an ideological stance that consisted of writing the story of dispersion; writing in the exiled linguistic form, Western Armenian; and writing in the genre least developed by their predecessors, the novel. Through the novel, known as the "genre of time," they sought to understand the ruptured sense of time that the genocide and their dislocation had created. One aspect of their literary agenda called for a rejection of narrating the past. Their works of fiction are devoid of any explicit account of the genocide, raising questions about the artists' response in the wake of a catastrophe. Why would writers who had lived through the genocide refuse to write about their experience of an event that is often seen as an identity-defining moment for the larger collective? What does their refusal say about the intersection of historical trauma and aesthetics? And more specifically, how can we read the absence of the genocide in their fiction?

Chapters 2 and 3 will answer these questions through close readings of some of Menk's most important fictional works. In the meantime, it is important to note that since the Menk writers were the first generation to come to adulthood in dispersion (orphanages or refugee camps), critics often turned to their works with the expectation of finding representations of the traumatic events of massacre and deportations.[41] Yet in their critical pieces and their fiction, the writers remain resolutely committed to both theorizing and aestheticizing their experience in the aftermath of catastrophe, focusing on the crisis of survival in exile. In other words, they narrate the present. Their deliberate avoidance of the past can be understood within the framework of first-generation trauma theory (Caruth, Felman, Daub), which asserts that traumatic experience produces a temporal gap, causing a crisis of witnessing and thereby a crisis of self. Based on the Freudian concept of trauma and memory that emphasizes the necessity of re-creating through narrative recall of the experience, this model maintains that traumatic experience damages a person's sense of a coherent self by locking them in the futile act of trying to bring the trauma to language. In literary criticism, this results in the view that trauma is unrepresentable. Best articulated by Cathy Caruth in *Unclaimed Experiences*, this theory claims that trauma is locatable not in the original violent event, but rather in the individual's inability to cognitively assimilate the event in their consciousness. "The way it is precisely *not known* in the first instance," says Caruth, is what comes back to haunt the survivor later.[42] In other words, this theory argues that trauma is known only belatedly, through repetitive reenactments or flashbacks that speak to the mind's inability to otherwise represent the event: "The historical power of trauma is not just that the experience is repeated after its forgetting, but that it is only in and through its inherent forgetting that it is first experienced at all."[43]

The works of the "orphaned generation," though devoid of explicit memory of the catastrophic events of the past, characterize the crisis of survival in the aftermath of the genocide and address the paradox of representation inherent to the experience of catastrophe. The novels, in particular, are informed by notions of interrupted time, impossible testimony, and displaced loss that ultimately represent the catastrophe as a loss of patriarchy. For instance, the almost-autobiographical fictional narratives of Shahan Shahnur's *Nahanchĕ Aṙants' Erki* (The Retreat without Song) (1929), Zareh Vorpuni's *P'ortsĕ* (The Attempt) (1929), and Hrach Zartarian's *Mer Geankʻĕ* (Our Life) (1934) present the lives of male protagonists who are faced with the impossible task of replacing their lost fathers within the surviving family structure. Just as the characters' move toward fulfilling this task is always coupled with the inability to succeed, the narratives struggle between the need to claim the father as dead (and therefore lost) and the inability to place the loss in language (creating a hauntingly absent figure). Moreover, the central characters of these novels face chronic illness, impotence, unemployment, and depression, hinting at feelings of shame, guilt, and a crisis of witnessing related to both their survival and their inability to reinstate the family structure. Within a similarly gendered articulation of the catastrophe as the loss of patriarchy, the fictional narratives of Menk develop the literary trope of incest. Works like Zareh Vorpuni's "Vartsu Seneag" (Room for Rent) (1929), Nigoghos Sarafian's *Ishkhanuhin* (The Princess) (1934), and Shahan Shahnur's "'Buynuzlĕ'nerĕ" (The Cuckolds) (1932), told from the perspective of the brother, unquestioningly imply the brother's position of authority in their postpatriarchy setting. They treat incest as the figurative representation of the collapse of the social network that was in place prior to the rupture of 1915. The reconstitution of patriarchy presents itself as the imperative mandated by the absence of the father, yet as something that is impossible to achieve because of incest.

While these narratives of lost patriarchy and incest can be problematic if adopted as sources for national allegory, they make a case for representing the catastrophe indexically, via its aftermath. In Menk's literature, we find stories about survivors' belated experience of trauma, characterized by the antithetical desires to relive and to repress the past calamity, to speak the catastrophe and to recognize the inability to do so. In the critical writings, in contrast, questions about the representation of historical trauma go untreated. For these writers, the forging of a new transnational literary orientation did not encompass the development of a unique aesthetic to depict the historical catastrophe, nor did it raise ethical concerns about the intersection of beauty and trauma, in the vein of the discussions of aesthetics that followed the Jewish Holocaust.[44] In their fiction, their aestheticization of trauma does not recognize the realm of literature as analogous to testimony, but treats it, rather, as a place where the story of impossibility (of bearing witness) can be explored and inscribed. Testimony, here, speaks to the historical concept of witnessing, which, while relying on accounts of the outside witness, focuses equally on the "inside witness," whose narrative is used to reconstruct the historical archive of an event. Thus, the Menk writers' rejection of the past as a narrative strategy is in many ways a move against history. "Literature's task is not to write history," claims Shavarsh Nartuni, in his review of the Boston-based *Hayrenik' Monthly*. The literary journal ran serial segments under titles such as "Remembrances," "Memories of an Armenian Revolutionary," "Pages from a Recent Past," and "Lived Days." Through these short works of both fiction and nonfiction, the journal, affiliated with the ARF, sought to cultivate a nationalist narrative of return to the lost homeland.[45] Seeing this approach as nothing short of propaganda literature, Nartuni wrote, "*Hayrenik' Monthly*'s notion of literature is not guided by a forward-looking political world view, which is why the longing (nostalgie) for the world of the fatherland leads its writers and readers toward retreat from all revolutionary desires (défaitisme)."[46] Menk, therefore, framed its dismissal of the past not within the context of catastrophe, but rather as a progressive, modernist move that embraced the innovative potential of art.

Generational Antagonism

Menk's notion of new and radical literary production called not only for contemporaneous writing, but also for discontinuity from the Western Armenian literary tradition developed in Constantinople prior to World War I. The group's self-conscious break with pregenocide traditional ways of writing can indeed be read as a modernist move. But the adoption of the discontinuity model was not done simply "in the name of pure art," as a later critic, Vahé Oshagan, claims in categorizing the group as a failed attempt at modernism.[47] Rather, Menk's proclamation that the old literary traditions were dead was also informed by a political view that recognized the imbalance of power in the production of knowledge in the world. In other words, the confrontational stance against the writers of the previous generation was very much an Orientalist critique: the Menk writers accused the pregenocide intellectuals of showing a false closeness to the cultures of the West. They explicitly blamed the pregenocide writers for their present calamitous situation, believing that the earlier generation could have prevented their current crisis of identity if they had armed the orphaned generation with an awareness of a genuinely Armenian literary tradition. Instead, in their work, Shahnur argues, "one could find poor, miniature replicas of all kinds of literary manifestos taken from big nations."[48] For Menk, the previous generation's Eurocentrism was detrimental to any notion of survival for the Western Armenian tradition, because it had produced nothing original. Accordingly, it was in part to blame for the orphaned generation's crisis of literary identity in dispersion.

In a similarly accusatory tone, Nartuni wrote, "We will once again come forth in order to reveal the destitution of those writers, who came to Europe and sold us imitation Western goods. Our political failure is the result of a false literary orientation. It was our old literature, which came from Europe, that ruined our home. Now, we're in Europe, and every day, we see where those goods came from."[49] Nartuni's claim echoes Shahnur's accusation of a lack of authenticity. Here, however, Nartuni moves beyond culture to link the idea of national literary identity directly to political consequences. If we read the "ruined" sense of home as the historical calamity of 1915, the connection between literature and genocide is not made entirely clear. Repressed in this passing accusation is the orphaned generation's futile search for accountability. As noted in many oral history accounts, survivors' attempts to work through past trauma often lead them to turn blame inward, either onto themselves or on the community's political and intellectual leaders, asking, "How could we have let this happen?"[50] For the orphaned generation, this inquiry often led to a questioning of the pregenocide political leaders' choices, especially their cooperation with the Young Turk regime and their faith in the possibility of reform through diplomacy. From the postgenocide vantage point, the collaboration of the Armenian leaders—particularly the ones affiliated with the ARF—with the Young Turks during the 1908 constitutional reform was seen as evidence of credulity. Although most historians frame the ARF and Young Turk cooperation as a "cautious rapprochement,"[51] survivors wondered whether a more skeptical and cautious approach could have prepared the empire's Armenian population for their ultimate fate and whether that particular outcome could have been avoided altogether. The pregenocide leadership's confidence about reforms was rooted in a belief in forging a democratic process of change in the empire and the late-nineteenth-century rise in national consciousness among Armenians, both inspired by the French Revolution. Given that the majority of intellectuals of the pre-1915 generation in Constantinople were educated in Europe, Nartuni's comments could also refer to the import of the nationalist ideologies that gave shape to the various Eurocentric schools of literary production, such as Romanticism and realism. In the years immediately following the massacres and deportations, many of the surviving leaders, trained in these schools of thought, formed the governing body of the short-lived Armenian Republic (1918–20). Now expelled from Soviet Armenia, they were active participants in the process of reinstating the classical political institutions of the empire in dispersed communities. As an avant-garde movement, the Menk project strove to set itself apart from the community-building agenda of those individuals whom the Menk writers deemed failed figures. Conflating intellectuals and political leaders, as well as literature and politics, Nartuni's accusation presents antagonism to the previous generation as one of the foundational pillars of Menk, indicating that the disruption of prewar traditions is essentially what gave rise to the group's formation.

Regardless of the antagonism, or perhaps because of it, the generation of surviving writers was actively engaged with the work of Menk and published responses to the Menk project that incited an exchange between the two camps. This engagement offered the young writers a chance to more articulately voice their literary theory. Among their critics was Zabel Yesayan, who was most vocal in demanding a clear ideological platform. Yesayan, after fleeing arrest in Constantinople in 1915, took up residence in Paris, where she had been educated in the years prior to the war. By 1931, having visited the Soviet Armenian capital a few times, she had adopted a stance favoring Yerevan as the sole Armenian literary center.[52] Commenting on Menk's lack of an avant-garde group platform, she demands, "What is your position? What's your generation's manifesto? What 'newness' do you offer to the literary, intellectual world? What enables you to boldly call yourselves 'new'?"[53] Yesayan's cosmopolitan background and her new insistence on aligning Armenian literature with the Soviet East further complicated the generational confrontation by adding to it the question of literary belonging. According to Sarafian, this reaction was nothing new: "For twenty years, our country hasn't been able to understand which side it belongs to, east or west!"[54] While distinctly rejecting the Eurocentrism of the past, Menk sought to place its "new" transnational Armenian literature within its broader decentered view of world literature. The Menk writers rejected Soviet Armenia as the central node for their literary production, mainly because their commitment to a new brand of literary production was informed by their experience of exile, which they sought to write in their exilic language. Calling out Yesayan's gaze toward the Soviet project, Shahnur claimed, "We stand on the side of Turkish Armenians, community Armenians. We believe in Little Armenias."[55] For him, what defined Menk's platform was the group's commitment to representing dispersion. He refused to abide by Yesayan's limitation of the literary platform to artistic form and focused instead on content. He argued that their literature must encompass the realm of the social and therefore that it must narrate their migrant experiences at the margins of French culture. It was only through this mode of self-exploration, he believed, that the group would eventually develop its own aesthetic.

As part of Menk's concerted efforts to distance itself from the previous generation's Eurocentrism, Nartuni wrote, "What a great testament of the ignorance of our past writers, who thought of French literature as universal and instructed us as such. No, we want to learn the literature of all nations."[56] Their displaced and exilic condition emphasized the distance and alienation that existed between Armenians and the French and erased French literature's appeal as universal, creating a space for the literature that they produced from the peripheries of French culture. Their identification with cultures of the East aligned them not with the Soviet East, but rather with imperialist Europe's imagined Orient. They saw themselves as Europe's other, proudly claimed the "Asian" designation, and provided a harsh critique of Orientalist narratives of the East, particularly against French writers Claude Farrère and Pierre Loti. Moreover, they forged their literary identity through and against their displacement. They developed a literature that confronted the uneven cultural milieu engendered by their forced dislocation from East to West. While their fiction remained rooted in the immigrant experience, their critical writings recognized contemporary European trends in art. In their journal, in addition to reviewing contemporary Armenian-language publications, they reviewed the works of American writers like Sinclair Lewis, Ukrainian Marxist thinker David Riazanov, and French thinkers such as writer Georges Duhamel, philosopher Frédéric Paulhan, and psychoanalyst Charles Baudouin. Though clearly familiar with contemporary literary trends, Menk writers claimed to reject these influences on the form of their Armenian-language prose, framing their output as "resistance" writing,[57] free of European artistic tendencies. In this way, they resisted both the West and the Westward-looking Armenian literary tradition of the past generation as part of their literary platform.

The surviving generation of writers responded to being rejected by the orphaned writers with cynicism, mocking their platform as naive. Two camps emerged in response to the Menk writers' antagonism toward their elders: one that argued for the centrality of Soviet Armenia and another that argued for the centrality of Western Armenian traditions. Like Yesayan, critic Costan Zarian, an Eastern Armenian writer who moved to Constantinople in 1914 and published the short-lived literary journal *Mehean* along with colleagues Hagop Oshagan and Taniel Varujan, delivered a harsh criticism of Menk's call for a new, transnational literary orientation: "They ask whether Armenian literature is going to be national or international. So, in fact, what they say is that we are prepared to sing; yet we do not know if we should sing European operas or 'a violet beneath the tree.' Excuse me, but first allow yourselves to test your voices. Let us hear how high your register can reach, let us see whether your vocal chords are strong or agile, whether you can outreach the vastness of a large hall, and then we can discuss what it is that you will sing."[58] For Zarian, Armenians, who now lived as refugees and exiles in European centers, lacked the necessary familiarity with their immediate surroundings to speak from a truly transnational perspective.[59] Furthermore, he deemed the efforts obsolete, dismissing the possibility of the creation of a language community outside the Soviet Armenian Republic. In Zarian's vision, the Western

Armenian form of the language could not produce literature in a diasporic setting, since the language was no longer practiced in all facets of life.[60] Accordingly, he believed that Western Armenian writers must contribute to the process of forging a nation through literature by contributing to the standardization of a single linguistic form, that is, Eastern Armenian.

Hagop Oshagan framed his response to the orphaned generation differently. His dismissal was not of Western Armenian production in exile, but rather—and more severely—of the writers' claim to Armenianness. For Oshagan, the young writers grouped around the Menk project "have ceased to belong to our nation. That nation, which they have not known during their most formative years or they have known only through a horrific calamity." Oshagan took specific issue with Menk's refusal to align itself with the pre-1915 literary tradition. Menk's transnational gaze, its refusal to narrate the calamitous past, and its insistence on providing immigrant accounts of cross-cultural encounters rendered its works "new," as the authors themselves claimed, but outside the parameters of what qualified as Armenian: "For us, what they have given us is foreign."[61]

Toward Literary Transnationalism

Menk's literature, which resolutely narrates the present and therefore the genocide's belated trauma in the aftermath, was read by the surviving generation of writers and by later writers who came out of the Beirut school as works that encouraged forgetting and were deemed insufficient for engendering *genocide memory*. But as members of the group suggested in their journal and other publications, producing such memory was never Menk's aim. Rather, the group considered the forging of collectivity to be its primary objective. More specifically, the writers once again highlighted the idea of newness as the guiding principle for their objective. They wanted their proposed collective to be formed around a new memory constructed through literature, a collective memory of the *aftermath* experience, and, therefore, an *immigrant's memory*. In the early years of dispersion, in which survivor responses varied radically with regard to remembering or forgetting the past, the idea of gathering around a new transnational literature seemed a little premature, if not impossible. But for Menk, new literature was proposed as a means of repairing the damaged sense of "wholeness" that served as an obstacle to the collective conceptualization of the catastrophe. The trauma of the genocide and the physical dislocation of the population, which tore apart the community's social networks and destroyed the connections that held society in place, also eradicated its collectivity. In addressing their acknowledgment of this loss, the cosigners of the inaugural announcement of *Menk'* articulated their immediate goal in the following way: "By searching in each person inspirations, concerns and common traits of children belonging to the same people, to open the path, to search, and in time, to give shape to a general manifesto, which, while giving freedom to each individual, corresponds to the needs of the Armenian culture."[62] Grounded in the notion of "search," Menk's idea of postgenocide collective was compromising, flexible, and changeable. It was a pluralistic notion of community, seeking not to infringe on individual freedoms and meant to inspire collaboration. It was based on the conscious conflation of political and literary identities. It was, therefore, a move toward literary transnationalism that overrode the importance of continuity of tradition with contemporaneity of content. Menk's claims of discontinuity from the past meant turning its attention to the immigrant experience across dispersed communities.

The crisis of immigrant identity became one of the central concerns of Menk and formed the basis of its literary orientation toward a "new" literature. In this way, literature was given the dual testimonial function of recording the immigrant population's collective experience of scattering and inscribing the stateless language's vitality in exile. For Shahnur, this meant giving literature an inward gaze: a role of internal reflection that would begin a period of self-awareness. Defending the group's platform, he wrote, "I jump from a social issue to a national one, because for us today, at this moment of crisis, there need not exist anything aside from the preservation of the Armenian people. For us, words like 'pre-war bohemian' have no significance. Social issues, humanity, working class . . . these, before all else, mean . . . all eyes toward Armenians."[63] Even in the realm of literature, concerns regarding the physical, economic and cultural survival of the dispersed Armenian population had to take precedence over aesthetic questions, according to Shahnur. In fact, he gave the artist the central role of not only recording the experience of the genocide's aftermath, but also critically examining the political and aesthetic orientation of prewar traditions to forge a new collective memory of that experience.[64]

The group's commitment to recording the immigrant experience was coupled with a desire to chronicle its struggle with language vitality in dispersion. Consequently, on the aesthetic front, Menk imposed a single constraint on its authors' writing: to produce in the Western Armenian linguistic form. As a result, Western Armenian gained two new, somewhat contradictory, designations, as a marker of both the orphaned generation's crisis of forgetting and its crisis of belonging. On the one hand, Menk's work highlights the threat of linguistic assimilation by representing the survivors' quest against the forgetting of their mother tongue. On the other hand, their literature testifies to the potential of writing in an exilic language in dispersion and marks Western Armenian as a symbolic, transnational territory.

Many of Menk's fictional or poetic narratives depict their generation's anxieties about loss of language. Nartuni's "Longing for the Armenian Language" consists of diary entries that document the narrator's struggles with lack of practice in his native tongue. Lamenting, he exclaims, "And, like an abandoned instrument, my Armenian has contracted to the corners of my mind. Like boiled bones, white and bare, my words have turned to chalk. I slam them, one against the other, hoping to find their sound. Alas, it's in vain."[65] The remaining entries record the narrator's efforts to bring his native tongue to life: daily self-imposed language exercises, anxiety-ridden dreams of speaking in Armenian, and a search for speakers in the streets of Paris. Similarly, Shahan Shuhnur's protagonist in *Nahanchě Aṙantsʿ Erki* (The Retreat without Song) struggles to revitalize his mother tongue to no avail. At the end of the novel, the protagonist, Bedros turned Pierre, struggles to remember the words of the Lord's Prayer in Armenian as he grieves over the dead body of his French girlfriend, Nenette. In the novel's final chilling lines, the long narrative about an orphaned survivor's process of assimilation into French culture finds resolution in linguistic concession. Displayed on the novel's final page are the repeated broken Armenian lines of the Lord's Prayer that Bedros cannot remember and cannot complete. They are followed by the French words of the prayer, which Nenette's child offers to Bedros to repeat and recite as a final act of retreat. In a slightly different approach, Sarafian also takes up the topic of language loss in his collection *Brom-ēt'ēagan* (Promethean) (1946). He devotes a poem to the surviving copy of his family's Haigazaian dictionary, a seminal work of classical Armenian published by three monks of the Mekhitarist Congregation on the island of San Lazzaro, Venice, in 1836. Meditating on the handwritten notes in the margins, the narrator wonders longingly about the many hands that have flipped through the pages of the book over the years and dwells on the figures of his dead father and brother. The physical book and the unused Armenian words it contains merge in the form of a relic, drawing the narrator near with its mystical charm and unlocking a chain of memories: "And my old memories, which carry the fallen dreams of history, of futility, dragged across many countries, give off an internal light amid this darkness."[66] Instead of focusing on the language's endangerment, Sarafian frames the exilic language as "magical," thereby highlighting its poetic potential. He endows the Armenian language with the capacity to safeguard the identity of Armenians in dispersion.

In general, Sarafian frames dispersion positively and celebrates the transnational literature it will enable for Armenians. He claims that a "pan-national spirit" has arisen as a consequence of World War I, owing to the forced encounter between cultures.[67] He is particularly interested in the *possibilities* that this intersection of cultures offers to national literatures. For Armenians, the intersection with new cultures refers to involuntary deportation and dislocation, of course. Although these events mark an occasion of great loss, Sarafian argues that they can also serve as an opportunity for innovative literary production. He writes, "This generation needs to acknowledge the exceptional fortune that the national misfortune gave them: emigration. What miracles can be accomplished through the conjoining of multiple communities within a main web!"[68]

Sarafian's call for Armenian writers to regard exile as a productive space,[69] one that could be conducive to the creation of art and the development of pan-national literature, presents us with a model of transnational literature that slightly predates the latest waves of globalization by which theories of transnationalism are legitimized. Perhaps Sarafian's "pan-national" can find a parallel in what Françoise Lionnet and Shu-mei Shih have called "minor transnationalism," recognizing the need to go beyond the binary model, which "presupposes that minorities necessarily and continuously engage with and against majority cultures in a vertical relationship of opposition or assimilation."[70] For Lionnet and Shih, the transnational space is a site of exchange, imbued with the potential to produce hybrid culture. In other words, culture is produced though processes of hybridization among networks of minoritized cultures, without the necessity of mediation from a center. While this model of minor transnationalism recognizes the obsoleteness of a center, here understood as the majority culture, Sarafian's call for a decentered, pan-national literature understands "center" as the nucleus of a diasporic space. Therefore, his plea for cross-border literary exchange refers to the forging of a horizontal network among various Armenian communities dispersed throughout different countries, thus making a diasporic center obsolete.

Even though Sarafian, from his Parisian locale, sought to explore intersections among Armenians, the French, and other immigrant groups, his desire to conjoin "multiple communities within a main web" referred mainly to the launch of an Armenian literary transnationalism. In literary theory, the category "transnational" has replaced the idea of the international to shift the focus of critical discourse from national powers to social, political, and cultural connections that transcend borders and geography. Literary transnationalism, therefore, often refers to movements that have permeable boundaries and reject the assimilationist and universalizing efforts of postnational border politics. In the case of Western Armenian, Menk's proposed literary transnationalism not only rejects the majority culture's centrality, but also refuses to recognize an Armenian national center. As such, conceptually, it reflects what social scientists such as James Clifford have called the lateral model of diaspora. The distinction between the lateral and vertical models of diaspora forms the basis of the main tension around which the field of transnational studies has developed over the past several decades. In early attempts at definition, diaspora was understood as forced or traumatic dispersion from place of origin, while later iterations approached it through a looser, broader understanding of dispersion. In the vertical, centered model, an ethnic minority is considered a diaspora insofar as it demonstrates a commitment to a homeland, real or imagined, and to other transnational communities that share the same connection. The lateral model recognizes ethnic minorities that are transnationally connected but not bound by a center, marking a clear distinction between dispersion and diaspora.

Within these models, Menk's project of gathering can be seen as the forging of a network of dispersion rather than of diaspora. With its decentered vision of literary production, it sought to suspend the narrative of return to a fixed place of origin, and thereby avoided the centrality of a mythical homeland. Yet it still aimed to inscribe what Avtar Brah has called a "homing desire."[71] In other words, what held together Menk's transnational network of literature was a desire to transform the writers' displaced locales into diasporic nodes of belonging. In exile, the writers of Menk tried to establish their "new" literature on a symbolic, transnational soil and turned to Western Armenian as a place of belonging. Sarafian writes, "It's necessary to create a spiritual homeland and think like an 'Armenian' in all these foreign countries, which have served as our source of despair and great opportunities at the same time."[72] Accordingly, literature functioned as a space that transcended the border politics of physical space and was marked by the potential to both construct an Armenian transnational identity and convert "foreign soil" into places of Armenianness. The establishment of a spiritual home through literature did not entail a return to the past or a revival of notions of cultural purity. Rather, the writers of Menk turned their focus to the present. For them, Armenianness came to mean the current Armenian immigrant condition.

Immigrant Memory

The group's literary identity was informed by the lack of political identity facing the refugees in France. Menk's pronounced emphasis on newness, as the guiding logic of their literary output, was in part a product of their generation's crisis of belonging, marked by the lack of naming and identification. In the absence of proper names for the historical catastrophe they had survived, the dispersion they were experiencing, and the civic status they held within the host society, their literature's thematic explorations documented the immigrant experience in France. Approximately sixty-five thousand Armenian immigrants entered France during the 1920s. Although most immigrants in France kept close ties with their country of origin, the Armenian immigrants had no nationality and presented themselves as orphans of the nation, in both the administrative and the literal senses. The prewar French Armenian community, which was created out of privilege, had given way to a community of forced exiles, who lacked a clear identity and sought a new definition.

For France, the naming of the Armenian refugees presented an administrative problem and launched a long-winded debate regarding identity cards. From the point of view of the French state, the "stateless" refugees needed to be categorized in relation to recognizable nations, and an Armenian nation simply did not correspond to such a classification. An independent Armenian Republic had existed for a short period from 1918 to 1920, but had just fallen short of receiving international recognition. At the end of the First World War, in 1920, a peace treaty known as the Treaty of Sèvres was signed by the Allied powers and the Ottoman Empire. The treaty, which aimed at a remedy for the recent collapse of the Ottoman government, sought to divide the Ottoman Empire among the victorious powers. Accordingly, Armenia was to be recognized as the Democratic Republic of Armenia, with borders that also included the region known as western Armenia.[73] Since the signing took place in the absence of an Ottoman parliament, which had closed down that very same year, Turkish nationalists rejected the terms of the treaty. At this time, having emerged victorious in wars against the Armenians, the Greeks, and the French, the Turkish National Movement had been gaining political recognition and soon developed international relations with the Soviet Union, forcing the nullification of the Treaty of Sèvres by the signing of a second treaty called the Treaty of Lausanne in 1923. As a result, the Republic of Turkey emerged as a new independent nation, claiming much of historic Armenia as its eastern borderlands. Concurrently with these losses to the west, Armenia was being invaded by the Red Army from the east, making way for the establishment of Soviet rule in eastern Armenia.

The issuing of identity cards raised the question of belonging for the Armenian immigrants, as well as for the state officials involved in dealing with the refugee problem in the administrative sense. The naming of stateless refugees posed a problem that created discord between the immigrants and their host country. On July 17, 1925, the French interior minister, in a circular[74] addressed to all governors in France, announced the nonexistence of the "nationalité arménienne." Since all Armenian provinces were now part of either the Soviet Union or Turkey, the prime minister proposed that Armenian immigrants be labeled either "Citoyens d'Union Sovietique d'origine arménienne" or "Turcs . . . [or] de nationalité turque, d'origine Arménienne." The minister further proposed that in the case that a refugee did not accept Soviet rule or could not provide an adequate Turkish passport, they should be labeled a "réfugié russe d'origine arménienne" or receive a document called the "certificat d'identité pour Arméniens de Turquie." These latter two categorizations would appear on an entirely different form of documents, known as the Nansen passports, which were internationally recognized identity cards first issued by the League of Nations to stateless refugees. Designed in 1922 by Fridtjof Nansen, by 1942 they were honored by governments in fifty-two countries and were the first refugee travel documents. Approximately 450,000 Nansen passports were issued overall, helping thousands of stateless people to immigrate to countries that would have them. Although Nansen himself was a fervent advocate of solving the Armenian refugee problem, the League of Nations eventually refused to include Armenians in the eligible category for receipt of the Nansen passport.

During the debates regarding the terminology used on travel documents and identity cards, Armenian immigrants in France voiced their discontent with the label given to categorize them. Many outright rejected the documents, creating dramatic scenes in police stations all over France. Exiled from a place that no longer existed and belonging to a people that had no nation-state, the Armenian refugees in France proposed that they be recognized according to their ethnic origins. They proposed the omission of prefixes such as "Turc" and "De nationalité turque" and wanted to be labeled simply as "D'origine arménienne." In a *Harach* editorial, Shavarsh Misakian reports on the various incidents of protest against the terminology of the identity cards and voiced the community's discontent by saying, "We are not Turks! We have our own particular name. Having been defeated or being weak does not justify the forgetting of our origins, along with a number of other historical rights."[75] The expression "We are not Turks!" weighs heavy on the page. It is not simply a correction of a false identification, but rather a refusal to be identified as the perpetrators of their genocide, the consequences of which have forced them to become homeless. Aside from rejecting Turkishness, the proclamation reads almost like an accusation, aimed not at the Turks themselves, but at the international community that is unable to recognize the reasons for the Armenians' forced exile. Five months after talks about the proposed "D'origine Arménienne" label, Harach's front page reported the news of its acceptance by the French government, citing a leaked source.[76] The announcement was made prematurely, for the decision never went into effect. In 1927, the League of Nations exempted Armenians from qualifying for the Nansen passport, and, as a result, France could issue only identity cards that assigned valid, internationally recognized states to the refugees.

By the late 1920s, all signs of the debate regarding identity cards had disappeared from the front pages of the French Armenian newspapers. At this point, the community seemed to be trying to come to terms with its refugee status. In 1928, Levon Chormisian began to publish a series of articles titled "Exile and the Armenians" that demonstrates the community's attempt at theorizing its condition. Chormisian concludes the first essay in his series by saying, "To have a homeland, but no home. . . . To love your country, but to be an exile. . . . Here is the soul's suffering that each one of us possesses."[77] "Homeland" in Chormisian's passage refers to the Soviet Armenian landscape, which becomes incorporated into the exile's imagination as a place of possible return. Yet this possibility could not settle the feeling of homelessness for the refugee, whose "home" remained within the borders of Turkey. At the same time, in these early years of dispersion, the Soviet Armenian government made no attempts to facilitate the repatriation of Armenian refugees within its republic, making the host country the exile's only haven. And thus, paradoxically, through the process of being administratively accepted into the country of the new Other, the Armenian refugees had to find language that claimed their "otherness." In a sense, then, for Armenians in France, the process of legal assimilation became a process of coming to terms with nonbelongingness.

The Limits of Menk's Attempt

In a 1978 interview published in *Pakin*, Zareh Vorpuni remembers with distaste the humiliating process of publishing his first book in 1931, during the early days of dispersion and in the absence of legitimate publishing houses. He recounts the unwritten protocol by which young writers mailed a copy of their book to prominent wealthy leaders of the community in order to receive a monetary gift in return. He recalls his discomfort with this exchange and his inability to welcome the compensation, seeing his actions as a form of begging. For Vorpuni, the missing institutional support hints at something beyond the displaced community's lack of resources: the lack of appreciation for the arts and the homelessness of Armenian-language literature in the postgenocide configuration of Armenian society. He follows his narrative with an anecdotal account of a conversation he shared with Shahnur, who similarly complained about book sales. One day, on their way to Montparnasse, as they cut through the gardens of Luxembourg, Shahnur suggested gathering all their books, burning them, and placing a plaque in the garden that read: "Here lies a literature that had no people."[78]

Addressing the lack of Western Armenian readership, Vorpuni and Shahnur's conversation demonstrates their acute awareness of the history of forgetting that followed the group's years of activity. When this group of orphaned youth emerged on the Parisian intellectual scene, embracing the "newness" of their exilic situation and proposing a new kind of cultural production that attested to that condition, not surprisingly, they were met with skepticism by the older generation of their contemporaries. In later years, as the genocide became politicized, another generation of readers greeted them with a new skepticism, one that entailed the accusation that Menk had not recorded the traumatic past and the story of the silent decade. Yet in the Menk generation's novels, it is within the silence regarding the past and the insistence on recounting the present that an indexical representation of the catastrophe is recorded as a revivified moment of the aftermath years.

As a group and as a periodical, *Menk'* did not last beyond 1933. When it dissolved, both its distant and its immediate goals were still unrealized.

While the journal's call for solidarity and cooperation as an immediately attainable objective did not reach as far as "all corners of the world," it did serve to bring together many of the prominent young Parisian writers of the time. Having shared locality and a desire to produce literature in the Armenian language as their sole common traits, the writers of Menk found it difficult to develop a sustainable group identity sufficient to continue functioning as a body. Krikor Beledian classifies their story of dissolution as an absent history, arguing that because the group did not leave behind official archives, we are forced to come to conclusions based on biased testimony that individual members of the group offered in later years.

What we are left with is an incoherent image of a group torn by irreconcilable tensions among its key members. The initial fissure seems to have occurred between the publication of the second and third issues of the journal. From one issue to the next, Sarafian, Shushanian, and Topalian handed over their editorial responsibilities to Shahnur, Beshigtashlian, and Frenkian, and Nartuni became increasingly absent. In a 1952 interview, Nartuni singles out Shushanian as the main cause of strife among the group, claiming that the writer, who often reacted passionately to discussions, was disliked in the community even prior to the group's formation.[79] In his biography of Shahan Shahnur, Krikor Chahinian notes Shushanian's reciprocal hatred of Nartuni.[80] Shahnur, who was in charge of editing the final two issues of the journal, is also often framed as a central node of conflict. In an interview published in 1986, Vorpuni claims that the journal "fell victim to individual fights," highlighting tensions between Shahnur and Nartuni and Sarafian's general dislike of Shahnur's work.[81] While the reasons for the personal hostilities remain unclear, it is also hard to assume that loyalties to differing political parties caused the conflict. Nartuni and Shushanian, after all, were both members of the ARF.

Bebo Simonian presumes that the main discord occurred around the publication of Shahnur's short story "'Buynuzlĕ'nerĕ" (The Cuckolds) in the third issue of the journal. The story presents incest as a form of revenge: a means of reversing the crime of the genocide. In it, volunteer soldiers in the Armenian Legion of the French Army during World War I come upon Turkish siblings working in a field in Cilicia and force them into sexual relations as the soldiers look on. Simonian contends that this story enraged not only members of the group like Shushanian, but also the general reading public, who deemed the story line an insult to Armenian values and called it "trash literature."[82]

In fact, the topics taken up by Menk writers in their fiction were often seen as too audacious. The themes of incest ("The Cuckolds," *Room for Rent, The Princess*), pornography (*The Retreat without Song*), nonmarital offspring (*Our Life*), suicide (*The Attempt*), and homoerotic desire (*Three Friends*) were not received well by the communities of Armenian readers in dispersion and were seen as an attack on conservative Armenian Christian values. Beyond the group's internal politics, therefore, the group's disbanding could also have been influenced by the lack of public support.

The outbreak of World War II, shortly after the group's breakup, facilitated the story of forgetting that surrounded Menk's legacy for decades to come. During the tumultuous decade that followed, the Parisian intellectual scene lost its status as a place of gathering and activity for the orphaned generation. Ohan Garo (1890–1933), Paylag Mikaelian (1905–36), and Vazken Shushanian (1903–41) died young of illnesses. Sema (1901–40) died fighting for the French at Flanders. Misak Manushian (1906–44) was executed by the Nazis for his involvement in the French Resistance. Lass, or Louisa, Aslanian (1906–44), one of the few female novelists at the time, disappeared in Auschwitz along with her husband. Shahan Shahnur retreated from Armenian community life and published French poetry with Gallimard Press under the pen name Armen Lubin. Kevork Kegharkuni moved to Bulgaria to head an Armenian-language school in Plovdiv. Nshan Beshigtashlian moved to Beirut and continued his writing career there. And while many others, like Vorpuni, Nartuni, and Sarafian, remained in France, most of their later works were published by printing houses in Beirut, which after the war gained prominence as the Armenian diaspora's intellectual and cultural center.

Menk's commitment to "Little Armenias" celebrated dispersion differently than did the later cultural narrative of the genocide, which cultivated the notion of victim diaspora to perpetuate the idea of return and build communities in the image of a nationalist project. In the following chapters, we shall see why the later cultural narrative, containing the idea of a unified future homeland as its foundational trope, excludes the literature of the Menk generation. Menk, which celebrated communities in dispersion, proposed a theory for transnational literature, refused to give a mimetic representation of genocide, and nevertheless offered a profound literature that aestheticized the experience of the catastrophe in its aftermath, did not survive the intellectual *center*'s move to the Middle East. I suggest that the disregard the Menk generation received as a viable model of literary production following World War II could have contributed to the long-term vitality of Western Armenian, currently recognized as "definitely endangered" within UNESCO's Atlas of World Languages. In an article penned on the genocide's one hundredth anniversary, contemporary French Armenian writer Krikor Beledian argues against framing Western Armenian's status as endangered. Rather, still recognizing the dwindling number of its speakers, readers, and writers, Beledian claims that the language remains intact, albeit "unpeopled," hauntingly echoing Shahnur and Vorpuni's projection.[83]

2

Interrupted Time

Patrimony of Absence and the Emergent Novel

"In time, poetry has surrendered to prose," writes Shahan Shahnur, in a *Harach* article called "Menkʻ." Defending the group's desire to develop a "platform" through literature, he claims, "Within literary genres, poetry and the novel should be placed at opposite ends of the spectrum, for poems have the least platform, whereas the novel has the greatest. The platform of the previous generation was poor or non-existent, because their novel was weak."[1] In asserting the novelistic genre's ideological capacity, Shahnur simultaneously underscores Menk's preference for prose over poetry and distances the group from the pre-1915 generation of Armenian writers, whom he accuses of failing to develop the genre. He believes that for the new generation of writers, the novel has taken precedence as a form of writing that, in its contemporary sense, requires its authors to take an ideological stance, which consists of writing the story of dispersion; writing in the exiled linguistic form, Western Armenian; and writing in the genre least developed by their predecessors, the novel.

Although most critics agree that the nineteenth-century Armenian novel was weak, it was a popular genre adopted by many writers as a means of spreading nationalism. Used in this way as an ideological platform, the Armenian novel of the nineteenth century grew out of a process that called for the democratization of Ottoman subjects. As in the West, its rise was inspired by notions of sympathy and sovereignty, what Debjani Ganguly calls the "discursive rubrics of the eighteenth century."[2] Congruent with efforts to modernize the Armenian language in both the Eastern and the Western forms, the development of the novel spread ideas of sovereignty

73

by inviting the readers to turn a spectatorial gaze on their shared suffering caused by existential angst, gender inequities, or state-sponsored injustices. The novels of Arpiar Arpiarian, Srpuhi Dusap, Hagop Baronian, Dikran Gamsaragan, and Krikor Zohrab broach the topic of the social by examining the laws and conventions that govern the private and public spaces that their Armenian subjects must navigate as they test the boundaries of community and belonging.

Marc Nichanian, in contrast, problematizes the very possibility of a pregenocide sovereign Armenian subject and argues that in the Western Armenian literary tradition, the genre of the novel properly belongs only to the postgenocide diaspora.[3] Proposing that the Armenian national liberation movement of the late nineteenth century be seen as a symptom of the impending disaster, he claims that the extended, synchronous notion of time, which is an inherent quality of the genre, had already lost meaning among Armenians of the Ottoman Empire during the decades preceding 1915.[4] He argues that the dread and premonition of death that the Armenian writers lived through during the late nineteenth century damaged their sense of durational time, and subsequently the concept of continuity inherent to the existence of a community. Calling to mind Benedict Anderson's discussions of time and nation formation, Nichanian claims that belonging to a collective is forged by this notion of ongoing time, wherein people build associations with the past and present, comprehend the "meanwhile," and envision possibilities for a continuing future. While he argues that the pre-1915 novel lacked an understanding of the concept of durational time that is inherent to the genre, he views the attempts of the post-1915 novel to represent the ruptured sense of time produced by genocide and dislocation as legitimate functions of the genre.

Indeed, at the heart of Menk's gravitation toward the "genre of time" was the authors' desire to address lost continuity and lost time. The group explicitly privileged prose as a stylistic tactic that accommodated its aesthetic and ideological needs.[5] Their novels, which they recognized as contributing to a new body of literature that belonged to the experience of dispersion, confront the notion of community. They often grappled with the Armenian exile's difficult dual socialization process in the public and private spheres: in the face of poverty and racism in the capitalist societies

of postwar Europe and in the face of loss within the surviving family structure. Turning to the novel, a genre that exemplified the modern sense of
temporality and nationhood, the young writers of Menk sought to record
the contradictions of fictionalizing the experience of community when it
was stripped of its markers of national belonging. The Parisian milieu that
provided the backdrop of their writing demanded a continuous confrontation with the loss of home and the subsequent encounter with a new
cultural and spatial Other. Their Armenian protagonists, feeling marginalized, gravitate toward their kin, only to face the realization that they
belong to a collective that is now dispersed transnationally. To capture
their new transnational belonging, the Menk writers chose to write exclusively in Western Armenian. Thus, written in a language that would never
again return to the place of its origin, the literature of the Menk group creates an imagined territory, defined by its simultaneous detachment from
and commitment to the specificities of its place and time of emergence.

During the interwar years, the generation of orphaned writers in
dispersion produced three emblematic novels that scholars often group
together. Beyond the proximity of their publication date, Shahan Shahnur's
Nahanchě Aṙants‘ Erki (The Retreat without Song) and Zareh Vorpuni's
P‘ortsě (The Attempt), both published in 1929, and Hrach Zartarian's *Mer
Geank‘ě* (Our Life), published in 1934, all address the confrontation with
loss through a patriarchal understanding of alienation and assimilation.
In other words, they narrate the genocide as a loss of patriarchy. In an
article that compares these three works, Krikor Beledian suggests that in
dispersion, the Armenian novel does not deal simply with the categories
of inside/outside when developing the theme of alienation.[6] According to
Beledian, the novel of the dispersion does not develop the idea of temporal
rupture caused by a break in genealogy distinct from the idea of spatial
rupture caused by dispersion. Instead, the two are conflated in the case of
Armenians living in the genocide's aftermath and in the novels that represent their experience. The break in genealogy and the break from home
result in family brokenness, complicating the inside/outside dichotomy.
Consequently, the orphaned male survivor in exile is left with three categories of "outside": the past Turkish Other, the host country's new Other,
and the inside, familial, Other.

While Beledian's categories of Othering conflate spatial and temporal ruptures, I argue that in Menk's novels, displacement (space) is subordinated to genealogy (time) when presenting the break in the concept of community. Even though the novels are set in the authors' contemporaneous French locale, they highlight the effects of dispersion by developing the trope of the absent father without explicitly narrating the story of loss that displaced Armenian families. Indeed, the genocide was gendered in its execution: men were targeted in round-ups and massacres, while women and children were deported via desert routes. So, contrary to expectation, these orphaned writers of 1915 do not describe the spatial rupture that occurred during the genocide. They are curiously silent, in other words, about what happened during the genocide. Rather, they represent the rupture implicitly, through a *temporal* reference concerning genealogy, by fictionalizing the broken family structure through the trope of the absent father in the genocide's aftermath.

It is through this explicit silence about and implicit confrontation with the past that French Armenian literature forges an understanding of time as discontinuous in the new context of the dispersion and represents the trauma of the genocide indexically. That is to say, Menk's prose literature locates the genocide's trauma in the aftermath of a survivor's experience. It is through the context of belatedness that their works, situated in Paris of the 1920s and '30s, point to the catastrophic experience of 1915 without explicitly narrating it. This indexical representation of trauma in literature gives voice to the experience of the catastrophe by addressing the two-fold paradox intrinsic in its definition: *the need to represent and mourn is coupled with the impossibility of representing and healing.* This framework I use to read the Menk generation's novels is informed by first-generation trauma theory's conceptualization of catastrophe as being experienced belatedly, in a different context than the original occurrence. It is this understanding of trauma as a continuous and belated confrontation with absence that plays out in the novels as the narratives' simultaneous confrontation with the *drive toward* and the *impossibility of* catastrophe's representation.

This chapter examines the strategic value that Menk writers attributed to the genre of the novel, which was thought to provide the largest platform for developing their understanding of diasporic time as interrupted by catastrophe's asynchronous nature described above. It is also precisely for this reason that the Menk generation's novels were excluded from the literary canon that emerged in the Middle East after World War II. The later literary canon would uphold a more explicit account of the genocide as a central marker of diasporic identity as expressed through literature. Here, rather than historicizing the genocide as an intelligible trauma sealed in the past, the Menk generation's novels represent the unsettling and often paralyzing experience of catastrophe. Rather than presenting a uniformly organized Armenian diaspora, their novels take place in unfixed communities of dispersion. I focus on Zareh Vorpuni's *P'ortsĕ* (The Attempt) (1929) and Hrach Zartarian's *Mer Geank'ĕ* (Our Life) (1934) to discuss the Menk generation's implicit representation of the genocide as a loss of patriarchy. These autobiographical novels present the lives of male protagonists who are faced with the impossible task of replacing their lost fathers within the surviving family structure. Just as the characters' attempts are always frustrated, the narratives struggle between the need to claim the father as dead (and therefore lost) and the inability to place that loss in language (creating a hauntingly absent figure). Through the figure of both the failed successor and the failed witness, these novels address the paradox of representation inherent to the experience of catastrophe.

Menk's literary archive is often overlooked as a viable response to the genocide because the Menk members did not seek to historicize the story of genocide and dispersion in a coherent, chronological fashion. The group is often criticized for failing to comply with the mandate to record eyewitness accounts. In 1932, for instance, Simon Vratsian claimed, "The new generation's main deficiency, their Original Sin if you will, is the danger of being cut off from the past. The past, present and future are linked together in a progenitive fashion: each time frame provides the other with a sense of continuity. It's impossible to understand today's realities without clearly recognizing the past."[7] This chapter makes a case for the value of their alternative approach, arguing that the aesthetic representation of genocide's trauma must be informed by notions of impossible testimony and interrupted time.

As discussed in chapter 1, Paris's influence as the stronghold for literary production in dispersion waned in the years following World War II. Only Shahnur's *Nahanchĕ Aṙants' Erki* remained popular after the Paris period; it was the only novel to be incorporated into the canon of Western Armenian literature instituted in the Middle East. Although I will address both the text of *Nahanchĕ* and its unique popularity in chapter 4, here my readings of the catastrophe's indexical representation will focus on *P'ortsĕ* and *Mer Geank'ĕ*. Both were the authors' first novels. They stand out in their preoccupation with the figure of the absent father, both within the narratives and in their paratextual dedications. In this way, they vividly exemplify the relationship between genocide's literary configuration as a loss of patriarchy and the novel's capacity to map out that loss as a temporal, genealogical break that defines the experience of dispersion. The Menk generation tries to reconcile the tragic loss of their fathers with the generative possibilities that the patriarchal order's demise in the Armenian way of life can enable, but later generations in the Middle East do not engage with the creative possibilities of this loss. In fact, they rely on and recultivate patriarchal notions of time to achieve their goal of instituting a national literature in exile.

Thus, loss and trauma, conceived through their belated iterations and the paradox of representation they call forth, are also embraced by the Menk generation as productive spaces that allowed for the development of the novel in the emergent post-1915 diaspora.[8] As discussed in chapter 1, these novels of dispersion, written in opposition to the pre-1915 generation's novelistic attempts, defy the eighteenth-century European novel's sentimental roots. While their autobiographical elements similarly attempt to combine fact with feeling, their invitation to the reader is not informed by eighteenth-century expositions on sympathy and spectatorship. In other words, they are not driven by the impetus to enable the witnessing of distant suffering. Can they be seen as serving a testimonial function if, having been written in Western Armenian, they speak only to a readership that has shared the experience of catastrophe? And if they do not seek to make the catastrophic experience of genocide legible, what can they tell us about the aesthetic limits of representing trauma? This chapter's discussion of *P'ortsĕ* and *Mer Geank'ĕ* seeks, on the one hand, to explain how the politically violent origins of dispersion informed the development of a new brand of literature. On the other hand, it shows how the eventual rejection of this new literature by the more organized diaspora of the post–World War II years points to a stateless culture's inevitable negotiations with dominant world literary paradigms. In many ways, it suggests that it is impossible for stateless literatures to elude international canonization and achieve literary autonomy by writing for an internal gaze. Ultimately, as I will discuss in later chapters, the dismissal of genocide's indexical representation and the embracing of mimetic representation intended for an external audience contributed to the decline of the novel in the Western Armenian language.

The Novel as Monument: Paratextual Dedications in *P'ortsĕ* and *Mer Geank'ĕ*

Zareh Vorpuni's *P'ortsĕ* and Hrach Zartarian's *Mer Geank'ĕ* are monuments erected in memory of lost fathers. Both authors mark the beginning of their first published novels with a dedication to their fathers who were killed in the genocide of 1915. Before launching their narratives and surrendering their authorial voices to their narrators, Vorpuni and Zartarian present their works as offerings to their deceased fathers. With the exception of the dedication, both authors avoid bringing to language the death of their fathers, and instead write their loss *through* absence. In other words, in an interesting opposition to their up-front recognition of lost fathers, neither author declares the father as dead within the fictional narrative. With this choice, they present the impossible struggle to replace the father as the central crisis of survival for postgenocide Armenians living in exile.[9] The contrast between the dedications' exclusive confrontation with the fathers' deaths and the novels' insistent avoidance of the topic demonstrates the authors' competing desires to remember and memorialize, on the one hand, and to forget the past, on the other. The contrast also parallels the surviving son's commitment to replacing the father, coupled with his inability to do so.[10]

Vorpuni devotes the opening page of the novel to the following dedication:

To you
My father . . . this first erection
of my mind and thoughts . . . as a grave
for your tombless bones,
and
a resting place
for your wandering soul.
                    Your son,
                    Z. M. Eoksuzian
                    (Vorpuni)

Vorpuni presents his first novel, his written word, as a site of memory. His father's lost body is left forever without a grave, leaving no trace that can serve as a marker of memory or a place for commemoration. Here, through the memory of the surviving son, language becomes a substitute resting place for the father. Further, much as the erection of a tomb transforms a dead body into a monument, the writing of the novel transforms the lost body into a literary construction. But although the novel has a physical representation in the form of a book, it belongs to the immaterial world of the imagination. Vorpuni's desire to hypostatize his father's "tombless bones" cannot find adequate fulfillment. Even in his material creation, the father's body cannot be recovered, and thus he exists only as a memory.

The novel's linguistic corporeality, however, serves as an offspring, a continuation of memory. The dedication is reminiscent of the epistolary genre in its form, offering a father-son frame through which it emphasizes continuity and preservation. At the beginning, with "to you, my father," Vorpuni addresses his father directly, both leaving readers out of the dedication and allowing them to witness the erection of the edifice, the novel. At the end, he subordinates his pen name, "Vorpuni," to his paternal last name, "Eoksuzian," which he spells out in the signature. More than an act of remembering the lost father, for Vorpuni, this dedication is an act of declaring himself a survivor. In his salutation, Vorpuni calls himself "your son" before spelling out his last name. He is the son, the carrier of a patriarchal lineage that was forcefully cut off. He is the son who survived that interruption and is here to claim his survival through writing. In this way, Vorpuni, like many other writers of the Menk generation, inadvertently inscribes Western Armenian literature as a patriarchal project, despite the more deconstructive critiques of patriarchal order that his fictional narratives offer.

Hrach Zartarian, in contrast, is more interested in revivifying his father's name than in claiming his own. Yet much like Vorpuni, he presents the novel as a monument dedicated to his father's memory. He writes:

> To Rupen Zartarian, my father . . .
> These pages, knelt down before his memory.
>   H.Z.

Rather than addressing his father, Zartarian directs his dedication to an unfamiliar reader. His implied first-person voice, which cannot declare itself with the pronoun "I," appears only in relation to his father, whom he claims with the possessive "my." Therefore, his inscription is addressed to the reader, whom he seeks to educate about his lineage. Zartarian first writes out his father's name, "Rupen Zartarian," and dispels any ambiguity regarding his relationship to that name by immediately adding "my father." In contrast to Vorpuni's dedication, where the author's full name is spelled out in conjunction with "your son," here the dedication does not emphasize progeny; it is the father's name that is fully spelled out and paired with "my father."[11] Zartarian further subordinates himself to his father by abbreviating his name as "H.Z." Although the novel is to serve as a site of memory or a symbolic grave for the lost father, it does not connote optimism about the future. In contrast to the "erection" of Vorpuni's edifice, the pages of Zartarian's novel are "knelt down" before the father's memory.

Whether through an emphasis on the surviving progeny or an accentuation of the lost father, both dedications attempt to recall the father in an effort to reinstate continuity. The dedications' difference in tone—one is triumphant and the other defeatist—does not persist in their fiction. Furthermore, the narrative of confrontation in the paratextual space of the dedications does not carry over into the novels, which remain silent about the past. Although the novels show autobiographical tendencies in describing the experience of the genocide's aftermath, neither author can narrate the father's death. Therefore, the lost father (of real life) is presented in his absence (in fiction), creating a literary absence that haunted an entire generation of survivors and became a recognizable trope in that generation's writing.[12]

Crisis of Responsibility in *P'ortsĕ*

Zareh Vorpuni began writing *P'ortsĕ* (The Attempt) at age nineteen, just ten years after the advent of the catastrophic years, which he survived along with his mother, brother, and sister. Published in 1929 in Marseille, *P'ortsĕ* was the author's first novel. It was intended as the first installment in a series that was to be called The Persecuted. Told from a first-person point of view and based on elements of Vorpuni's life, *P'ortsĕ* narrates the daily life of the eldest son of a family of genocide survivors living in Marseille during the 1920s. In the absence of his father, who perished in the genocide, the anonymous narrator[13] is expected to provide the family with income. Poor and starved, he throws himself into the city streets every morning with the task of finding a job. The port city occupies a central space in the novel, both as an escape from the demoralizing atmosphere of the family's apartment and as a place where the narrator's Armenian immigrant identity is tested against a multiethnic postwar French society. While the protagonist traverses the city with a strict purpose, his status as an outsider and a survivor prevents him from accomplishing the task at hand, ultimately stripping him of agency. His multiple failed attempts to find a job and assume financial responsibility for his family, along with one final failed attempt at suicide, give the novel its chilling title. In accounting for the crisis of responsibility that marks the surviving family's reconfigured dynamic in the absence of the father, *P'ortsĕ* locates the genocide's catastrophe in the aftermath experience. The novel represents the belated haunting of loss, loss of the father, and the unfair demands it makes on both survivors (individually) and the surviving family unit (the social construct that forms the organizing logic of the nation).

The opening scene takes place around the dinner table, with a representation of a broken family. The absence of a paternal figure underlies the scene, during which the narrator sets up the dynamic between the surviving family members. In light of this absence, the narrator, his mother, his sister, and his younger brother negotiate and adjust their positions in the family through a silent exchange of gazes. The absent father, though not mentioned, dictates the disrupted interfamilial relationships, for it is his paternal responsibility that awaits redistribution among his survivors. Speaking of the uncomfortable intersection of gazes across the almost bare dinner table, the narrator says, "None of us looked at each other's face. We sat with our heads hung low. The shame which we felt within our souls was beyond description. And when, by chance, our gaze met, each in the other's eye, mixed with a kind of grudge and hatred, it would search for the one responsible for this unfortunate situation."[14] The passage begins with a description of the family members' deliberate avoidance of one another, despite their physical proximity. It introduces the quest for responsibility as the central crisis that dictates the family members' affective response to each other: shame, grudges, and hatred are presented as the dominant feelings served at the dinner table.

Many theorists present shame as a feeling induced by the gaze of another.[15] Yet in *P'ortsĕ*, shame seems to be self-induced. It occurs in the presence of others, while each person looks inward. At this early point in the novel, the family's extreme poverty is the only contextual frame offered by the narrator that could substantiate their feelings of shame. The historical contexts of genocide and dispersion are alluded to in passing, but these allusions suggest that the family's poverty is the result of exile and link their shame to the abrupt reversal of their pre-1915 living conditions. If the state of poverty is the object of shame, or shame's external representation, then the family members' turn inward suggests a need to find responsibility for that "shameful existence" within themselves. It is, of course, a futile task, since the family's physical removal from their home during the deportation was a forced action executed systematically by an external, ethnic Other. Therefore, the internal search for responsibility takes the form of guilt, turning survival itself into a shameful act.

Ultimately, the crisis caused by the need to locate accountability produces a sense of *responsibility with no culprit* and induces feelings of guilt. Therefore, following the passage that describes the *self-motivated* search for a culprit within, the narrator turns the *family's gaze* inward and assumes the position of responsibility that he cannot fulfill. Vorpuni writes: "I was the eldest son of this orphaned, immigrant family. Therefore, my father's successor. The looks, incited by hunger, just like a snake waking up from a winter's sleep, would sometimes rise and be directed at me. Soaked in a heart-breaking plea, they would weigh upon my heart, and forgetting our situation's real, external reasons, the responsibility would come and sit on my shoulders."[16] The need to replace the father, in the hopes of repairing the damaged family structure, becomes a substitute for the imperative to identify the culpable party outside the self or, in this case, outside the family. This impossible imperative, which has produced feelings of shame and hatred, now takes the form of guilt. As traditionally understood, guilt refers to actions in the past. Here, it is a feeling produced in the present moment upon realizing the paradoxical bind of responsibility: the narrator must replace the father, but he cannot do so. In the passage, there is no explicit declaration of the father's death. Rather, the loss is implied in the proclamation that the family is "orphaned." "Orphaned" refers to the absence of the father, for the mother is present at the family table. This declaration not only affirms the patriarchal tradition that guided familial and community life prior to dispersion, but also avoids acknowledging that the father's death was a murder. Further, it distances the narrator from the absent father, since it is not he who is orphaned, but the family. As a result, the proclamation that he is his father's successor, which is subordinated to an ambiguous absence that evades responsibility, refers to an impossible, though necessary, task.

Due to post-1915 dislocation, the external, ethnic Other responsible for the family's current situation has no visible presence in France. Thus, the futile attempt to locate responsibility produces a series of affects that reveal the survivor's confrontation with the trauma of the past. In addition to the contradictory demand for responsibility, the narrator experiences a conflict of remembering. This paradox indexically represents the past trauma, which is defined by the simultaneous necessity and impossibility of confronting it. For the most part, the text avoids going backward in time to reveal the events of the narrator's past life with any specificity. Usually, the events of the past are implied or otherwise evident through the context, but they are not explicitly narrated. Descriptions of the narrator's present imply a past catastrophe as the origin of the current conditions. For example, the narrator describes his orphaned Armenian family, now living in France, and refers to other Armenians living in similar conditions, indirectly suggesting that a shared experience caused their dispersion.

Though we may attribute the novel's silence about the past to the author's conscious refusal to discuss the genocide, the language of his narrative at times betrays his defiance.[17] There are a few scattered moments of "opening" when the otherwise consistent avoidance of the past is weakened. The text displays momentary lapses of resistance, during which the past begins to surface to the level of language, only to immediately retreat back to either silence or ambiguity. In other words, the few instances of remembering always occur alongside a resistance to remembering. At the only point when the past is mentioned as a specific historical experience, the narrator presents the act of remembering as an excavation of the past. Here, he attempts to recover from the cause of his family's current conditions, for which he feels responsible. The following passage, which describes his work of memory, comes immediately after a discussion of self-degradation, within which he claims to be the object of his mother's hatred:

> Once my thoughts were seized by that complicated question, they would transform into a thousand and one roots and would begin to indiscriminately excavate the core of the issue, just as a mouse, upon receiving the scent of his food, begins to stubbornly gnaw at the worm that stands in his way. And just like that, my conclusions would emerge in the same way, slowly, like mushrooms, from this systematic process. I would take into consideration all qualifying conditions. The war, the horrible and inhumane massacre, the alienation, the spiritual and material impoverishment of mankind, his style of life, withdrawn, like that of a turtle in its shell, man's fear and contempt for his kind, his self-worship. And still, all of the seasons of human society's economic organization, where a man is to another nothing but a productive machine, a means for exploitation, each man concerned with securing his personal life.[18]

A series of alternating active and passive constructions runs through the passage and constitutes the act of remembering as a "systematic process."

Because feelings of incompetence and self-degradation initiate the process, the narrator's thoughts are presented as outside his control. He is "seized by that complicated question," which refers back to the problem of responsibility for his family. The narrator finds the distance between himself and his mental faculties enabling. His thoughts do the work of excavation that he is otherwise incapable of. Their work of digging into the past involves working though obstructions of memory, as the metaphor of the "gnawing" mouse demonstrates. The narrator, while detached from the work of excavation, embraces the objects it recovers. The product of this memory work is "mushrooms," which are proverbial for rapid growth and rapid decay. Much like the surfacing of these fruited bodies above ground level, the past quickly (and only momentarily) arrives at the level of language as the embodiment of a concealed memory that remains beneath the surface. The arrival is described as taking place on its own. Therefore, the work of memory consists of the passive acceptance of things that surface as the consequence of an otherwise uncontrolled but systematic process.

Upon this momentary recovery of the past, the narrator shifts his attention from the internal process of excavating (his thought's movement) to an external process of articulating what was found (his observation). This transition is marked by an assertion on behalf of the first-person "I," pointing out the only place in the passage where the narrator acts as the subject of the sentence. He states, "I would take into consideration all qualifying conditions." While he actively considers the possible reasons for his family's current situation, and consequently his inability to claim responsibility for repairing it, he presents the list of past events (the recovered memory) as something other than lived experience. He immediately forfeits the position of the "I" as subject to the events themselves, without specifying his relationship to them. The events in the list are referred to in reductive, general, and ambiguous language and do not warrant the process of excavation more tediously described above. In addition, the list of historical moments moves between universal and particular experiences of distress. For example, World War I is referred to as "the war," followed by "the horrible and inhumane massacre," which is particular to Armenians who lived in the Ottoman Empire. Without specifying his or his family's encounter with that experience, he proceeds to the next item, "alienation."[19] Although alienation is the result of the experience of dispersion particular to the Armenians, once again its precise significance remains ambiguous, since there is no mention of the word's relationship to the preceding phrase.

Alienation, in other words, is not presented as the consequence of the deportations that accompanied the massacre of Armenians. Though the following conditions listed in the series, like "fear" or "contempt," are loosely relevant to the experience of genocide particular to the Armenians, they are also general conditions of distress characteristic of the confrontation with modernity in the early part of the twentieth century. In fact, the conditions mentioned in the last sentence of the passage no longer refer to the "recovered" past of the narrator's memory, but rather describe his present condition. He prefaces the sentence with "and still," blurring the distinction between past events and present injustices, and in particular "society's economic organization, where man is to another nothing but a productive machine, a means of exploitation." Indeed, the narrative often digresses into a critique of labor in France, whose postwar industrial economy relies on immigrants for exploitative purposes. During a very brief interlude when the narrator is employed, he refers to his band of coworkers as "prisoners," mechanically painting parts for a transatlantic shipping company, and mocks the French manager who idly chaperones them.[20] The machine imagery, repeated elsewhere in the text, is not only a familiar trope used to describe the postindustrial or modern condition, but also indicates the narrator's postgenocide incapacity to reclaim his selfhood, which in his case is inherently tied to the demands of patriarchal order. His presentation of the loss of humanity as the core of his present condition reinforces his need for distance from past events and highlights his inability to remember and narrate the particularities of his own experience of the catastrophe, despite his desire to do so. Here, what we see in the catastrophe's representation is an understanding of trauma that is characterized by an impossible mourning, the limits of which are defined by the nature of the event and not by the adequacy of the survivor's response.[21]

In P'ortsĕ, then, the narrator is consciously confronting a past that is simply not retrievable. His crisis of responsibility takes the form of a series of unsuccessful attempts. The novel's title hints at the narrator's attempt to reinstate patriarchal order in the aftermath of the genocide. The task consists of claiming financial responsibility for his near-starving family and of securing genealogical continuity; in other words, it concerns work and sex. While recognizing the sense of inevitable failure that dominates both realms, the narrator incessantly moves toward a confrontation with these impossible tasks, marking the aftermath experience as an unavoidable contradiction, a paradox of being.

With regard to assuming financial responsibility for his family, the narrator's search for work is continuous but resigned. While we hear of his morning visits to multiple factories, the novel's narrative dwells on his wandering, whether down city sidewalks or through the imagined space of his daydreams. We find him staring longingly at sweet delicacies in bakery windows, roaming the marketplace, people-watching on park benches, and fantasizing about becoming a movie star. The one time he finds employment, he maintains it for less than a day: he faints, falls, and injures himself during his lunch break. The second "work" sequence takes him to the home of a movie director, to whom he makes an elaborate pitch to be hired as an actor. Neither the exploitative work of painting for a shipping company nor the fantasy narrative of acting in French films is presented as a sustainable form of employment. In both instances, flashes of his past as a student interrupt the narrative to remind him of his loss, the displacement of his present circumstances, and the impossibility of his task of reinstating patriarchy in dispersion.

Of his daily wanderings in search of work, the narrator says: "My senses had lost their capacity for feeling, my mind was deprived of its ability to command. Leaving in the morning and running to the factories and the docks had become instinctual. It seemed to me like that was my first obligation of the day that I was preconditioned for that march and its shamed return. It was like I was a machine, whose springs were wound in such a particular way that they would halt exactly at the doorstep of our home. And link-by-link, the chain of these days of misery would grow."[22] Stripped of feeling and the ability to command, he relies on instinct to guide him through his daily routine. The passive sentences present his losses (of mental and emotional capabilities) as happening *to* him, outside his control, yet somehow with his consent. The task in this passage is the fulfillment of his familial responsibility to find work, which signifies patriarchal succession. What produces the loss of senses and of command is the recognition of the succession's impossibility, which leads to the underwriting sense of consent that runs through the passage. The narrator knows he will not succeed, but he throws himself out into the streets anyway, going through the motions mechanically. The narrator, therefore, is not a victim with a pathological relationship to the lost object. He recognizes the loss of his father, which is what mandates his daily attempts to take his place by finding a job. But he also knows that it is a task that can never be accomplished, for the catastrophic loss entails the loss of the right[23] to mourn. The performativity he's involved in, therefore, is of unavoidable, impossible mourning.

In addition to assuming financial responsibility, the narrator feels responsible for securing the genealogical continuity of the family. The reinstitution of patriarchy inherent to this task requires the narrator to address the unequal gender and generational dynamic that is now present within the family structure. To claim the position of head of the family, he must reframe his relationships with his mother and sister, both of whom present a prohibition of coupling. If he takes on the position of the father, what roles must his mother and sister play if they cannot be paired off with him? The repressed frustration of this interdiction plays out in aggressive acts toward women he meets in the streets. On three separate occasions, the narrator sexually assaults women from similarly underprivileged socioeconomic backgrounds, and he rapes a homeless girl in the final sequence of the story. Along these lines, a triangle of jealousy emerges in the narrator's home. His sister's new romantic relationship with a neighbor drives him mad with jealousy and makes her happiness painful to watch. Around the same time, their younger brother also aggravates the narrator by bringing home stolen food, challenging the narrator's position as head of the family. What follows is an instance of conflation. The sister is momentarily revealed as an object of the narrator's repressed sexual desire. Upon hearing her singing, he claims that he hates her and instantly recalls the fish seller at the marketplace, who slapped him earlier in the day for his unwelcome sexual advances. The passage then oscillates between the soothing sound of his sister's voice and women he was attracted to during his wanderings that day. Lying in bed, he muses:

> How beautiful was the fish seller. She had trout-like sweet reddish lips. My mind once again turned to my sister's song. Her gentle and affectionate voice attracted me, rocked me, like a nap of sweet dreams. With my sister's song, the girl from the hair salon stood smiling in front of my eyes. Her cloaked body was milky white. My arms instinctively raised themselves toward the girl from Figaro. "Laura!"
>
> At night my body was tense . . . a tremor passed through my thighs and shook me, followed by some sort of laxness, which kept me asleep until morning.[24]

It is the sister's voice that allows him to recall the attractive yet equally unattainable women he has encountered throughout his day. Her singing voice penetrates the walls of their apartment and fills the solitude of the narrator's room, where he lies tensely on his bed. The final lines, which conclude the chapter, suggest an act of masturbation as a form of release. While his conflated desires find temporary resolution here, the life drive remains unfulfillable in the face of the mutually exclusive patriarchal mandates of financial responsibility and genealogical continuity.

Within this dual struggle for responsibility, the competition among the siblings is aggravated by the presence of the mother, who appears frail and on the verge of death throughout the novel. She is neither old nor ill, but suffers from hunger and the stress of survival. Toward the end of the novel, the mother suddenly dies, pushing the narrator to the edge of despair. This loss of the matriarch, which the narrator attributes to his own inability to provide for the family and which Beledian refers to as "matricide,"[25] further paralyzes his will to make attempts at life. He can no longer struggle with the crisis of his situation: the urge to succeed his father and his inability to do so. To pay for his mother's funeral, he decides to sell the collection of cherished books from his school years in Istanbul that he has been holding as a last resort. But this attempt fails as well. He is tricked and robbed by a group of prostitutes, who greet him outside the pawn shop and guide him to a restaurant with the promise of a good time in a hotel room somewhere. "I don't know how I went," he claims. "They took me by the hand." Passively, the narrator follows them, hands them his money, and fruitlessly awaits their return. After this final defeat, he flees his situation altogether, not with the intention of moving on, but in preparation for one final attempt: suicide. Death appears to be his only option, and it seems to take over from the inside. He explains, "A sense of poisonous hopelessness had directed all my blood to my heart and it would try to choke me to death."[26] This poison is the loss of all hope, an absolute resignation. He runs mechanically through the streets of Marseille, without any control of his movements, giving himself up to the darkness of the night. Eventually, he catches a train to Paris.

The contradictory demand for responsibility, which defines his struggle with survival as the eldest son of the family, persists. Even in these final moments of acquiescence in *P'ortsě*, the narrator cannot break free from the interdiction of mourning. Although he abandons the series of attempts that gives the novel its title, his resignation to the absolute hopelessness described above is not left unchallenged. He evades responsibility and instead blames the unfair conditions of life. He claims, "Life, like the wheels of a car, would rotate around me. The same movement, the same indifference and negligence everywhere. The contented voices of people would wear on me. And this overall sense of indifference, as though directed at me, would point to my death sentence. . . . I was simply an animal lost in the corridors of life."[27] Whereas before his mother's death the narrator referred to *himself* as a wound machine that operated mechanically outside his control, here "life" is described as rotating mechanically, independent of his control. Life simply "happens" around him. This distancing allows the narrator to address critically everything this outside life contains. For the first time, the narrator adopts a condescending tone toward people in general. The "contented voices" of French society are presented as a source of exhaustion. This pronouncement marks a slight shift in his sense of responsibility, almost a splitting: people outside the family circle now share the blame owing to their indifference. The French, in particular, become culpable for their refusal to bear witness to the narrator's pain.

Yet as in the earlier instances of locating responsibility, the French are inadequate substitutes for the people responsible for the narrator's orphaned and displaced condition. As a result, their indifference becomes the source of his self-destruction when it is redirected toward him. This death warrant, as the final form of unclaimed responsibility, leads the narrator to his final attempt: suicide. Whereas the earlier efforts at assuming responsibility had respectively produced feelings of shame, hate, and guilt, this last search, characterized by resignation and the sharing of responsibility with the French, produces feelings of exhaustion and a desire for death. Like all of the previous attempts, this final attempt fails. In the final passage of *P'ortsě*, the narrator, who has fled to Paris, stares into the waters of the Seine, unable to jump in:

> And suddenly, amidst all this, both dominating and stupendous, so unexpected, the apocalyptic mirage of my father, with my father's kind and serious face, in the radiant weave of the river's waves, which was now slowly turning to blood, as a symbol of the blood which once flowed through his veins.
>
>   And once again, this time with a more forceful strike, life shattered my will.[28]

The sudden appearance of his father's face prevents the narrator from committing suicide. Though momentary, this clear vision is a tangible recollection and does not suffer from the conflict of remembering discussed earlier. The narrator refers to it as a mirage that appears outside his control. Yet in the context of this distancing (with which the reader is all too familiar at this point), the image represents a precise and explicit memory. In the water's reflection, the narrator can see his father's face in detail, looking both "kind" and "serious." This memory strengthens his drive to live. His claim that "life shattered my will" does not place life in opposition to the will, but rather expresses that in that moment, his will to live supersedes his will to die. The narrator here abandons figurative language. The river's flowing water is not simply likened to blood; it turns into blood. Blood, which generally symbolizes life, is presented specifically as the blood that once flowed through his father's veins. For the narrator, jumping into the water would mean locating death within the father, an ultimate recognition of loss. His rejection of the father's blood allows him to claim his life for himself by reviving the figure of the father as lost, rather than absent.

P'ortsĕ, which began with Vorpuni's paratextual recall of his father, ends with the narrative's reinstatement of patrimony in the form of life. The narrator then turns around, moves away from the shore, and walks into a foreign city. While the will to live overrides the death drive, the question of what postcatastrophe survival entails remains unanswered. The novel suggests that lost patriarchy is irretrievable. Moreover, the will to live comes at a price: abandonment. In the final scenes, the narrator recedes into Paris, having left his family, and by extension everything Armenian, behind in Marseille. Regardless of Paris's cosmopolitan makeup, his move into this city is a withdrawal from the mandates of his Armenian survivor's identity and a move toward assimilating into the host society. The novel suggests that the experience of dispersion cannot sustain the continuity of patriarchal tradition and that postgenocide survival often demands cultural retreat. Therefore, in reconfiguring the genocide as a loss of patriarchy, *P'ortsĕ* indexically represents the genocide's trauma as both located in the aftermath experience and consisting of impossible mourning and a paralyzed notion of responsibility for the male survivor, who must now reimagine his identity within the family unit.

For Vorpuni's contemporaries, this literary representation of postgenocide life was too bleak. They saw it as forgoing the opportunity to cultivate a sense of hopefulness among its readers, as other works of fiction could do. In the initial reviews, critics criticized the protagonist's narrative arc, chastising Vorpuni for developing a character who continues to make amoral choices in the face of hardships. A. Hagopian, for instance, listed the author's "pathological" tendency to linger on "life's ill-ridden aspects" as the novel's central weakness. Along the same lines, K. Fenerjian claimed, "Why Vorpuni has chosen to roll his unfortunate young protagonist around in moral degradation remains incomprehensible to us."[29] Ultimately, their criticism identified the novel's failure in Vorpuni's inability to exploit literature's constructive capacity and to recognize it as a space where the rupture caused by genocide could be repaired. In this way, the early critics dismissed the novel as an earnest but failed "attempt," oddly echoing the work's title.

Crisis of Witnessing in *Mer Geank'ě*

Over the few decades following the publication of *P'ortsě*, a cluster of novels published in France became recognized as the orphaned generation's unsuccessful attempts at prose. These novels were deemed too demoralizing to belong to the diaspora's literary canon, which had emerged in the Middle East and was being taught in schools there. The list included *P'ortsě*, Shahnur's *Nahanchě Aŕants' Erki* (The Retreat without Song), Zartarian's *Mer Geank'ě* (Our Life), Shushanian's *Amran Kisherner* (Summer Nights), and Sarafian's *Khariskhēn Heŕu* (Far from Anchor). Grouping these novels together, Alexander Topchian wrote that they reflected "the hopeless crisis of national retreat," a period that, according to him, ended in total concession to the powers of assimilation. What these novels shared, in fact, was an honest portrayal of life in displacement and in the aftermath of loss, without embellished narratives of hope and survival. Their representation of Armenians in dispersion, while difficult for many readers and critics to accept, confronted the irreparable nature of the genocide and subtly suggested that the disrupted sense of national time would never be repaired.

Of the novels listed above, Hrach Zartarian's *Mer Geank'ě* most closely resembles *P'ortsě*'s effort to represent the postgenocide sense of the rupture of time by reconfiguring the genocide as a loss of patriarchy. Although orphanhood and familial structure are once again central to the story, the novel's meditation on responsibility is not entirely grounded in the family's economic hardship. Rather, social hardships produce the struggle of survival for this group of Armenians living in exile in Paris. In other words, the obligation to take the absent father's place does not present itself in the form of financial responsibility, as it did for the narrator of *P'ortsě*. In *Mer Geank'ě*, the protagonist's task is to ensure his younger brother's upward social mobility to "the realm of the French!"[30] In this novel, the protagonist's particular struggle with fulfilling this responsibility introduces a literary discussion of witnessing that nuances the absent-father trope so familiar in the prose of Menk. Arsen, the narrator and protagonist, considers his own life wasted because of the displacement. He therefore sacrifices the remainder of his youth to secure a livelihood for his younger brother, Dertad, convincing him to abandon his habit of stealing, care for his neglected and sick former love interest, raise his unwanted child, and arrange a marriage for him. In these efforts to allow Dertad to live an ordinary French life, meaning a life unburdened by the genocide, he assumes the role of active witness to his brother's life and ultimately becomes a passive witness to his own. *Mer Geank'ĕ*, then, depicts the impossibility of mourning by exploring the survivor's simultaneous compulsion and failure to bear witness. I argue that the collapse of the witness in the aftermath of the genocide is linked to the survivor's inability to bear witness in the originary moment of trauma. In *Mer Geank'ĕ*, Arsen's struggles to claim the father as lost reveal the exile's crisis of witnessing and reinstate the impossibility of continuity. As with *P'ortsĕ*, the novel suggests that the genocide's aftermath experience is marked by the rupture of the preexisting patriarchal order that can no longer be repaired.

To establish his responsibility for his younger brother, Arsen acknowledges the absence of the father within the family structure. Much like the narrator of *P'ortsĕ*, however, Arsen has difficulty claiming the father as dead. In the opening pages of the novel, he delays the allusion to losing his father and instead presents the dynamic between the surviving family members: his mother, his younger brother, and himself. The novel begins with a discussion of his brother's habit of stealing precious metal from his employer, an Armenian jeweler. It also alludes to their mother's deep concern about her son's actions and the narrator's honest work as a tax preparer. Then, about fifteen pages in, the narrator suddenly interrupts to announce the father's absence and to briefly talk about the past. He writes, "Let me say immediately that my father is dead. Well, in reality, he is not dead. He has ceased to be a part of our family."[31] Hurriedly, as though unburdening himself of a difficult truth, Arsen says that his father is dead. The verbalization of this truth seems to be burdensome, for he immediately retracts his sentence. In fact, he claims the opposite with certainty. We are left to understand that his father is still alive, but simply no longer part of the family. In the pages following this dual declaration, Arsen makes the story of the missing father even more ambiguous, essentially privileging absence over loss.

The narrator's incongruent statements, which demonstrate the common difficulty that the orphaned generation of writers faced in bringing the father's death to language, are never resolved. Instead, he settles for an alternative somewhere between avoidance and confrontation. Arsen's inability to declare his father's death runs parallel to the declaration that he is a witness and therefore the bearer of the responsibility to replace him. This simultaneous avoidance-declaration shapes the novel's treatment of responsibility around a discussion of witnessing vis-à-vis the traumatic past. Arsen recounts his family's experience of the genocide in the following manner: "Only I have seen the horrible scenes of immense delirium and have become a friend to my mother and a father to my brother. At the time of the Great War, we lost my father during the deportation. My mother worked in an orphanage in Greece during the ceasefire. Along with my younger brother, all the other orphans used to call her 'mother' and went crazy over her. . . . It has been my mother's continuous dream that I become a great man. So many stories . . . I neither want to, nor feel the need to record them here. It became necessary for me to put my spectacles aside, to crumble many illusions, to resign from education and . . . to mingle with people, people, people."[32] After the statement "we lost my father during the deportation," his family's separation from the father is never mentioned again. But even here, Arsen avoids claiming absolute loss: he implies separation and disappearance without explicitly declaring murder or death. Most of the passage focuses on the shifting roles the surviving family members have had to take to compensate for the father's absence in the aftermath. For Arsen, the conditions of orphanhood and exile have forced him off the path to becoming a "great man." More precisely, the mandate to assume the role of his father has meant forgoing his education and career. In these lines, he links this mandate directly to his having been old enough to witness the catastrophe. Like the narrator of *P'ortsĕ*, Arsen must fulfill this role, knowing well that it is an impossible task. This paradoxical bind produces a semi-incestuous relationship with his mother, whom he continuously places on a pedestal. He never marries and continues to live with her as the "friend" he claims to be. Together they raise Dertad's "illegitimate" son, an act that ultimately severs their ties with him. Dertad, who according to Arsen was too young to witness or remember the "scenes of delirium," is free of responsibility and succeeds in making a new life for himself in France.

Through the contrasting characters of Arsen and Dertad, Zartarian's novel distinguishes between the responses of witness and nonwitness survivors. This distinction emphasizes the originary moment of violence and dismisses the possibility that the aftermath experience of exile and displacement may be a trauma that hinders the process of mourning. Instead, the initial forced departure from home gains singular significance: it is *the* catastrophe. During a moment of emotional breakdown, he recounts to his mother the path of persecution and exile: "Agn to Istanbul, Istanbul to Edrineh, Edrineh to Selanig, Selanig to Izmir, Izmir to Istanbul, Istanbul to the Caucasus, the Caucasus to Greece, Greece to France."[33] While this list is not new to his mother, who was in his company during the journey, it situates Arsen as the carrier of this memory, forever wounded as a result. "What am I?" he concludes. "A nameless idiot, a wretched itinerant."[34] Arsen, who has a conflicted relationship with his memories as a survivor, is fated for a life of impossible mourning. But as Robert Eaglestone reminds us, "The pathology of trauma is not the event itself or the distortion of the event in memory." Rather, building on Cathy Caruth's deconstructive approach to trauma, he argues that trauma lies in the structure of its experience and its reception. As mentioned before, for Caruth, "Trauma is not locatable in the simple violent or original event in an individual's past, but rather in the way that its very unassimilated nature—the way it was precisely *not known* in the first instance—returns to haunt the survivor later on."[35] Arsen, therefore, is haunted by his experience of the genocide in ways that his brother is not.

Regardless of Arsen's admitted entanglement with memories of a traumatic past that he has witnessed, *Mer Geank'ē* keeps silent about the details of his experience. With the exception of ambiguous statements like "horrible scenes of immense delirium," the novel remains committed to narrating Arsen's present. The exceptional, rare moments of remembrance occur immediately following an act of witnessing some aspect of Dertad's life. Confrontation with the past's trauma, therefore, is always mediated through an act of witnessing the present. For example, Arsen is present when Dertad breaks up with his French girlfriend, Elise, whose heartbreaking pleas call up a chain of past memories. Sitting in the doorway of his bedroom, Arsen silently follows the action taking place in the living room. Elise, obsessively in love with Dertad and pregnant with his child, has come to make a final appeal for Dertad's affection. He no longer desires her, however, and has moved on to pursuing the daughter of a wealthy Armenian, a development I will address later. Refusing to let go, Elise continuously modifies the terms of her conditions, finally asking for a mere prolongation of their friendship. While her pleas leave Dertad cold, the desperation of Elise's tone, as she begs to hold on to a relationship long lost, pierces Arsen's emotional shield. From his position of witnessing across the hallway, Arsen claims to have entered a new realm of emotional angst: "That was the highest point of shock, beyond which any event, no matter how tragic, would be unqualified to bring me the same profound agitation. I can say that it was in that very moment that the period of my emotional decadence began. . . . And yet my life has experienced so many colorful moments of crisis. . . . I have seen my mother's face." Right after declaring he has reached the pinnacle of emotional excitement induced by the pain in Elise's voice, Arsen begins to remember his own past pain. Beginning with a memory of his mother's face, Arsen recalls a series of painful memories of familial life prior to the rupture of 1915 and ends with an account of a few images from the deportation. He says, "Oh, what have I not seen during the deportation. So much roaring agony right at my feet, women throwing themselves into the water. . . . Ruined and deserted villages, in one corner of a cottage, I have seen a dead, forgotten little boy."[36] This brief passage is the only place in the novel where the narrator has an explicit memory of the years of massacre and deportation, or what I referred to earlier as the originary moment of trauma. This opening in the narrative that allows the past to intrude momentarily on the present is made possible by an act of witnessing another's pain. The fleeting encounter with the past, though necessary, never achieves a full return to the moment of the catastrophe, a moment that was lived but not integrated into consciousness. In *Mer Geankʻě*, Arsen becomes locked in acts of compulsive witnessing. They ultimately paralyze his progress in life, turning him into a passive witness to his own.

In Vorpuni's *Pʻortsě*, the physical survival of the already incomplete family unit is threatened by their extreme poverty in Marseille. In Zartarian's *Mer Geankʻě*, it is the process of social integration into French society that threatens Arsen's family in Paris. In the context of this threat, the task of fulfilling the father's role means ensuring the reproduction or continuity of the paternal order, in terms of both lineage and cultural heritage. Therefore, Arsen's preoccupation with making Dertad a reputable bachelor for the Armenian immigrant community requires certain negotiations with French culture. It is not preservation that Arsen seeks, but rather a compromise between old Armenian traditions, modified according to the conditions of dispersion, and French traditions, which are seen more generally as exemplary of a Western worldview. More specifically, this compromise translates into economic success coupled with an Armenian marriage.

The novel introduces the theme of stealing to symbolically distinguish between the two brothers' approach to integrating within a Western society. Stealing is presented as a particular form of assimilation into French society that Arsen deems threatening to the process of transference he seeks to protect. In *Mer Geank'ĕ*, stealing is continuously referred to as "taking." When the novel begins, Dertad has developed a habit of stealing small amounts of precious metal from his workplace. This pattern of behavior has become a major source of stress for both the mother and Arsen, throwing the latter into a mode of compulsive investigation and questioning in the hope of correction and repair. When confronted by Arsen, Dertad presents stealing as "the absolute order" that guides all struggles in the world. He insists that his brother fails to understand that in the modern world, all types of people, ranging from government officials to artists and from French to English, steal. By situating his actions in the context of Western capitalism, Dertad justifies them as wise and progressive. Although Arsen shares his brother's hopes of economic success, he is committed to achieving it through honest hard work. For Arsen, who has given up his hopes of becoming a "great man" for the sake of providing for the family, economic mobility is the ultimate attestation to survival and resistance, as long as it is based on effort and merit rather than charity and corruption.

Suspecting that his brother continues to steal while claiming not to, Arsen obsesses about finding proof, which he believes can be obtained through the act of witnessing. He explains:

My brother continued to *take*. How did I know? I had no proof. Yet for me, it was an absolute certainty. Not by means of assumptions or interpretative analysis, no. Having these types of certitudes would occur to me often. I would wake up in the morning, and without any reason, I would know that I was to see a certain someone on that particular day. It's extraordinary. One day, I am going to give my testimony, with interesting details, to a psychological or a metaphysical society. The proof is that one morning, I woke up, and I knew the truth. Nothing could change my conviction. What remained was for me to establish it. Here's yet another uncompromising demand that cannot be satisfied by mere conviction, without proof.[37]

Arsen knows, without any proof, that his brother is continuing to steal. This sense of instinctively knowing something to be true allows him the opportunity to discuss the problematic relationship between truth and evidence, which he will attempt to resolve by inserting himself into the equation as a witness. At the beginning of the passage, he claims to know "with absolute certainty" that his brother is stealing, equating that knowledge with fact. He denies that it is merely his opinion, since he has not arrived at it through "assumptions" or "interpretative analysis," thereby ruling out the process of deductive reasoning. As a result, his knowledge defies logic and therefore begs further justification. To provide additional validation for his conviction, Arsen declares that he has experienced multiple instances of this type of knowing—he claims to be clairvoyant. The desire to give testimony of his capacity for instinctual knowledge attests to his privileging of experience as an alternative to proof. Since he has experienced multiple occurrences of clairvoyance, he is a witness to the act. The giving of testimony turns him from an insider into an outside witness, one who can document an experience in the form of hard evidence. This idea of experience as evidence, mediated by an act of witnessing, resonates with this specific instance of Arsen's clairvoyance: he knows the truth about Dertad's stealing. He claims to have *known* upon waking up one morning but feels compelled to "establish" it as a truth that others can believe with the same certainty. Here, the verb "to establish" is used synonymously with the verb "to prove," limiting the definition of "truth" to something that must be proved or provable. Accordingly, Dertad's stealing, which

Arsen *knows* but has not *experienced*, requires an act of witnessing so that it can produce proof and thus be transformed into a "truth."

Arsen's compulsive witnessing not only fails to produce proof, but also fails to assert experience as evidence. Rather than reconciling truth and evidence by presenting experience as an alternative form of proof, his acts of witnessing complicate these categories. In the pages following the above-quoted passage, Arsen, hoping to resolve the problematic relationship between truth and evidence, stages a witnessing of his brother's stealing. Every evening, upon Dertad's return from work, Arsen listens for noises from his brother's room, which is adjacent to his. He becomes convinced that the noises he hears indicate that his brother is depositing stolen precious metal into a drawer. Obsessed with the idea of proving what he *knows* to be true, he begins climbing out the window and peeking through the window of his brother's room every night. Hoping to *experience* his brother's stealing as a spectator, he makes the trip out his window ten times, with no success. On the eleventh attempt, he trips and takes a two-story plunge. The resulting leg injury leaves him disabled for the rest of his life. Thus, the novel discusses the categories of truth, evidence, and the witness *literally* in the context of Dertad's stealing habit. Figuratively, Arsen's attempt to prove what he knows to be true presents "ownership of knowledge" as the crisis of witnessing for the postgenocide survivor. On the one hand, witnessing is a necessary act to prove something is true; it is a way of logically establishing an event. On the other hand, in the case of a catastrophe, the knowledge it places in the hands of its witness is debilitating, because it is knowledge that defies logic and thus cannot fit into the discourse of proof. Arsen's concurrent need and inability to witness Dertad stealing lead to his debilitating injury. Similarly, his need to confront the past he has witnessed and his inability to do so prevent him from reclaiming his "lost first youth." Ultimately, the memory of the traumatic past, as a form of knowledge that Arsen lives with, is the source of a paralysis that hinders his forward movement in France. In this case, "forward movement" refers to marriage and procreation, or, in other words, the ability to restore the disrupted patriarchal genealogy and order.

Through his inability to put an end to Dertad's stealing habit, Arsen reexperiences a collapse of witnessing.[38] The collapse in the original moment of trauma is caused by the witness's inability to do two things: first, as Dori Laub argues, to "step outside of the coercively totalitarian and dehumanizing frame of reference in which the event was taking place, and provide an independent frame of reference in which the event can be observed,"[39] and second to intervene on behalf of the victims. In the aftermath, the initial powerlessness to observe and intervene complicates the witness's inability to understand or prove the catastrophic scenes. This powerlessness translates into inaction in the present, causing a secondary collapse. Arsen, who is locked in a cycle of attempting to prove the unprovable through acts of compulsive witnessing, is performing the collapse of the witness. The physical injury he incurs during the fall is a metaphor for the incapacity of the witness-survivor and the stagnant life this inadequacy can engender.

After his fall and Dertad's marriage, Arsen lets go of his position as active witness in his brother's life and dwells on his physical and emotional disabilities. Rather than viewing them as conditions unique to himself or as conditions brought forth in the context of his immediate familial circle, he assigns injuries to all Armenians living in exile: "One's lungs, another's heart, another's uterus, another's kidneys, and everyone, everyone, everyone's nerves. Let all Armenians, without exception, go through physical examination. The doctor will drive all of them straight to the hospital, some for a short period of time, others indefinitely. . . . Plagued with all kinds of untimely illnesses, old age has designated a sixty-year-old's worn-out organs to a youth of twenty or thirty. Young, young, their hair falling out, their teeth rotted, their eyes dimmed, their hollow faces."[40] This passage follows Arsen's complaint about living in shame and being unable to look people in the eye. Here, self-criticism mingles with a critique of the collective. Arsen indiscriminately attributes an illness or a disability to all surviving Armenians. Although the illnesses he ascribes to them vary in their target body part (lungs, heart, uterus, kidney), the condition of sick "nerves," meaning psychological pathology, is common to all. As his tirade progresses, it becomes apparent that the illness he confidently metes out is comparable to his own disability, epitomized by his leg injury. Like him, his Armenian peers suffer from lost youth. He describes Armenian youth in their twenties and thirties as having emaciated bodies characteristic not only of elderly people, but also of those individuals who are impoverished of the will to live. With their hair fallen out, rotten teeth, dimmed eyes, and hollow faces, the survivors of Arsen's generation are presented as ghosts, occupying the space of the living without agency of their own.

Although the conditions of poverty characteristic of immigrant life contribute to physical emaciation, Arsen's portrayal of his generation's ghostly appearance also symbolizes the feelings of shame that accompany the collapse of witnessing. Just as the narrator of *P'ortsě* feels shame in the presence of his family owing to his inability to claim responsibility, Arsen feels shame in the presence of the French because he cannot act as an active witness. The term "active witness" is itself a paradox, hinting at the "collapse" that occurs when no action is taken. In truth, there can never be an active witness in the case of catastrophe. The traumatic nature of such an event cannot be fully understood by the witness, either in the moment or in retrospect. As an experience that defies logic and meaning making, the self-shattering scale of a catastrophic moment does not permit action in the form of intervention during the initial witnessing. Through acts of compulsive witnessing in the aftermath, the witness tries to reproduce the originary moment of inaction in order to correct it with action. Even retrospectively, since logic cannot be assigned to an experience of catastrophe, the originary moment remains incomprehensible and unsalvageable. The inability to move forward in the new life, symbolized by Arsen's physical injury, is a form of inaction in the present.

Essentially, what the survivor-witness cannot reconcile is the stark contrast between the space of the present and the space of the past trauma. The French, as inhabitants of the new space, are outsiders to the originary moment of the catastrophe. Their presence calls attention to the survivor's status as witness and provokes the secondary collapse of witnessing, producing disability and feelings of shame. Therefore, what Arsen perceives to be his failure as an active witness is also the source of the shame he feels in the presence of the French. To address the shame induced by the encounter with the French, *Mer Geank'ě* once again relies on the metaphor of stealing. As we saw earlier, the novel presents stealing as a form of integration that enables progress. Whereas Dertad's stealing allows him to economically integrate into French society, Arsen remains committed to honest work and does not achieve economic mobility. Nevertheless, for Arsen, living with the French as an equal implies stealing from them. When his mother refers to a rich ancestral past in an effort to motivate Arsen to become a "great man," Arsen bursts out in anger: "Our ancestors, you give our ancestors as an example. Our ancestors ate in fear, drank in fear, coupled in fear, gave birth in fear—it would have been better if they hadn't—worked in fear. For them, living had become like stealing. And I, too, as I now live, I think that I'm stealing. I think that I am not human. I am amazed when a *garçon* serves me. I think that the truth is going to surface and I will be disgraced."[41] Arsen links feelings of shame regarding life, or life in the presence of others (and specifically members of another ethnic group), to being Armenian. In claiming that inferior living is a condition of living as an Armenian, he implicitly recognizes historical circumstances as sources of his shame. His ancestors lived in fear because they were subordinate subjects of the Ottoman Empire. Much like them, Arsen, now living in a host country, feels that living is a right denied to him. Living, therefore, feels like stealing, which causes him shame. Immediately after recognizing his life as a life of stealing, Arsen degrades himself to "not human." He is amazed that waiters serve him in restaurants, for he believes they do not recognize his deception. The process of dehumanization that accompanies his self-regard not only produces shame, but also perpetuates fearful living: he is afraid he will be recognized by the French as less than human.

For Arsen, "living as stealing" is a hereditary condition, passed down by his Armenian ancestors. Thus, he negatively identifies with his own ethnic group, which was victimized on the basis of ethnicity. Further, having accepted and internalized inferiority, he negatively identifies with the host ethnic group, the French, since he cannot be their equal. This dual negative identification with Self and the Other (in the collective sense) parallels the collapse of witnessing both in the originary moment and later in the context of the host country. In other words, the collapse consists of the inability to bear witness both from the inside, surrounded by fellow members of the victim group, and belatedly from the outside, in the presence of the French.[42] For Arsen, active witnessing, in the form of intervention in his brother's life, results only in disability. Subsequently, he practices a form of passive witnessing, performed in the same compulsive manner as was the search for proof in the case of active witnessing. After Elise's death, Arsen and his mother decide to bring little Dertad to their home and raise him. The elder Dertad, who now has a son with his Armenian wife, disapproves and eventually severs all ties with his mother and brother. During the years that follow, Arsen and his mother develop a habit of watching the elder Dertad from a distance. They locate a window-front table on the second floor of a restaurant directly across from Dertad's workplace. They regularly sit at this table in the evening, waiting to get a glimpse of Dertad as he closes up the shop and heads home. The spying becomes a ritual of its own, performed in complete silence.

As an extension of this silent, passive witnessing of Dertad's life, Arsen becomes a passive witness of his own. His physical disability finds a figurative counterpart in the form of paralysis in life. The novel concludes with an overwhelming sense of disappointment: "I was always convinced that had things been this way or that, had this or that thing finished and the other started, I would reclaim my first youth. I was confident in this and didn't care that the days, full of events, were passing, passing. I would let them pass. I used to think that I had found a lifelong job that I had to stick to. In the meanwhile, aside from that job, whatever the days were filled with, however they passed, was not of concern. I would remain an indifferent spectator to it all. I was passing through a tunnel. Once I came to the open, under the sun, I was going to find my first youth."[43] At this point, Arsen has fully distanced himself from his own life and watches it as a "spectator." Rather than being presented as lived experiences, the various events that make up daily life are described as passing in front of him, outside his control. Yet he seems unable to let go of the idea of finding his lost, first, youth. The prospect of its rediscovery, though, comes as a pathetic excuse that reinforces his stagnancy. The temporary quality he assigns to his condition creates a sense of false hope that only fortifies his passive stance. The novel concludes with Arsen stuck in his "tunnel" in perpetuity, highlighting the alternative to the assimilationist path of his brother. The novel suggests that in both cases, the reinstitution of pregenocide patriarchal order remains impossible for the Armenian survivor, who must now reimagine the concept of family in dispersion.

In Zareh Vorpuni's *P'ortsĕ* and Hrach Zartarian's *Mer Geank'ĕ*, what is at stake in the crises of responsibility and witnessing is the prospect of continuity, which is threatened by the absence of the father and the pre-genocide laws of patrimony that his figure represented. The novels' protagonists struggle to cope with ruptures in continuity and to reconfigure their place in the family unit. French Armenian literature of the inter-war period is largely testimonial, and it relies heavily on the trope of the absent father. In the texts discussed in this chapter, this trope is developed through the problem of unclaimed responsibility and the collapse of wit-nessing. Its source lies in the break in continuity caused by the genocide. In other words, these novels reconfigure genocide as a loss of patriarchy by suggesting that patriarchal order could no longer be the organizing logic of the Armenian family and, by extension, the Armenian community in dispersion. The massacre of an entire generation of men and the deporta-tion of women and children engender certain patterns of dispersion and familial reconstruction. For young survivors, especially the ones who move to Western countries, the attempt to reconstruct an Armenian fam-ily requires pitting the pre-1915 patriarchal model of their society against other models that are often seen as forms of cultural assimilation. This necessary reconfiguration, aside from being a sociological issue inherent to processes of diaspora formation, presents itself as a philosophical issue that is intrinsically related to survival. As Marc Nichanian puts it, the Menk generation's novel is driven by the following question: "What does it mean to be a son in the diaspora, after the catastrophe?"[44] Most poignantly developed in the literature of Vorpuni, Zartarian, Shahnur, and Sarafian, this patriarchal formulation of the postcatastrophe experience was the by-product of the predominantly male intellectual scene of Paris. By using the literary trope of the absent father, the orphaned writers produced works that represent the genocide's trauma indexically, as experienced in their present. Rather than narrating the father's death, they narrate the pressures of his absence. More generally, rather than narrating the massa-cres and deportations, they narrate the aftermath. The authors' insistence on presenting patriarchy as irreparable and their refusal to make the story of genocide legible would serve as a reason for their exclusion from the diaspora's post–World War II nationalist literary canon.

Menk's novels, thus, are not diaspora novels. Rather, they are novels of dispersion. Written in an exilic language, they depict the breakdown of national categories in the aftermath of genocide. While their autobiographical elements gesture toward testimony, they are aimed at a readership that shares the authors' experience of dispersion. As I asked in the opening of this chapter: What, then, do they tell us about the aesthetic limits of representing trauma, when they deliberately evade the originary moment of catastrophe? Trauma studies' intersection with questions of literary representation is informed by the discussions of aesthetics that followed the Holocaust. From a psychoanalytic perspective, what is traumatic about the experience of genocide is the impossibility of integrating it into conscious thought, which results in an interdiction of mourning and hence of representation. Language, as a system of meaning making, cannot adequately represent an event that by its nature defies meaning. Others argue that the Holocaust and other instances of mass violence can be described just like any other historical event. Those scholars who take this position usually hold that narratives can have a testimonial function, especially when they are committed to facts. Others still, in the spirit of Theodor Adorno's 1949 famous claim about the barbarism of writing poetry after Auschwitz, find it unethical to render the horrors of the Holocaust beautiful and therefore pleasurable. They argue that doing so constitutes a betrayal of the victims of genocide. Informed by a psychoanalytic view of traumatic rupture, my reading of the Menk generation's novels shows the possibility of a postgenocide aesthetics maintained through indexical representation, as told through the context of belatedness. By reconfiguring the genocide as a loss of patriarchy and thus suggesting that diaspora time is interrupted time, Menk's novels depict the trauma inherent in the experience of surviving a catastrophe.

In *Unwanted Beauty*, Brett Kaplan makes a case for the necessity of aesthetic pleasure for the post-Holocaust mechanisms of survival and memorialization. Her dual interest in trauma's belated haunting in both surviving and future generations (what Marianne Hirsch has termed "post-memory")[45] and the importance of keeping historical traumas at the forefront of cultural consciousness suggests an interesting departure point for comparing the literary responses to the Armenian genocide and the Holocaust.[46] The Menk generation's novel insists on providing a testimony of the present in order to capture the trauma's belated haunting, which plays out through various interdictions of mourning. In writing the story of the aftermath, the Menk generation offered an implicit, indexical representation of the genocide's trauma. But their refusal to narrate the genocide explicitly did not comply with the demands of the post–World War II cultural narrative that emerged from the Middle East. The legal response of the international community and Germany to the Holocaust in the face of Turkey's historical amnesia politicized the question of genocide for Armenians, who began demanding recognition and reparations on various public platforms. Congruently, the increasing authority of survivor testimony in what Annette Wieviorka has called the "era of the witness" altered the function of the arts within this new political framework of the genocide.[47] Over the decades, literature and the arts were made to contribute to the development of the diaspora's cultural narrative by offering literal and testimonial representations of the catastrophic years as a means of providing proof and strengthening the genocide's archive. In this sense, both survival and memorialization were placed in service to the fight against denial, sealing the question of aesthetic pleasure under this political mandate.

The literature of interwar Paris serves as a repository of post-1915 literature that is not burdened by the politics of denial, and thus is free of what Nichanian would call the game of proving one's own destruction.[48] Here Nichanian refers to the destruction of an existential category, for engaging in the discourse of denial requires the victim to continuously reclaim a position of victimhood. The work of the Menk generation remains largely untranslated and inaccessible, for diaspora institutions have not reprinted or republished them. Yet they present us with an alternative archive for understanding the complexities of aesthetic representation in the aftermath of genocide. Their works situate the meaning of testimony within the complicated relationship of trauma, survival, speech, language, and memory, and ultimately guide us toward an understanding of catastrophe that is no less horrifying than any understanding we could reach through mimetic representation.

3

Lost Bodies

Incest and Postpatriarchy Configurations of the Nation

In the immediate aftermath of the genocide and its deportations, the daily newspapers that emerged in large refugee-center towns quickly took on the role of institutions, actively participating in and facilitating the reconstruction of social networks. In its early years, the Parisian daily *Haṙach* printed a "Search" column on its back page. Nestled among quotidian announcements about public events, newly established restaurants, inexpensive teas, and "reputable" doctors, the "Search" column serves as a reminder of the dim reality of refugee life. With this column, the newspaper provided a forum for its readers to search for missing relatives. The short narratives of the "Search" column are generally formulaic. The first half consists of information about the person being "sought" in the following order: name of town of origin, full name, name of father (and sometimes name of mother), and place and time last seen or heard from. Since many of the missing persons would have been young children at the time of the last known contact, the father's former profession is often given to aid recall. Next, the narrative gives information about the "searcher" (name, address, and often the relation to the one being sought). Invariably, the narrative ends with a request that reads, "We ask that newspapers abroad reproduce [this announcement]."[1]

What I have referred to as the "Search" column bears a title in the passive construction *gĕ pʻndṙui*, literally signifying "is being searched for," much like various types of "Wanted" ads. The ambiguity of this passive voice, aside from emanating a haunting tone, places emphasis on the sought, rather than the searcher, as an adequate English translation of the title, such as "Seeking," might highlight. Despite the subordination of the searcher's identity, the announcement has a dual function: it is both a call for kin and a declaration of survival. In her call for the missing, the caller announces herself as living. In this way, the "Search" column, which also appeared in other Armenian community newspapers at the time, illustrates the dispersion.

The dispersion was an experience not only of the physical scattering of a people, but of the loss of patriarchal order within which the family unit operated and the idea of the nation was constructed before the genocide. Isolated survivors needed to resituate themselves within a new social structure, now in the absence of father figures and of the paternal law that once dictated the limits of social relations, especially within the family. While this change may have liberating, imaginative possibilities from the perspective of both modernist and contemporary gender politics, with the backdrop of immense loss of life, it was seen as detrimental to collective survival. The massacres, particularly of an entire generation of males, and the forced dislocation of Ottoman Armenians had caused a collapse of the social network that held the members of society in place. As a microlevel representation of the larger system, the family also experienced a collapse that eliminated the marked distance that once existed between kinfolk. One result was that the relationships between generations (parents and children) and between siblings were radically restructured. In exploring the generative possibilities of their situation in the genocide's aftermath, Menk's orphaned generation of writers turned to the literary trope of incest, a recurring theme in their works.

As the "Search" columns of the 1920s newspapers indicate, during the decades following the genocide, Armenians in dispersion sought reunion with lost family members whose survival was uncertain. Owing to the passage of time since the initial separation, it was conceivable that siblings or other relatives could meet without recognition. For the generation of orphans, then, incest was a real-life possibility, however unlikely. Furthermore, with the collapse of the social order and the subsequent breakdown of familial and societal distance between members of the same group, the survivor stood before any fellow Armenian in a new proximity that evoked feelings of both familiarity and strangeness. Referring to the newfound strangeness among kin as a "perversion of human relations," Krikor Beledian examines the theme of incest in Sarafian's work to suggest that the genocide produces a process of internal othering, whereby Armenian survivors feel estranged from each other, and, thus, renders postgenocide desire "catastrophic."[2] In building on Beledian's notion of internal othering, my discussion of the incest trope shows how this unprecedented nearness among siblings was presented as being simultaneously attractive *and* repulsive, creating both a desire for the "same" (the Armenian who resembles the self) and a gravitation toward the new Western "Other."[3]

This chapter examines how the Menk writers portrayed these ambiguous feelings of familiarity and strangeness through the theme of incest. The gendered mode of the genocide placed the male authors of Menk in the position of being the "first generation" and solicited a literary response that examined gender roles within a new frame. Their narratives of incest, told from the perspective of brothers, unquestioningly imply the brother's position of authority in the postpatriarchy setting. The reconstitution of patriarchy presents itself as an imperative mandated by the absence of the father, yet it is impossible to achieve because of incest. In their fiction, the Menk writers explore the inevitably ambivalent, incestuous, and violent nature of postgenocide sexual desire. The idea of incest as a trope directly linked to genocide reaffirmed the Menk generation's commitment to representing the past trauma only indexically, through the narration of the present. Once again, the past event itself does not constitute the context or the site of genocide's trauma. Rather, the genocide's trauma is shown to be experienced belatedly, and located in postwar Paris. Consequently, their definition of catastrophe as an experience of belated trauma and their treatment of the incest trope as a symbolic reference to that experience of catastrophe contributed to the rejection of their works as viable forms of representing the genocide. When, following World War II, the political demand to narrate the past explicitly as a form of proof mandated that literature contribute to the making of a national discourse in exile, similar explorations of trauma's aesthetic limits were deemed either profane or inconsequential.

Zareh Vorpuni's short story "Vartsu Seneag" (Room for Rent) (1934) presents its protagonist's simultaneous attraction to his sister and to a Frenchwoman, creating a love triangle that was a familiar trope in the literature of this generation. Nigoghos Sarafian's novella *Ishkhanuhin* (The Princess) (1934), explores the possibility that siblings may romantically encounter each other without recognition. Whereas Vorpuni treats incest as a metaphor for the survivor's identity crisis in the face of a new Other, Sarafian emphasizes the corporeality of incest. In Sarafian's work, the collapse of the "nation" is displaced onto marked bodies that reveal their owners' identity only through sexual union. Shahan Shahnur treats incest in a radically different way. His short story "'Buynuzlě'nerě"[4] (The Cuckolds) (1932) presents incest as a form of revenge: a means of reversing the crime of genocide. Here, volunteer soldiers in the Armenian legion of the French Army come upon Turkish siblings working in a field in Cilicia and force them into sexual relations as the soldiers look on. In all three texts, incest is treated as a figurative representation of the collapse of the social network that was in place prior to the rupture of 1915.

In the first essay in the series Totem and Taboo, called "The Horror of Incest," Freud traces the dread of incest in what he calls "savage" tribes. His aims are the following: to define "totem"; to demonstrate that totem bonds are stronger than blood ties, for the prohibition of incest applies to members of same totem groups; to argue that the fear of incest is an infantile feature, for a child's first love object is incestuous and consequently forbidden and repressed; and, thus, to claim that the fear of incest bears a striking resemblance to the mental life of a neurotic patient. As a result, Freud views incest as an inherent fantasy turned into a universal taboo, the origins of which we may never know, since the "real reason" must belong to the unconscious realm.[5] In his 1912 magnum opus *The Incest Theme in Literature and Legend*, first presented at Freud's Psychological Wednesday Society meetings, Otto Rank examines how incest is treated in literary works, which he sees as products of individual psyches that should be analyzed in biographical terms. Tracing the theme from its first appearance in the works of Sophocles all the way to Ibsen, Rank follows Freud in noting the presence of the incest fantasy and sees literature as the space where the taboo surrounding incest is broken, allowing the fantasy to emerge into the open.[6] If we are to take from Freud and Rank the understanding of incest as an innate fantasy repressed over time to become a universal taboo, established in the service of protecting the sanctity of a family, a group, a tribe, or a people (in other words, as the precondition for culture), then it is worthwhile to ask whether the Menk writers' turn to the theme of incest was an attempt to reinforce the taboo in order to reaffirm the lost paternal law and order.

Post-Freudian critics approach the incest motif otherwise. Incest in Romantic literature is often interpreted either within a religious framework that suggests alarm at the breakdown of sexual morality or within a psychoanalytic, Oedipal framework wherein incest, like doubling, repetition, and revenge, enacts "a doomed oedipal struggle against the priority of the father over the son and of the past over the present and the future."[7] Incest in modernist and postmodern literature produces varied critical responses that move beyond the Christian collective body or the concept of family. Taking as her departure point the secularization of community, for example, Christina von Braun sees the nightmare-fantasy of incest as containing within it the fear of otherness, as exhibited in nineteenth-century anti-Semitic texts, and reads it as an indicator of the changing concept of the self through which Aryan racial theory was developed.[8] In a similar vein, the incest motif appears in American and Spanish American literature from the nineteenth century onward. Efraín Kristal argues that this motif may be seen as a fictional vehicle that explores the perceptions of shifting societies as they transition from hierarchical to more egalitarian models. He cites, for instance, many examples from early American novels that deal with incest and reads the motif as reflecting anxieties about European heritage in postindependence America.[9]

In Menk's writings, the theme of incest underscores the problem of generation that characterizes the genocide's temporal and spatial dimensions. In the absence of their fathers and in the face of their people's dispersion, the orphaned male survivors confront the questions of regeneration. Their anxieties around procreation, on the one hand, and anxieties around securing the continuation of culture, on the other, find literary representation in incest. Incestuous relationships, if understood as a universal taboo, should not produce progeny. Therefore, for many survivors, the genocide resulted in a problem of regeneration. As they saw it, gravitating toward the ethnic Same would result in incest and limit offspring, while gravitating toward the ethnic Other would endanger the continuation of Armenian culture because of the pressures of assimilation.

Despite the Menk writers' desire to move away from the imperatives of their fathers and explore their community's new anxieties of otherness, the Menk literature on incest revivified old social and cultural taboos, which in time forged new *literary* taboos. Writing openly about sex in general, and incest and homosexuality[10] in particular ultimately led to their rejection. This rejection solidified the emergent literary taboo that limited the future literary production of the diaspora. This taboo consisted of a new negative interdiction: the *not* writing of the past and the *not* preserving of pre-1915 traditions. The Menk writers have been criticized for not writing about their people's immediate past and for focusing too heavily on "non-Armenian" elements of their current reality. Hagop Oshagan, one of the few surviving literary figures from the pre-1915 era (the fathers' generation), summarized Menk's efforts thus: "As such, we should not see in Menk a reactionary stance, the forging of national identity, or efforts to create Armenian depth and thought, and we should not be taken in by the noise that would inevitably arise around that. Rather, we should view these boys in a truer light. They have ceased to belong to our nation.[11] That nation, which they have not known during their most formative years or they have known only through a horrific calamity."[12] After World War II, Armenian literature produced in the diaspora assumed the role of national preservation, relying on ideas of cultural purity. Oshagan's dismissal of Menk's literature is founded on this discourse of purity. Although the recurring appearance of incest has stigmatized the literature of Menk as a literature of taboos, and thus as "literature of the Other" or "literature of the non-Armenian," my earlier suggestion regarding the reaffirmation of paternal law derives from a different kind of reading. By conceptualizing the collapse of the pre-1915 Armenian social network through the breakdown of the family, the works of Vorpuni, Sarafian, and Shahnur represent the genocide indexically, via its aftermath. Ultimately, their efforts succeed in giving the experience of the catastrophe of genocide another name: incest.

The Armenian Sister in the Brother's Regime

The catastrophe that befell the Armenians of the Ottoman Empire at the turn of the twentieth century consisted of genocide and dispersion, and it occurred against the backdrop of the First World War. As a result, it has been classified as a phenomenon characteristic of modernity.[13] The postpatriarchal nature of the genocide in the Armenian context intersected with the postpatriarchal nature of the twentieth century in the modern context. Many psychoanalytic critics, such as Juliet Flower MacCannell, view the modern period as an era in which society was formed by the superego and dominated not by fathers or elders, but by sons. For MacCannell, the Enlightenment-era paradigm of replacing patriarchal order with the model of liberty, equality, and fraternity was designed to mask the substitution of the Oedipal order of traditional society with the more tyrannical regime of the brother.[14] Menk's representation of the genocide as a loss of patriarchy parallels the modernist gesture of reconfiguring patriarchy from the perspective of the son. If understood within the framework of the "regime of the brother," the formulation of the genocide as incest, as an extension of the loss of patriarchy trope, underscores two main shifts in the societal order that the orphaned writers of Menk fictionalized. First, the new regime entails the suppression of the sister, who replaces the mother as the primary Other that must be rejected for the brother to claim his "manhood." Second, taboos, like that of incest, have an expanded function that limits relations within the group at large. Therefore, in the case of the Armenians, the genocide, both as a catastrophe and as a *modern* phenomenon, is seen as destroying the father and patriarchy in the metaphorical as well as the practical sense. Consequently, the brother occupies his position of power both inevitably (as a progressive governor) and forcefully (as one deprived of any choice other than to replace the murdered father). The sister, then, becomes a figure of ambivalence: she is an Other that must be rejected for the survival of the regime and must be nurtured for the reinstitution of the lost patriarchy. Furthermore, the laws, prohibitions, and taboos that are necessary to maintaining order are no longer intergenerational, but intragenerational. The sister is no longer defined as a figure within the family structure, but rather as a figure within the larger group.

All young Armenian women become sisters and cannot be seen as love objects, causing a crisis for the brother's regime in dispersion.

In Menk's literary works, the orphaned Armenian male's conflicted representation of the figure of the sister is further complicated by the presence of the Frenchwoman. Zareh Vorpuni's short story "Vartsu Seneag"[15] (Room for Rent) explores the triangular dynamic between a "brother," a "sister," and a French prostitute. The story is a third-person narrative about Dikran, a young Armenian man living in solitude and working in a factory in Marseille. When the story begins, he is on his way to a rental office in search of a larger apartment to accommodate both himself and his sister, who is about to arrive from the orphanage where she has grown up. Overcome by both enthusiastic anticipation and anxiety about the task at hand, Dikran hurries to the rental office after work, hoping to get there before it closes. The crowded streets of the city threaten to distract him from his aim. As Dikran recalls overlapping images of his long-lost sister from both memory and photographs, a Frenchwoman he encounters functions as both a substitute for his sister and an obstacle to reuniting with her.

Throughout the story, much of Dikran's longing for his sister is driven by the dual quality of strangeness and familiarity that she represents. It is this ambivalence that allow Dikran to conflate his sister's smile with the smile of the stranger on the street, leading to a replacement of his yearning for his sister's love with the yearning for the affection of a Frenchwoman. To remember his sister, Dikran concentrates on a photograph she has recently sent:

> His field of vision was entirely captured by an absent face. He could see a head walking in front, her face turned toward him, and smiling, with sisterly, undying affection. That vision was a distant memory, derived from a family photograph, and successively come to dissolve into another photograph. An already mature girl clad in a simple orphanage uniform, underneath which protruded a chest, round with womanly agitation. Large eyes full of a sweet gaze revealed an obvious desire for life, although upon them was the stamp of a life lived in fear and conformity.
>
> Plump cheeks conveyed the presence of a natural pinkness, regardless the black and white of the photograph. Life had struck her head, her shoulders: they were turned in, upon themselves, like violets

blooming beneath the shade of thick, sun-blocking leaves. Regardless
of all these pressures, youth, through many sly paths, had managed to
arrive and settle in her chest and cheeks.[16]

This passage introduces Dikran's sister, whose conquering presence in
Dikran's field of vision is emphasized through her physical absence. The
recollection overlaps photographic images from various stages of the sister's life that reinforce the temporal and physical distance that has kept
them apart. The sister's smile that Dikran recalls in the streets of Marseille
is not from a memory of a real experience, but from a memory of a family photograph from a distant past—a time prior to 1915, when the family
existed. The passage then describes the image of the sister in an orphanage, suggesting the recollection of a newer photograph taken in the years
after 1915. A process of dissolution marks the shift from the family photograph to the newer photograph, leaving an ambiguity about the succession
of time as it is preserved in Dikran's memory. As a result, the memory of
Dikran's sister brings multiple pasts to the foreground of the short story's
narrative. The process of recollecting these pasts causes them to become
conflated, suggesting a parallel between the postgenocide collapse of order
and the temporal collapse in the mind of Dikran. The sister, as a memory,
is both near and far, both familiar and strange.

The sister is also recalled as both a child and a woman. As the remainder of the passage presents the image of the recently received photograph, the language oscillates between describing the sister as a deprived,
orphaned girl and a maturing young woman. A tone of brotherly recognition of maturity gives way to a more sexually charged language as Dikran
focuses on the womanly chest bulging underneath her uniform. The narrative's temporary abandonment of a sisterly image for a womanly one
distances her from Dikran and presents her as an object of desire, though
not without tension. She is both visibly oppressed, for she bears "the stamp
of a life lived in fear," and "full of desire for life." Dikran's ascription of
youthfulness to localized body parts like her chest and cheeks further
attests to her desirability.

Regardless of the attention paid to various body parts, it is the smile
on his sister's face that pierces Dikran and prompts the simultaneous

recollection of two photographs. What remains unclear is whether the smile, or what Roland Barthes would call the "punctum" of the photograph,[17] is evoked by the recognition of a similar smile in Dikran's real-world frame of vision. Although the narrator will later explicitly describe Dikran's recognition of a French woman's smile within the crowd walking in front of him, here the language appears intentionally ambiguous. Immediately following the recollection of the photograph, which highlights the womanly qualities of Dikran's sister, the narrative becomes self-reflexive: "In one word, she was a stranger who received the right to live in Dikran's soul, thanks to the other photograph of a small child—who had been his sister—and thanks to the reconstruction of the past with no return, evoked by the flood of memories now resurrected by her. Vartanuuush . . . It sufficed to simply utter her name. A simple movement of the lips, the hushed pronunciation of syllables—'hushed' so that those walking next to him would not know—and a subsequent vibration in his ears. An entire world awakened, relived, and filled the heart of the young man, whose life had suddenly gained new meaning and direction."[18] The "stranger" in the opening sentence of this passage may just as easily refer to the sister as to the French woman on the street. Through this ambiguity, the sentence hints at both. On the one hand, it appropriates the figure of the French woman as a nonstranger: it draws her near as someone who "received the right to live in Dikran's soul." On the other hand, it turns the adult sister into a stranger. It distances her by claiming acknowledgment of familiarity long lost: the "small child" in the family photograph "had been his sister," whereas the young woman in the recent photograph is a "stranger." The ambiguous usage of the term "stranger" allows for a combined reading: *both* the sister and the French woman are *both* strange and familiar to Dikran.

The estrangement of the sister as an adult, suggested by the dual meaning of the word "stranger" at the beginning of the passage, is immediately followed by an outpouring of nostalgia, as though to counterbalance Dikran's momentary betrayal of his kin. The progressive identification of his kin as a "small child" and then as a "sister" finds resolution in the proper name "Vartanuuush," which is uttered in an emphatic, elongated manner through the brother's "hushed" lips. Here, by adding an element of sensuality to the nostalgic recall, the narrator, having previously focused on the sister's body, now calls attention to Dikran's body. Dikran's "awakening" no longer alludes simply to the emotional world, but encompasses the visceral domain as well. He seems to rouse from a period of dormancy: the tension between the past and the present and between the simultaneous familiarity and unfamiliarity of the sister calls him back to consciousness.

This call to consciousness gives birth to a revived and new Dikran. The promise of a womanly presence in his everyday life allows him to envision a future where his domestic life is governed by paternal law. Still in his role as brother, he fantasizes about claiming a position as husband or father: "Dikran is now the father of the family. He races up the stairs, his nostrils full of the savory aroma of food. His sister stands there, just like an open rose found in a modest garden. His sister smiles. Her smile fills the apartment with light. The walls laugh. And the warmth of the laughter passes through all the furniture, which momentarily rattles with life. But before all else, it passes through Dikran's soul. 'Hurry, quick! The food will get cold.'"[19] Describing an imaginary future, the narrative uses the present tense to assert Dikran's position as the head of the household. The sister, though described in the role of mother of the family, is not explicitly referred to as such. The narrative continues to recognize her as the sister, but sexualizes her to better accommodate her to the role of domestic partner, that is, wife. The "open rose" imagery not only presents the sister as an object of beauty, but also emphasizes her sexual maturity. Her smile is once again stressed to suggest her reciprocation of her brother's affection and to position her as the source of light and life in this vision of the future. These effects are reinforced by her compliance with the traditional patriarchal order. At the end of the vision, she calls Dikran up the stairs with promises of hot, freshly baked food, in the role of a wife or a mother cheerfully performing her domestic duties.

In Dikran's present reality, the "stranger" of a previous passage, who was both the sister and a stranger on the street, now becomes "a woman." Dikran finally recognizes the presence of an external Other, smiling at him in the present moment. This woman walks in front of Dikran; she is described as a mythical flower fleeing capture, and she continues to appear and disappear within the dense crowd on the street. The unambiguous identification of a Frenchwoman is interrupted by the recollection of his sister's letter, recently received. Now it is the sister who is an obstacle: the remembrance of her letter is presented through direct speech. In this singular instance, the sister gains a voice. The narrator recounts the letter: "'Dear Dikran, I still cannot believe that only ten days keep us apart. My letter, via airmail, will find you in a couple of days. I am entirely overcome by a single thought: our meeting. Ten years, just imagine! You were a young boy back then, when you amazed your little sister with a thousand and one wonders. Almost like an all-powerful god. It seemed to me that there was nothing in the world you couldn't do. Even more so than father.' Here the recollection halted. The rest vanished into a fog, while the words at the bottom of the page became magnified: 'Your loving sister, V. Sahagian.'"[20] Like Dikran, the sister is curious about finding her brother as an adult, rather than the "young boy" she remembers. However, the letter contains none of the conflation of past and present that, in Dikran's earlier recollection of the sister, hinted at time's collapse after the genocide. Rather, the sister's letter reconstructs time. The past that separates the siblings is no longer an ambiguous realm. The sister clearly articulates and limits the time remaining before their reunion ("ten days") and the time that has elapsed since their last encounter ("ten years"). Although the sister does not suffer from an impossible present and operates with a more conventionally organized notion of time, she, too, displays incestuous desire. She openly and powerfully expresses her childhood infatuation with her older brother. This past desire for her brother puts her in a position of awe and submission, in accordance with the role of the feminine figure within the patriarchy. Furthermore, her desire for the brother overshadows the "primordial Elektra" desire for the father, as she claims that Dikran seemed capable, "even more so than father."

The momentary recall of the father (through the sister's letter, and thus the sister's memory) causes a sudden halt in Dikran's act of remembering. The remainder of the letter fades away, reflecting Dikran's inability to face the loss of his father. Although the latent sexual desire seems to be reciprocal, the destruction of patriarchy and the subsequent collapse of time and distance do not drive the sister's desire for her kin, because her desire predates the loss of the father. For Dikran, therefore, incest is inherently catastrophic. The desire for the same is inextricably tied to the imperative to take the father's place, a task that both must be attempted and is impossible to complete. The name of the father mentioned in the sister's letter reminds him of the impossibility of the task. The interrupted memory-narrative jumps to the end of the letter, bringing the sister's signature to the forefront in a "magnified" manner. Yet this time, the sister is not referred to by her proper name, "Vartanush," but rather by her paternal name "Sahagian." By reducing Vartanush to the initial "V" and inscribing the family name instead, the sister reinforces the familial blood ties that join her to Dikran. In turn, by the magnification of this signature in his memory, Dikran strengthens his commitment to the task at hand, which is now redefined as the reconstitution of patriarchy.

The acknowledgment of the stranger's smile and the subsequent recall of the sister's letter together complete the circle of desire. First introduced through still photographic images, the sister now gains a voice to express her desire for Dikran. Similarly, the stranger, who was first introduced ambiguously through Dikran's fixation on the sister's smile in the photographs, now has a face that emerges out of the still frame of the photograph, becoming an active agent in Dikran's present. She is no longer a disembodied smile that he feels drawn to, but rather a smiling woman who is attracted to him. After recognizing them as two distinct entities, Dikran brings them back together and places them within a frame. The narrator explains, "Dikran searched his thoughts for the two women's faces. He found them and placed them side by side, in an oval-shaped frame. He hung it on the wall of his mind."[21] Dikran intentionally collapses the two figures into a singular photographic image. The Armenian sister and the Frenchwoman are placed "side by side" and reflect back to Dikran the opposing objects of his desire.[22] Furthermore, in his conscious merging of the two, he appropriates them as his own. As figures belonging to his fantasy, they neither exist separately from one another nor exist without him. In fact, they become locked in a triangular relationship, forcing the temporal categories of past, present, and future into a similar bind. Because the past contains a catastrophic and irreparable loss, the present becomes impossible in the face of a nonexistent future. Neither the Armenian sister nor the Frenchwoman can secure the continuity of the lost patriarchy. As their figures become conflated and torment Dikran, therefore, the past and the future, both marked by loss, blend and impose themselves on the present.

The story ends with a violent disentangling of the two figures. They can no longer coexist in their triangular relation with Dikran. In the rental office, Dikran sees the Frenchwoman once again. She claims to be there for the purpose of listing her apartment for sale and convinces him to follow her to what turns out to be her hotel room. Once there, Dikran finally realizes that she is a prostitute. We are told that as though waking up from a dream, "Dikran shuddered. The woman had finally been unmasked."[23] The smiling stranger ceases to be the present-day substitute for the love the sister can offer. She is doubly unmasked: first as the sister's substitute and then as a lover. In her dichotomous relationship with the sister, the prostitute personifies French culture for Dikran. She is strange, and intoxicatingly attractive in her strangeness. Yet she promises no future beyond the temporary pleasures of the flesh. Her sexuality serves only to divert Dikran away from the task of reconstituting the lost patriarchy, which now can be accomplished only with the help of the sister. Distraught, he throws some money on the bed and runs out into the streets without the services he has paid for, having failed to secure an apartment.

The unmasking of the Frenchwoman leaves the image of the sister intact but shatters the triangular relationship: "It seemed to him that the oval frame containing the two beloved beings had fallen from the wall where it hung in his mind, and shattered into pieces; pieces which he now trampled underfoot. The desire to run, to flee urged him on." Here, the sister is the sole object of desire. In Dikran's mind, she continues to exist undamaged and now appears as a singular image, yet still internally divided between lover and sibling. Back in his room, lying in bed, Dikran falls asleep to a parade of images of his "sister's face," which he recognizes as a "mature woman's face."[24] The Armenian female, first seen as a sister, is distanced and once again becomes a woman. She is necessary for the process of reconstituting the patriarchy. In this sense, the story suggests that incest, as a consequence of the genocide, also becomes the only means of repairing it. For suggesting the unthinkable, "Vartsu Seneag" was marked as taboo literature, offensive to the sense of moral righteousness that the postgenocide generation wielded to assert its survival.

Postgenocide Sexual Desire and the Inevitability of Incest

Nigoghos Sarafian's short novel *Ishkhanuhin* (The Princess), published in 1934, is the story of an accidental incestuous encounter between siblings. *Ishkhanuhin* stands out as an exception both in the author's literary career and in the novelistic genre developed by the Menk generation. Known as a poet, Sarafian confined his endeavors in prose to prose poetry, such as *Vēnsēni Andaṙě* (The Forest of Vincennes) (1988), and journalism.[25] In 1932, he published a novella in serial form, *Khariskhēn Heṙu* (Far from the Anchor), in *Hayrenik' Monthly*. *Ishkhanuhin* was his only freestanding edited novel.[26] Although it was published in the same year as Zartarian's *Mer Geank'ě* (Our Life), *Ishkhanuhin* does not appear in the triad of early novels produced by the Paris generation.[27] Considered weak because of its haphazard formal composition,[28] this novel differs from the other three mainly because its narrative centers on an orphaned female survivor. It is an early attempt in Armenian literature to imagine the life of the Armenian women who at a very young age were saved, bought, or stolen by Turkish or Kurdish men during the genocide. Often referred to as "cryptic" or "hidden" Armenians, this particular group of survivors has recently captured the attention of scholars and memoirists[29] who tell the stories of an older generation of women with hidden Armenian identities in Turkey. Sarafian's novel is one of the first literary attempts to fictionalize a survivor's chance encounter with one of these lost girls.

Set in the 1920s, *Ishkhanuhin* reaffirms the Menk generation's commitment to representing the past trauma only indexically, by narrating the present context of the aftermath. Central to the genocide's indexical representation in this novel is the suggestion that the genocide is catastrophic insofar as it renders desire incestuous in its aftermath. By using the trope of incest, Sarafian configures the genocide as a loss of patriarchy to propose the impossibility of postgenocide sexual desire. The novel takes place along the northern shores of France, where the young and beautiful Aïshé[30] vacations with her husband: an older Turkish pasha by the name of Davud, notable for his gluttonous appetite for food and younger women. Although Aïshé considers herself a Turk, her true origins remain a mystery. In her nebulous early-childhood memories, she remembers her father leaving a mark on her shoulder, a branding in a foreign language that we later find out forms the letter *A* in Armenian. From the pasha's older wives, who all have been dismissed, she learns that he adopted her as a small child. She now remains the pasha's sole wife and most cherished love object (though the attraction is not reciprocal). Following a number of coincidental encounters with a young man on the beach, Aïshé begins to nurture a number of fantasies, which she realizes by sleeping with the young man.

Aram, the young man, is an orphaned Armenian living in Paris who has also come to vacation on the shore. Independent of his attraction to Aïshé, to whom he finds himself uncontrollably drawn, he has recognized Davud Pasha as his father's murderer and decides to seek revenge. During a romantic rendezvous, Aram reveals to Aïshé his family story and her husband's identity as a murderer. Amid this heart-wrenching revelation, Aïshé realizes that she is Aram's long-lost sister.[31] Overcome by the trauma of having committed incest and having been married to her father's murderer, she decides to guard this information from both her brother and her husband. She resolves to kill the pasha by inviting him for an afternoon drive and driving him off a cliff. The assassination attempt results only in suicide; the pasha is injured but remains alive. When he and Aïshé's body are transported to their beachfront home, Aram arrives at the scene along with a crowd of locals. Seeing Aïshé lying dead, he notices the mark on her shoulder and immediately recognizes her as his sister Araxi. He walks into the pasha's room, takes out a gun, and shoots him. With no time to turn the pistol on himself, he is tackled by the crowd and arrested by the police.

The story thus ends with a final tragic act that violates the law. The cycle of violence prompted by the genocide results in sexual violence in the form of both enslavement and incest and concludes with the murder of the perpetrator and the suicide of the victim. Aram, representing the Armenian survivor, is the only one who survives the novel. Although he has sought justice for himself, he is now criminalized by the new European Other, French society. As the death of his sister/lover reaffirms the impossibility of generational continuity in the aftermath of the genocide, the death of the perpetrator also eliminates his position as victim. Therefore, the novel's fundamental question concerns the significance of the survivor's physical survival (a question that would prove continuously destructive if posed within the framework of patriarchy). In other words, the novel's driving question is not only "What does it mean to survive the genocide?" but also "What does it mean to survive as sexual beings?"

Although Sarafian places Aïshé at the center of the novel, his representation of female sexuality remains undeniably a construction of the male imagination. In fact, the novel begins with a long description of Aïshé's naked body moving across the sea. The opening lines read, "Who would ever believe . . . A Turkish woman plowing through the Northern Sea, standing naked on a wooden board, just like a fairy princess on a magic carpet."[32] As the narrator's invocation suggests, the story requires imagination because it challenges the limits of belief by presenting a Turkish woman out of context: she is an Eastern heroine on French shores. Far from her land of origin, she is introduced as a floating image, foreshadowing her lack of family roots. More specifically, the moving image of her naked body is paralleled with the boat pulling her, thus presenting her as a vessel for desire.

Here, at the beginning of the novel, prior to the intrusion of her past as Araxi, Aïshé embodies the emergent Turkish nation. As the open exhibition of her body suggests, she has adopted the progressive ideals of modern Europe while remaining proud of her physical attributes that mark her as being from elsewhere. She nurtures a sense of Turkish pride, but one that is based on an ahistorical identity. She is ashamed of her husband, who personifies Turkey's Ottoman past—which ironically contains the hidden history of her identity as an Armenian. Commenting on Aïshé's Turkish pride, the narrator remarks: "If the princess was ashamed of her white-haired husband, many mistook her for his daughter, she equally carried the pride of a Turkish woman. She often thought, and perhaps rightly so, that Europeans, eager for Eastern ideas, saw in her a heroine out of a Loti or a Farrère novel.[33] Aïshé was proud still, for her homeland reborn, where progress was moving at dazzling speeds. She herself, in her physical and intellectual demeanor, was proof of that."[34] Aïshé's shame about her husband goes beyond the vast age difference that separates the two; it is also caused by her husband's loyalty to the Ottoman past. He retains the title of pasha, an honorary title in the Ottoman political system granted to high-ranking officials. Although he has officially given up his harem in accordance with the tenets of the new Turkish society, he continues to have sexual relations outside his marriage to Aïshé, as is suggested by some of his encounters with the servants in his current vacation home. He enjoys a life of luxury owing to the wealth afforded by his rank, which he has acquired by naming his Armenian friends in Constantinople and contributing to their persecution during the final days of the empire. As the living trace of the Ottoman Empire, Davud Pasha is both a source of embarrassment for Aïshé and a basis for her Turkish pride, since it is on these imperial ruins that the modern nation of Turkey stands. This unacknowledged ambivalence in her alliance with Turkey, a nation founded on the erasure of its past, also encompasses her personal hidden past and origins, the ambiguities of which she dares question only in the private sphere.[35]

In the public domain, particularly outside the Turkish context, Aïshé carries "the pride of a Turkish woman." Now in France, she is well aware of how she is perceived by the locals. As their gaze induces feelings of shame for being married to a much older man, it equally fuels her sense of pride in being from a country that has embraced European modernity. She manipulates Europe's Orientalism in this regard. Her pride in modernity derives from her ability to offer counterevidence to Europe's view of the East as "backward." Here the narrator's own voice aligns with his representation of hers: the narrator reinforces the accuracy of Aïshé's perception that Europeans exoticize her and see her as a heroine from the novels of Loti and Farrère.[36] Her naked exhibition of her body manipulates their Orientalist views by preserving her image as a desired object, while it simultaneously exploits them by superimposing a new image of a "modern" Turkish woman.

In private, Aïshé's solitude enables her to question her own history and ponder her clouded memories of early childhood. The few foggy scenes of the past center on her father and his branding of a letter on Aïshé's shoulder at the moment of separation. This letter in a foreign language is the only visual trace of her life outside Davud Pasha's care. It is a reminder of her foreignness to herself, to her body. In her private chamber, she scrutinizes her image in the mirror: "And she kissed her, herself, like a stranger, extraordinary, with fervent ease, which spread like a vine, and swirled up the body. And it turned foreign, her own hand. It turned into the hand of the dreamt man and slid down her throat, where unfamiliar cries and pants were accumulating. And beneath her half-shut lids, she saw it, the desired gaze, familiar and strange at the same time."[37] Aïshé cannot fully possess her body as her own. The language of the passage oscillates between belonging and foreignness. Aram is the man she dreams about during these private moments, though he is still only a stranger she has encountered several times on the beach. Aïshé's fanciful submission, therefore, is an act of surrender to the realm of the foreign and the mysterious, which includes both the stranger and her unknown past. Sexual surrender becomes a means of confronting her forgetfulness, though unproductively. Although she dares to face the ambiguities of her origins in privacy, it is still the reflection of the other's gaze that she finds in the mirror. The "desired gaze," meaning her own gaze desired by others, looks back at her, doubly strange and doubly familiar at the same time.

Knowing and not knowing, as markers of familiarity and strangeness, eventually produce divisions in Aïshé's sense of self that lead to her self-discovery: she discovers that she is a victim. She feels attracted to Aram because, like her reflection in the mirror, he is both foreign and familiar. Upon their second accidental encounter, she already recognizes a certain familiarity: "She felt the fire of an infatuating intimacy, from his wide and smiling eyes straight to her heart."[38] Aïshé gravitates toward the stranger because his eyes promise intimacy, and therefore mimic her desire for the familiar in the foreign. Consequently, the physical joining of their bodies literalizes this self-reflexive gaze. In sleeping with Aram, she discovers her identity as Araxi.

While incest unlocks Aïshé's Armenian past and problematizes her Turkish identity, it creates a new "unknown," now for Aram. Aram does not know he has slept with his sister, for Aïshé decides to spare him the horror of this knowledge. Until the concluding moments of the novel, he perceives Aïshé as a Turkish woman married to the pasha, his father's murderer. Accordingly, his attraction to her is characterized by a perverse longing to become one with the perpetrator, on the one hand, and a subversive attempt to dominate the perpetrator, on the other. Aram desires Aïshé within the bounds of extreme physical and spiritual measures, yet his desire is impersonal. He reaches this state of infatuation before any introduction or exchange of words. In fact, they speak to each other for the first time only after their first sexual encounter. The exchange of personal information that follows is secondary. The only prior information that necessitates the union of their bodies is Aram's recognition of her as Turkish and Aïshé's recognition of him as Armenian. Hence, it is not necessarily the instinctive familiarity of an unknown familial bond that draws him to her, but a conscious search for familiarity and sameness in the Turkish Other.[39] Although they are not yet aware of how their personal histories are intertwined, they are aware that their national histories are shared histories, however unequal their intersection may be.

It is precisely in this regard that Sarafian's *Ishkhanuhin* fails Aïshé. Aram's male Armenian perspective overshadows her voice. The narrator's observations during Aram and Aïshé's first sexual encounter focus on Aram. Commenting on the contradictions produced by Aram's new proximity with a Turk, he says: "But that love is a tragic[40] one, for a boy who was picked out from the desert and who carries the revenge of fallen victims in his heart. Many generations are not going to be able to free themselves of the nightmare that an Armenian relives, upon coming face to face with that exclusionary Turkish race, whose customs and nature have not changed over the centuries." The narrator not only focuses on Aram's internal conflict in relation to his desire for Aïshé; by generalizing the situation, he presents Aram as representative of all Armenians across many generations. In fact, we never learn of Aïshé's reception of Aram as an Armenian. Her attraction is always devoid of politics, whereas Aram's sexual desire soon becomes synonymous with his desire for revenge. Aïshé's later unveiling as a victim has no dramatic effect on the reader, who by now recognizes the story as a masculine narrative about revenge. Whereas Aïshé has no recollection of her early childhood and has adopted Turkey as her place of national belonging, Aram carries an exilic notion of nation, founded on the memory of his lost parents. Aram, who was six years old when he was separated from his family, remembers his father's murderer and has recently identified him as the pasha. Following a long passage about the methods of conversion Aram's adoptive family subjected him to, the narrator concludes, "All this is enough, for the ripe mind of a boy, in whom the nation becomes erased, only to regroup under the memory of his parents." The family embodies Aram's sense of national belonging; it is its loss that he tries to avenge. Accordingly, he attempts to disrupt the marital tie that the pasha has established with Aïshé. Specifically, he uses sexual domination as the inverse of the pasha's past physical violence. In sleeping with Aïshé, he believes he is robbing the pasha of his wife and therefore exacting revenge on the one who robbed him of his father: "Aram felt content, with the particular satisfaction of a vengeful person, for having stolen from the Turk his most valued possession, his wife, for having denigrated his honor." By blemishing the pasha's honor, Aram strips him of his masculinity, of which he feels equally robbed as a result of his father's murder. Yet this problematic configuration of revenge as sexual violence succeeds only in repeating the original violence toward Aïshé. As an instrument of revenge, Aïshé is sexually violated by Aram in a way that mirrors her enslavement by the pasha. And Aram's need for revenge is not satiated, for "this conquest was unsatisfactory. Oh, only if the Pasha could suddenly walk in."[41] Aram feels that his efforts at revenge are inadequate because the pasha does not witness his sexual domination of Aïshé. It is from his position of domination that Aram reveals his intentions and tells Aïshé his story. This unmasking, both of Aram's intentions and of the pasha's identity as a murderer, becomes the final validation of Aïshé's victimhood. She was a victim of enslavement in the past and is a victim of incest in the present, and in both cases, she remains unrecognized.

Aïshé's lack of outside recognition as a victim is the result of the pasha's forced forgetting and Aram's need for revenge. While one tries to erase the past, the other insistently returns to it in an attempt to reinstate the paternal order. Consequently, both men silence Aïshé. Requiring no recognition from either man, Aïshé empowers herself by guarding the revelation about her identity as Araxi. She decides to spare her brother the truth and kill the pasha. Thus, self-discovery ultimately proves to be a twofold process: self-recognition (of victimhood) and self-destruction (by attempting to eliminate the perpetrator). Upon hearing Aram's story, Aïshé runs out of his room with no explanation. Soon afterward, she invites her husband for an afternoon drive in hopes of steering the car off a cliff. Before the drive, Aïshé returns to the mirror and gazes at her reflection. This time, she does not find her reflection attractive in its ambivalence of familiarity and strangeness. Rather, she struggles with the likeness that she now sees between herself and Aram. In striving to give a name to this newfound trace of her Armenian past, she calls out to her unknown father: "father . . . father . . . who are you, oh father . . . who . . . I, your daughter, I want to know at last."[42] Like Aram, she names the crime as the death of her father, whose absence begins to dictate her actions. Aïshé's attempt at revenge uses physical violence, the form of the crime committed against her father. But neither her father's murder nor her own enslavement is avenged through the attempted assassination, which results in suicide.

Sarafian's *Ishkhanuhin*, therefore, in identifying the murder of the father as the original crime of genocidal violence suggests that the survivor's trauma is located in the aftermath of the loss, precisely when it is experienced as inescapable and irreparable. For the Armenian characters in the novel, seeking revenge and restitution entails the reinforcement of the lost paternal law, which proves impossible. Aram's quest for revenge is carried out at the cost of his lover/sister. In other words, the perpetrator and the victim are inextricably tied to each other, for the attempt to kill off the perpetrator results in the elimination of the victim. In this triangular relationship, Aram is the only one who stays alive in the story to assume a third identity. He is a survivor who can neither avenge the father's death nor replace the father in the genocide's aftermath, placing him at an impasse that renders survival catastrophic.

The definition of the genocide as a collapse of the pre-1915 patriarchal order provided the conceptual framework for the development of the "absent-father" literary trope in Menk's literature. In identifying the father's death as the originary violence of the genocide, works like Sarafian's *Ishkhanuhin* explore the theme of incest as a mode of representing the survivor's perpetual trauma. In developing his theory of internal othering, Beledian summarizes Sarafian's novel as follows: "En effet, le meurtre du père introduit dans la relation amoureuse des rescapés un amour incestueux comme s'il supprimait la loi fondatrice de différences. Comment aimer ne deviendrait-il pas, désormais, une affaire incestueuse?"[43] What Beledian refers to as "the foundational law of difference" contains the laws of the familial domain and thereby, what Freud and Rank called the "universal taboo": the prohibition of incest. The works of the Menk generation seem to suggest that in the postwar Armenian case, defined by the patriarchy's precarious state, the son's Oedipal struggle for power is compounded by the traumatic legacy of the genocide, which dismantles the incest's prohibition. In this context, incest is no longer a repressed fantasy, rather an inevitability that must be confronted in any attempt that seeks to reconstitute the family or the nation in dispersion.

Revenge, Forced Incest, and the
Perpetuation of Sexual Violence

In the third issue of *Menk*', printed on May 20, 1932, Shahan Shahnur published a short story that generated a scandal both within the group and among its reading public. The publication of "'Buynuzlĕ'nerĕ" (The Cuckolds) not only contributed to Menk's dissolution, but also became the scapegoat used in attempts to defame the author and to label his work as "trashy" literature.[44] This story of incest, unlike those works of Vorpuni and Sarafian, which are set in France, takes place in the general region of Cilicia, where Armenian legionaries were deployed on behalf of the French Army during World War I.[45] The change of setting makes possible a shift in the power dynamics among the story's characters, placing the Armenian in a rare position of authority; in this case, it is authority over Turks. Like "Vartsu Seneag" and *Ishkhanuhin*, Shahnur's "'Buynuzlĕ'nerĕ" conceptualizes the genocide as a loss of patriarchy and, by extension, a crime of perversion, of incest. Returning to the scene of the original violence, Shahnur literalizes the crime committed against Armenians in 1915 as incest and reverses its direction: Turkish siblings become the victims of forced incest. It was this literalization of the catastrophe, and not the reversal of the victim-perpetrator roles, that the readers of "'Buynuzlĕ'nerĕ" found offensive. Revenge and its literary representations were never criticized in the post-1915 diaspora. Though Armenians in the diaspora did not necessarily approve of revenge, it was regarded as a legitimate response by survivors. The shock of Shahnur's story comes from its demand for recognition of something beyond revenge. To comprehend "'Buynuzlĕ'nerĕ" as a story about revenge, Armenian readers needed to confront and accept their own position as victims forced into incest.

Set in the Cilicia region, "'Buynuzlĕ'nerĕ" recounts the encounter between a group of Armenian legionaries and two Turkish siblings working in the field. Driven by a need for vengeance, the soldiers, led by their corporal, Avak (meaning "senior," and also used as a proper name), decide to force them to have sex with each other as they watch. A few months later, on their escape path from the advancing Turkish Army, the same legion stumbles upon a house in the middle of the night. After cautiously approaching the house, they find that the siblings live inside. Moreover, they discover that the brother has continued to rape his sister regularly. Though thirsty and tired, the soldiers decide not to stop there and leave without interfering.

Corporal Avak frames the story's third-person narrative. As the commander of the legion, he is the first to arrive at the scene when one of his soldiers spots two Turks in the fields, which lie below the main road that the legion patrols. Although Avak questions them for not taking the main road and accuses them of hiding, it is clear that the Turks, a man and a woman, are innocent civilians on their way home after gathering hay in the fields. Their nonthreatening demeanor and the donkey loaded with hay that accompanies them do not prevent the soldiers from finding them guilty of a punishable crime. They are guilty simply for being Turks, members of the ethnic group that perpetrated genocide against Armenians only a year or two earlier. The power now granted to the Armenians as a result of their temporary validation by the French Army enables the soldiers to inappropriately seek justice for a historical crime gone unpunished. Having surrounded the two Turks, the legionaries cheer their corporal on as he accuses them of being killers. In this scene of informal prosecution, the two Turks represent all Turks, and all Turks are equated with perpetrators and are therefore regarded as guilty of massacre. The exchange takes place mainly between the young man and Corporal Avak, who continuously addresses the former as "little Talaat," after Talaat Pasha, the Young Turk often referred to as the mastermind of the genocidal plot.[46]

This informal prosecution is carried out with an element of theatricality, not only because the accused are obviously innocent, but also because their verdict is predetermined. One of the legionaries, arriving late on the scene, cries out, "Boys, wait! Don't kill them yet! I, too, want to see." As this soldier assumes, the captives are destined to be killed for being Turks. Furthermore, the soldier's need to "see" the killing attests to the act's purpose of revenge. Much like the initial period of questioning, when the Armenians perform their recently acquired authority with exploitative measures, the killings are to be a spectacle, witnessed by an audience that awaits catharsis. In watching the murder of Turks, the Armenian soldiers will gain the satisfaction of avenging the deaths of their loved ones. From the other end, the two Turks beg for their lives, using a strategy based on the same loss of Armenian victims. They both swear that they did not harm any Armenians during the period of massacres. In fact, they insist that they saved a few Armenian orphans. Feeling helpless, the woman evokes the memory of the dead and asks them to spare her life for the sake of their lost souls. Rather than having a favorable effect, the woman's plea validates the soldiers' decision to kill. Indeed, it fuels their desire for revenge as they cry back in unison, "For the sake of the souls of our dead . . . rather than . . . for their souls . . . we should not forgive . . . we will massacre, just like you did to all of us . . . all of us, from young to old."[47] As stressed in the soldiers' response, the memory of the lost souls is overwhelming, and it demands a form of revenge that is equally vast and indiscriminate.

Although death is the initially desired form of punishment, the legionaries begin to contemplate other forms of violence more "suitable" for their victims, especially when they discover that they are siblings. One suggests cutting off their ears. Another jumps in to propose: "Just like what we did to yesterday's caravan, let's cut off the man's penis and put it in his mouth. And we all know what we can do to the girl."[48] With this suggestion, the forms of revenge being contemplated move into the realm of sexual violence. The idea of literally stripping the man of his masculinity and raping the woman contributes to the proposal that is eventually agreed upon as the best form of revenge: one of the soldiers suggests forcing the siblings to have sex with each other as they look on. The enthusiastic discussion of various options of violence and the ultimate decision to force incest depict the Armenian soldiers as capable of savagery, exposing the inherent contradiction in the concept of revenge. Shahnur now inverts the reasons the soldiers used to qualify these two Turks as "deserving" of punishment. The reasoning goes: all Turks were "little Talaats," since the crime of geno-cide was carried out with the help of ordinary people, who viewed Talaat's master plan as being in compliance with their civic duties as Muslim Otto-man citizens. That is, all Turks were capable of the crime and are therefore accountable for it. Although such essentialist categorizations are often the root cause of mass violence, here Shahnur emphasizes the nature of evil with a different intention in mind. Reminiscent of what Hannah Arendt called "the banality of evil" in reference to the Holocaust, Shahnur shows that all humans are capable of perverse crimes, even crimes that seem too horrendous to be carried out by ordinary people.[49]

The idea of forcing the Turkish siblings to have sex with each other does not seem to jar the legionaries, and the corporal immediately pro-ceeds to articulate this nearly unanimous agreement in a command addressed to the brother. Only one soldier dares to contest the decision. His protest speech, which goes unnoticed, gives the story its title. The opposing soldier argues that he has no wish to become a true *buynuzlĕ*. The narrator provides the following explanation soon after the soldier's protest: "It was true that the Turks of Cilicia had named them [the legion-aries] as such, but the reason for that was their military helmet, the edges of which were pointed upward just like horns. Currently, this one was not in the mood to plant real horns."[50] The narrator's supplemental explana-tion hints at the play of meaning Shahnur attempts to achieve with the story's title. The soldier does not want to become "horned," meaning he does not want to turn into a real beast by committing the grotesque crime. In other words, he does not want to lose his humanity. Meanwhile, he is aware that the Turks already refer to him as horned because of the shape of his military helmet. The play of meaning is between the word's literal and metaphorical meanings, if the word is taken to mean "horned." In its wider usage, *buynuzlě* also refers to a person who has been deceived. It is also used to describe Anatolian Armenians, who at the time of the story have recently been betrayed by their imperial Ottoman government. Once cheated and abused (*buynuzlě*), the Armenians now become the abusers and the executioners of a heinous crime (*buynuzlě-nere*, Armenianized). Ultimately, the Armenians revert back to the figurative *buynuzlě*. They are *cuckolded* by the French, who, after using the legions to their advantage, abandon them by signing a treaty with the Turks.

The soldier's protestations prove insufficient to stop the crime. Once the corporal gives his orders to the brother, the other soldiers not only look on, but also participate: one by one, they lay their coats on the floor, one on top of the other, and make the sister lie on top. Aside from adding insult to injury, this gesture implicates them in the crime. Revenge, therefore, is a *collective* crime. To institutionalize it as an imperative for all surviving Armenians, the legionaries walk away with a song of victory: "Let the black blood of revenge irrigate our soil, / Let the exiled Armenian renew his life."[51]

The story ends with the legion's accidental encounter with the siblings a few months after the crime of forced incest. Thirsty and worn out, and in retreat from the advancing Turkish Army, the soldiers spot a lighted house at night. They cautiously approach the house, and from their position outside the window, they become silent witnesses of their crime's aftermath: the continuation of incest. They discover that the brother, having institutionalized the violence earlier inflicted onto him, continues to rape his sister. Hence "'Buynuzlě'nerě" concludes with the perpetuation of incest, now under the abusive authority of the brother and with the sister as the true victim. It was not only Shahnur's equation of the catastrophic crime with the crime of incest, therefore, that shocked his Armenian readers and turned the publication of the story into a scandal. It was also, or perhaps even more, his suggestion that the victim group was perpetuating the crime in the aftermath through unequal gender relations and faulty sexual politics. Unlike Sarafian's insistence on staying within the frames of patriarchal laws as a means of reversing the damage of the genocide, this story's final image warns against the self-destructive patterns that may emerge from that approach. The final scene of the sister's rape tarnishes the idea that kinship is the precondition for the family and the nation. It also implies the impossibility of familial reconstitution for survivors of the genocide, especially if the process of reconstruction is founded on notions of patriarchy, the absent father, and a new regime of the brother.[52]

PART TWO

Centering Western Armenian
in Post–World War II Beirut

4

Tradition Resurrected

National Literature in the Diaspora

Although the Menk generation of writers committed themselves to writing in and about the present, they eventually found avenues for inscribing personal memories of their traumatic past. Well after the group disbanded in 1933, most of the orphaned generation abandoned their resistance to narrating the past: Zareh Vorpuni in his 1964 novel *Ew Eghew Mart* (And There Was Man), Hrach Zartarian in his 1954 novel *Orpats'ogh Martig* (Orphaned Folk), and Shahan Shahnur in his journalistic essays published as a collection in 1967 as *Zuyk mĕ Garmir Dedragner* (A Couple of Red Notebooks) all revisit the past. While for many in that generation these returns to the past occurred later in life, Ghevont Meloyan is an anomalous case. One of the eldest members of the Menk group, Meloyan was already an accomplished writer before 1915, and his work reflects a more direct engagement with the genocide. In fact, in 1910, in the immediate aftermath of the 1909 Adana Massacres, Meloyan reflected on the impossibility of keeping silent and evading representation of catastrophe in literature. He remarks on the futility of resisting an articulation of the past by saying, "Why do you remember? Why do you speak? Why do you write? Why do you publish? . . . Keep silent and forget. . . . You said and you left, friend, friend of my lived days. . . . But when the pharos of memory burns incessantly . . . it does not leave you to rest. The flame of the past sparkles, the blades of memory sink down in my brain—I write so I won't turn mad."[1] As a signatory in 1931, he undoubtedly found that his views corresponded with the group's proposed literary identity in dispersion. Prior to joining Menk, however, his postgenocide literary reaction was closer to that of the surviving generation of writers. Like Aram Andonian and Hagop Oshagan, Meloyan attempted to represent the events of 1915 in literature, in the immediate aftermath of the catastrophe. Moreover, he executed his creations with the specific purpose of informing an international audience, an aim shared by the historical memoirs produced by second- and third-generation Armenian writers of North America.[2] With this purpose in mind, Meloyan wrote his work in French, the language that Menk rejected, just as it rejected representations of the past.

In 1918, Meloyan wrote *Arménouche*, a five-act play in French about an Armenian survivor of the genocide and a German soldier who has witnessed the atrocities inflicted on a young Armenian woman during the deportation marches. The German soldier, Oscar Muller, experiences a crisis of responsibility because he did not intervene. He finds and rescues the woman, Arménouche, now mad and living in a brothel in Germany. Oscar's conversations with his mother narrate Arménouche's story. On their journey through the desert, the Ottoman gendarmes attempted to rape Arménouche; they killed her infant before her eyes and forced her to drink his blood. This chilling scene haunts Oscar, for he was a silent witness to the crime. His belated efforts to help Arménouche are in vain. She is beyond saving and commits suicide at the end of the play. Although Meloyan manages to give an explicit account of the genocide's trauma, he does so indirectly. By shifting the focus from victim to witness, Meloyan presents his play as a story about international responsibility. Indeed, the play gained international acclaim. It won first prize in a competition organized by the Geneva-based La Société des Amis de l'Instruction and was performed onstage in Geneva in 1920 and in Paris in 1948.[3]

Meloyan later translated the play into Armenian, but it was the play's original language of publication, French, that made possible its widespread circulation. Rather than placing Armenian art on an international platform, *Arménouche* placed the Armenian *story* of 1915 on the international stage. For the Menk generation of writers, however, the question of their literature's "international" and "national" potential remained invariably tied to the Armenian language and not to the Armenian story of 1915 per se. They chose to write in Western Armenian and consequently were aware that their work did not contribute to a national literature or cater to an international audience. Although they have been criticized mostly for failing to record the past, I propose that the Menk writers have been over-looked also because of their attempt to redefine the concept of national literature, which has been understood as a problem ancillary to the genocide.

While the Menk generation propagated a decentered model for transnational literature that was free of the concept of return, the older surviving generation (like Costan Zarian and Simon Vratsian) called for the resurrection of the national model centered on an imagined homeland. Developed initially within a series called Azkayinn u Michazkayinĕ Kraganut'ean Mēch (The National and International in Literature) in Zuart'nots' and in conversation with articles published in Harach (1929–31), the discussion about the new scope of Armenian literature turned into a "we" versus "you" debate, positioning the younger generation on the side of dispersion and the older generation on the side of some version of homeland. The literary output of Paris in the 1920s and 1930s reflects the younger generation's outlook, which they cultivated in nuanced conversation with writers of the surviving generation. But the years of the Second World War and the Nazi occupation halted literary activity in France, allowing writers in the Middle East to lay claim to the dominant discourse in dispersion. Their outlook resembled that of the older generation. This chapter examines how the initially complex debate regarding literature of the dispersion collapsed into a binary argument about two conceptions of homeland and eventually became a call for a return to a pre-1915 notion of national literature. In this vein, this chapter outlines the post–World War II shift from dispersion to diaspora and, more specifically, suggests that the concrete language of diaspora was forged through literary discussions. Within the framework of national literature, the idea of an undisrupted past-present-future became essential to the cultural narrative of diaspora, which attempted to historicize the genocide and its dispersion in order to reconstruct the damaged notion of continuity.

Turning to Beirut, this chapter traces the critical response and emblematic status given to a 1929 novel by Menk member Shahan Shahnur, Nahanchĕ Arants' Erki (The Retreat without Song), in the decades following its publication. By examining the misreading and mistranslation that made possible this acclaim, I interrogate the role of diasporic nationalism in the post–World War II diaspora's effort to preserve cultural and literary traditions. I propose that the Menk writers have been overlooked because of their attempt to redefine the concept of national literature, as the extraordinary treatment of this novel demonstrates. As we will see in future chapters, the refusal of diaspora's post–World War II intellectuals to engage with Menk's proposition for a new, transnational literary orientation ultimately limited the possibilities for Armenian-language literature produced outside the boundaries of "nation." After Menk, the stakes of producing literature in the Western Armenian literary form remained forever high.

Between Emblem, Exception, and Misapprehension: Shahan Shahnur's *Nahanchĕ Aṙants' Erki*

On May 12, 1929, *Haṙach* printed an ad for an upcoming novel that the newspaper would publish in serial form. As a preview of the novel, *Nahanchĕ Aṙants' Erki: Badgerazart Badmut'iwn Hayots'* (The Retreat without Song: An Illustrated History of Armenians),[4] the ad featured the following information: "A novel of life in our times, the first work of a young writer, will be revealed in *Haṙach*."[5] In fact, what the ad previews is not the novel's artistic merits or content, but rather the way critics and readers should receive it. The brief description of the novel already frames it as a representational narrative, one that will depict the contemporary lives of Armenians in dispersion. Moreover, the promise of the novel's "revelation" creates an air of expectancy for the work and its author, whose name is not even mentioned. The unnamed author is presented as a pioneer of his generation for producing some sort of a "first" in post-1915 literature. Simultaneously, the ad plays the secondary role of advertising for the periodical. *Haṙach* itself appears as a pioneer for staging the unveiling of this anticipated new brand of literature. The newspaper's founder and editor, Shavarsh Misakian, generally took great pride in introducing young new writers to the public via his newspaper, but he was also one of their harshest critics. Misakian's comportment toward the new writer is exemplary of the general response Shahnur would receive as a figure of innovation and controversy whose popularity made him an exception in Menk.

Nahanchĕ Aṙants' Erki tells the story of a young Armenian man from Constantinople, now living in Paris and working in a photography studio. It is an immigrant story that traces the Armenian's encounter with the French in a post–World War II Parisian setting, a thread that is developed through the protagonist's relationship with his French lover, Nenette. As the young man negotiates between Armenian and French identities, alternating between the name Bedros and its French equivalent, Pierre (to suit different cultural settings), the narrative exposes the vulnerability of the Armenian culture in dispersion. Bedros/Pierre's small circle of Armenian friends offers a colorful representation of the various active ideologies of the Parisian scene. They are eventually abandoned for Nenette, an ex-prostitute whose shady past includes involvement in a pornography ring. By contrasting elements such as God and taboo with sex and prostitution, the novel announces the death of Armenian nationalism and foreshadows the Armenian exile's silent "retreat" into other cultures.

The novel received an overwhelmingly favorable immediate response, although many older writers and journalists were critical of its overtly sexual content. The Parisian literary journal *Zuart'nots'* and Boston's *Hayrenik' Monthly* were the first to review the novel, soon after its appearance in *Haṙach*. They both introduce it as a first in the emerging literary tradition of the dispersion. *Hayrenik' Monthly*'s book-review section, authored by a critic with the initials N. D.,[6] declares *Nahanchĕ* "a true discovery for our new literature." It goes on to describe it as "a novel that bears the reflection of our destiny. It would hardly be an exaggeration to call it a novel that allows Armenian literature to make a new entry into European literature."[7] N. D.'s proclamation that *Nahanchĕ* is a groundbreaking work indicates a Eurocentric perspective that measures the novel's merits against European literary works and views it as matching their level of artistic production.

Kegham Fenerjian, a contemporary of Shahnur, also praises the novel's innovative qualities, but from a perspective internal to the Western Armenian literary tradition. Referring to both *Nahanchĕ Aṙants' Erki* and Zareh Vorpuni's *P'ortsĕ*, published the same year, he writes, "Similar works of the new generation reveal wisdom and self-consciousness about our national reality, which were tragically lacking in the previous generation."[8] Shahnur's and Vorpuni's 1929 novels are devoid of hope, nostalgia, and the triumphalism of pre-1915 nationalist literature. As a result, the depiction of the grim reality of exilic life after the genocide becomes a marker for the new wave of literature. In addition to their commitment to representing the present—however disconsolate it may be—the up-and-coming writers are also considered pioneers for breaking away from previous stylistic traditions in Armenian literature. In his book review, N. D. applauds Shahnur's "daring" efforts to finally cut off ties with the literary traditions of the past: "a rupture with the moral, artistic, and stylistic requirements of tone and expression. It is as though the author has completely erased our literary blackboard by writing this beautiful novel."[9] The comment regarding tone and expression refers to the novel's often colloquial language, which includes frequent interjections of Turkish and French words. It also refers to the "freedom of expression" with which the narrator narrates and the characters speak about issues previously considered taboo.[10] For its unprecedented literary and linguistic techniques, Shahnur's *Nahanchě* is presented as an emblematic first work of literature, an original creation that stands on a cleanly "erased" slate.

From its earliest days in print, the novel was read as a work whose significance would withstand the passage of time. With foresight, Fenerjian claims that "for future periods, this [*Nahanchě*] will be an important document about the generation of Armenians who have fallen into Europe, uprooted and self-abandoned, having surrendered to work and pleasure, and welcoming the danger of extinction bit by bit."[11] Shahan Shahnur's senior Arshag Chobanian was wary of the young critics' hasty classification of the novel as the foundational literary work of the dispersion era. In an article he published in his own journal, *Anahid*, Chobanian shies away from making absolute statements about the work and criticizes the language of "newness" that has been circulating in the novel's regard. He dismisses comments that have dubbed *Nahanchě* the novel that launched the literature of the diaspora,[12] arguing that contemporary Armenian literature has always been written outside Armenia, in places like Constantinople, Vienna, Tbilisi, and Moscow, well before the deportations of 1915. He says that what deserves to be called "new" in both Shahnur's and Vorpuni's first novels is that the works issue forth as "conceptualizations of the feverish psychology of a community, which, through its character and conditions, vastly differs from all other communities that existed either near or far from the homeland during the years preceding the Great War."[13] Thus, for Chobanian, they are novels of the genocide's aftermath, and hence are original works that are limited by their thematic content.

Although Chobanian recognizes *Nahanchĕ* as a significant contribution to post–World War I Armenian literature and commends Shahnur's talent in representing the essence of their time, his critical remarks outweigh the compliments. Whereas the novels of the Menk generation are usually distinguished from earlier Armenian literature for presenting the figure of the Other, Chobanian is particularly displeased with *Nahanchĕ*'s portrayal of the French. He expresses surprise at Shahnur's willingness to depict his French characters, particularly Nenette and Monsieur Lescure, in a derogatory manner. He quotes a passage from Shahnur's novel that portrays a photography studio as a brothel: "Previously, he had likened the store to a whorehouse, having been offended and terrified of the women's extraordinary audacity, lewdness, the paint, the clothes. Parisian women's lack of humility seemed foreign to him at first, but he grew accustomed to it bit by bit, and the initial curiosity with which he observed the falling off of dresses and undergarments soon faded. And thinking that there are no whores here, since all of the women looked alike, without searching further, he approximated the photography shop to a bathhouse."[14] For Chobanian, Shahnur's depiction of the French photography studio is both appalling and shameful. The shock of the immigrant experience is lost on this Francophile.

This passage describes the simultaneously repulsive and attractive qualities of the urban European woman, who in the world of Menk's male writers was seen as a vehicle for integration. Rather than criticizing the problematic patriarchal assumptions embedded within a literary trope that implies that the Armenian subject is strictly male, Chobanian finds the passage degrading for other reasons. His condemnation, lacking any gender critique, accuses Shahnur of discrediting and misrepresenting the integrity of French culture as a whole. He expresses utter contempt for the passages in the novel where Shahnur "insults an entire nation" through his characters Nenette and Lescure, emphasizing the targeted nation's "greatness": "and not just any nation, the French nation, the culture to whom our nation is so indebted, whose literature has been the sole guide to Shahnur himself in the process of finding his aesthetic voice and forging his style."[15] Chobanian speaks from something like a cultural vacuum here. Having arrived in Paris in 1895, his integration into French society was unlike the experience of the post-1915 generation, who arrived en masse and as refugees. Whereas Chobanian quickly established close contacts with the leading French intellectuals of his time,[16] Shahnur's generation was disillusioned with Europe. Rather than being viewed as representatives or cultural elites, the postgenocide Armenians in Paris bore the title of "immigrants" and the discriminatory treatment that came with it.[17] Chobanian could not grasp the element of shock that accompanied the encounter between Shahnur's generation of Armenians and the French, and he found their representation of this cultural tension in literature exceedingly offensive.[18]

For Fenerjian, the strength of Shahnur's *Nahanchĕ* lies in the position from which its story is told: a minority perspective that does not claim a false proximity to the majority group. He writes, "The immediate contact that significant masses of Armenians had with foreign people conveyed to us a state of self-consciousness, of which our past 'leaders' had not the slightest clue."[19] Once again, exile and displacement are viewed as productive (and here also constructive) experiences. Rather than interpreting the representation of French characters as degrading, he focuses on the opportunity for awakening and self-realization that the encounter between French and Armenian characters presents.

The passage he selects in this regard immediately follows the excerpt Chobanian quotes, which portrays the photography studio as a brothel. Fenerjian's passage recounts the first exchange between Bedros (who now goes by Pierre) and Monsieur Lescure, who stops by the photo studio where the former works and invites him to a restaurant. Over dinner, he informs Pierre that he owns a photo shop as well, one that he wants to invigorate and modernize with the latest techniques of the profession. He expresses his respect for and trust in Pierre's work ethic and in Armenians in general and offers to hire him to run the photo studio. Before taking his leave, he expresses yet again his faith in Pierre, but here he says "that he had great faith in Turks."[20] For Monsieur Lescure, the Armenian and the Turk, as ethnic minorities, are one and the same, regardless of their vexed history. Thus, what Fenerjian views as the novel's attempt to remind its Armenian reading public of the covert racism with which the French often regard immigrants, Chobanian would have interpreted as Shahnur's unjust stereotyping of the French as ignorant and insensitive to Armenian cultural history. Chobanian, who equates Shahnur's depiction of the French with Loti's and Farrère's depiction of Armenians and accuses him of reverse racism,[21] himself bears similarities to the Orientalist French novelists. In fact, rather than reverse racism, it is inverse Orientalism that frames his critical outlook.[22] Beyond the issue of the portrayal of the French characters, Chobanian expresses similar disappointment in *Nahanchě*'s uncensored sex scenes. He criticizes Shahnur for going "beyond the limit" that writers have always known not to cross.[23] Yet what we should notice in Chobanian's commentary is not his claim to preserve an aesthetic purity in literature, but rather the additional limitations he places on *Armenian* literature in particular. According to him, writers should know to leave out scenes that are not exemplary, "but especially those that are not exemplary for a people like the Armenians, who, having not yet reached the pinnacle of civilization's benefits and harm and having been weakened by tragic forces, have a great need for moral strength and purity of customs."[24] In other words, Chobanian claims that Armenians are not advanced enough and their literature is not developed enough to risk the possibility of damaging its integrity (in the eyes of the West, I would add).

Like the theme of incest in Menk's literature, *Nahanchě*'s overt sexual content has often caused the novel to be classified as literature *of* taboos by its traditionalist critics and as literature that *breaks* taboos by its admirers. With Shahnur, sex entered Armenian literature in a raw, nonornate form: it is at times simply organic, at other times pornographic and even repulsive. It is not unreasonable to assume that the provocation was intentional on the part of the author. The novel opens with the following passage: "But he was an already mature boy: proof that he could not distinguish between the words whore and God. He had embraced the girl from behind, and having slipped his arms under her armpits, he sank his nose deeper and deeper behind her ear, enraptured by her seductive scent. She was truly an opulent girl, evidenced by her breasts that were of the same depth as the young man's palms."²⁵ The juxtaposition of God and prostitute, which in later years was read in the context of the cultural encounter between Armenians and the French, appeared as an offensive insult that polluted the integrity of Armenian literature. Although some critics, like Chobanian, did not allow room for alternate interpretations, others accepted the sexually explicit content of the novel as representative of the times and redirected their criticism to the Armenian youth of Europe. In its review, the 1931 yearbook of the journal *Geankʿew Aruesd* (Life and Art) attributes the novel's "trashy" sex scenes to a "disease" of the modern era: the disease of delighting in the pleasures of women. The review applauds Shahnur's portrayal of young Armenian men's moral atrophy in light of their victimization, exile, and encounter with the West: *"Nahanchě Aṙantsʿ Erki* is a novel that perfectly summarizes the mental caliber and meditations of Armenian youth who took wing on foreign shores. Meditations that reveal the psychological state of us all: our need to search for persons responsible for our political defeats, to place our past and present under scrutiny."²⁶ Accordingly, the vulnerable, orphaned Armenian youth have succumbed to the lures of modern Western culture, however "detrimental" it may be to their own culture in exile. In addition to praising Shahnur's candid portrayal of the crisis facing young Armenians, the review scolds the critics who have railed against Shahnur's "boldness" in style and expression, arguing that this very boldness will become the distinguishing mark of the new generation of writers.

Whether read as a poignant representation of the community's crisis, as a warning against the loss of tradition and mores, or as a trashy novel that defaces Armenian literature, *Nahanchě* tells the story of assimilation, as its title suggests. The "Armenianness" of the protagonist Bedros *retreats* into French culture, aided by the figure of the French lover. Making a generalization about the fate of young Armenian men in dispersion, Shahnur writes, "Here or there, the victory remained the same. Always the same Nenette, the granddaughter of the Manons, the Ninons, or the Nanans. Some married, many lived with girlfriends. The Armenian Church was soon emptied out. The number of letters being sent out decreased, and of course, far away, mothers cried."²⁷ In this passage, assimilation is presented through a patriarchal framing: Armenian men assimilate into French culture through their relationship with French women. In a similar association, the passage not only presents Armenian culture as a male realm, but also equates it with the Armenian Church. The Armenian community is left occupied with the figure of the lone mother, as the remnant of the national, patriarchal structure, engaged in the act of mourning her loss. Furthermore, in juxtaposing the Armenian Church with the notion of free sexuality that marks the French realm, Shahnur's novel connects the question of the national identity of the diaspora to French women.[28] As figures of desire that represent both modernity and sexual freedom, French women are often portrayed in the literature of Menk as prostitutes, attractive and threatening at the same time. As in the novel's inaugural lines, *Nahanchĕ* frames its protagonist's "retreat" within the contrasting images of the church and the prostitute. Throughout the novel, Bedros oscillates between his Armenian name and Pierre, as he enters and leaves relationships with French women and particularly with Nenette. At the novel's conclusion, now irrevocably Pierre, he is unable to recall the Lord's Prayer in Armenian and begins to recite it in French, having left the Armenian Church, and thus its culture, behind.

I understand Bedros's retreat as a literary trope that deconstructs and explores a probable cultural paradigm, albeit through a patriarchal lens. Many others, though, themselves coming from a patriarchal framework, understand it as a wholly defeatist or pessimistic outlook vis-à-vis assimilation. Many of his critics rebuke his portrayal of the protagonist's character, pointing out that men like Bedros are few in France. In the "new" Armenian novel, they would rather see a "successful" character, one who has integrated economically without leaving the Armenian community. Not surprisingly, Chobanian voices a similar opinion. He expresses disappointment in the choice of protagonists in both Shahnur's *Nahanchĕ* and Vorpuni's *P'ortsĕ*.[29] But he develops his commentary under the umbrella of yet another common criticism of Menk's novels: the absence of the genocide. He writes, "It seems to me that both would have brought to life characters of a different constitution if the scene of the great catastrophe burned directly or at every instant in their minds, and if they felt that the primary burden that it placed on the shoulders of Armenian youth is to not doubt their race and to strive to fulfill the forging of forces comparable to or even stronger than those lost."[30] Although Chobanian's comment may be applicable to the novels' main characters and to their absence of memory, it refers more specifically to the novels' authors. Chobanian accuses them of failing to keep the memory of the genocide alive in their minds and of failing to understand the mandate that the great catastrophic loss imposed on its survivors. The mandate, which is defined by an imperative to succeed and flourish when it is addressed to the surviving generation, demands a more specific task of the writers of Shahnur and Vorpuni's generation: to write about the genocide.

In Shahnur's view, the mandate to present praiseworthy and exemplary characters as opposed to "failed" ones would lead Armenian literature straight to its death, for such literature would lose its representative authority and cease being art. Directly narrating the genocide, the catastrophic nature of which defies representation, would have the same effect. Nevertheless, the genocide is present in Shahnur's *Nahanchĕ*. Its experience is told through the story of its trauma's revivification in the aftermath, enabling the creation of a contemporaneous novel. Located in the space of the Other and within the ruptured time of the "afterward," the novel's setting mirrors the artist's milieu. Whereas within the novel the context of loss pushes Bedros into retreat and disappearance, it becomes a productive space for Shahnur, allowing for the creation of a work of art. The space of "Armenianness" (the realm of the church, traditions, and mores), in contrast, is devoid of meaning in the new context of the Other. For Shahnur, it is barren and cannot produce art. He proposes therefore that the novel of the dispersion, though written in the Armenian language, must contain within it the Other.

"A Man Who Has No Ararat in the Depth of His Soul": Shahnur, the Armenian Press, and the Polarization of the Homeland Debate

The figure of the Other, which to the Parisian writers meant the French in particular, became a defining trait of the literature of Menk's generation. In a 1935 article, Shahnur, the group's most outspoken writer, claimed that

Armenians have always lacked "intellectual greatness and maturity . . . not only to create, but also to be able to comprehend the Other."[31] These comments, which mark a sharp turn in the writer's career, mock his ethnic group's sense of selfhood, as negotiated against others, and its ability to represent that self aesthetically in the arts. The article in which these lines appear, "Azadn Gomidas" (Gomidas the Free), when it was republished in 1969 (thirty-four years later), accidentally instigated a heated discussion that unfolded in the pages of various journals and newspapers of Soviet Armenia and in the diaspora. The journalistic mayhem, a scene that Arpik Misakian describes as a "circus,"[32] placed Shahnur at the center of a controversy and branded him as a controversial figure, ultimately providing a new lens through which the writer and his novel *Nahanchĕ* are remembered and read.[33]

The reappearance of the 1935 article and the noise with which it was received present an exemplary case of the highly networked journalism of the Armenian diaspora in a rare moment of dialogical exchange with Soviet Armenia. The publicized controversy signals to the maturation of the post–World War II "geography" of Armenian diasporic space, which solidified its identity against Soviet Armenia and the competing notions of homeland that the Soviet reality created for Western Armenians living in dispersion. To examine the multiple layers of exchange, misunderstanding, and cynicism that escalated to a full-blown debate surrounding the figure of Shahnur, we must first untangle the distinct settings of the article's first (1935) and second (1969) publication. Shahnur wrote "Azadn Gomidas" on the occasion of Father Gomidas's death, which occurred in Paris in late October 1935. Father Gomidas (1869–1935), an Armenian priest and famous composer, is regarded as the founder of modern Armenian classical music. Following his 1915 arrest in Constantinople and deportation to a camp at Chankiri, where he witnessed the extermination of Armenian intellectuals and artists, he developed a mental illness that he suffered from for the rest of his life. His death in a psychiatric clinic in 1935 marked a great loss for Armenian survivors, for it was seen as a delayed reaction to the genocide and thus reopened the wound in a new locale, in the context of dispersion. By the mid-1930s, the internal politics of diasporan communities was sharply divided along political party lines, which only heightened the sense of wounded identity for Armenians in dispersion. Three political parties—the social democrats, or Hnchagian Party; the center-left-leaning Armenian Revolutionary Federation; and the center-right-leaning liberal party, the Ramgavars dominated Armenian political life throughout the dispersed communities. Because of its various structures and institutions of literary and journalistic production, the Parisian Armenian population was especially politically charged and was divided between loyalty to Soviet Armenia and loyalty to the concept of a unified homeland.[34] In the atmosphere of this political split and in the aftermath of Menk's failed literary attempt, Shahnur's 1935 "Azadn Gomidas" commemorates the life of Father Gomidas by singling out his achievements as one of the only significant contributions made by Armenians to world culture.

Although the article's grand generalizations are unfounded and emotive, the sense of collective cultural degradation that informs Shahnur's bitter tone is not based on exaggeration. What had begun as an upward movement toward the construction of communities through the reinstitution of predispersion social and political structure during the 1920s soon turned into destructive political feuds that developed along party lines. The tensions reached a new climax with the assassination of Archbishop Levon Tourian in New York City on December 24, 1933, of which several ARF party members were accused.[35] As a consequence of the assassination, the partisan divide caused a split in the Armenian Church between the catholicosates of Echmiadzin and of Cilicia, designating the former as the patriarch of Soviet Armenia and its diasporan loyalists and the latter as the patriarch of exiled Armenians who imagined a future unified homeland. Against this backdrop of heightened political opposition and cultural atrophy, Shahnur mourned the loss of Father Gomidas, one of whose most notable achievements was preserving cultural heritage through extensive efforts to gather and record folk songs from the countryside.

Shahnur's "Azadn Gomidas" and other articles that express a similar sentiment regarding the decay in Armenian cultural and intellectual life, published in the Ramgavar newspaper *Abakay*, elicited an antagonistic reaction from many writers and critics active in the French scene and abroad. In addition to figures from the older generation like Chobanian and Tekeyan, Shahnur's Menk colleague Rafael Zartarian and his brother Hrach Zartarian showed hostility toward Shahnur, to the point of physically attacking him in the restaurant Floria.[36] His withdrawal from Armenian intellectual circles as a result of these disagreements coincided with his advancing illness,[37] forcing him to spend most of the next two decades in hospital beds. During this time, he moved away from writing Armenian-language literature and prose and began to develop his French-language poetry, published under the pen name Armen Lubin.[38] Shahnur's return to the Armenian literary scene in the 1950s was largely facilitated by the efforts of Arpik Misakian.[39] Consequently, *Harach*, the newspaper that introduced him as a writer, became his "home" periodical. After the Beirut publications of *T'ert'is Giragnōreay T'iwĕ* (The Sunday Issue) in 1958 and *Zuyk me Garmir Dedragner* (A Couple of Red Notebooks) in 1967, *Harach's* press published Shahnur's final Armenian-language works: *Azadn Gomidas* (Gomidas the Free) (the revised and expanded version of the controversial article) in 1970, *Pats' Domarĕ* (The Open Calendar) in 1971, and *Gragĕ Goghk'is* (Fire at My Side) in 1973.

Among the Menk writers, Shahnur was unique in his venture into French literature. This move produced two distinct responses in his Armenian audience. On the one hand, it increased his popularity, or even "validated" it, since many Armenians believed that being revered by the French implied international success. On the other hand, many were critical of his ideas regarding Armenian literature, sensing betrayal and abandonment in his move away from Armenian-language production.[40] The duality of Shahnur's reception, instigated by his oscillation between Armenian and French, is best represented in the episode over the republication of "Azadn Gomidas." In 1969, on the occasion of the one hundredth anniversary of Father Gomidas, the Beirut-based *Sp'iwrk'* (Diaspora), a weekly periodical edited by Simon Simonian, published Shahnur's 1935 article without the consent of the author or any mention of the article's origins. As previously mentioned, "Azadn Gomidas" commemorates Father Gomidas's achievements by debasing Armenian cultural, artistic, and literary accomplishments in very general terms. The article's opening lines, for instance, read, "I think that the world would not lose anything if the Armenian disappeared from its surface, in terminal extinction."[41] Although since the article's initial publication in the 1930s diasporan communities had developed along the same polarized trajectory, divided by loyalty to Soviet Armenia or to the idea of a future unified homeland, these lines offended Armenians from all camps, including intellectuals in Soviet Armenia. Now removed from the violent and heated context of the 1930s, and with the view of Shahnur's career in retrospect, these lines were read as an indication of a diasporan Armenian's loss of "Armenianness."

The controversy was ignited not by critics of the diaspora, but notably by a writer from Soviet Armenia. Following *Sp'iwrk'*'s 1969 republication of "Azadn Gomidas," poet Vahagn Davtian published a letter addressed to Shahnur in a Soviet Armenian weekly publication. This open letter, which appeared in *Hayrenik'i Dzayn* (Voice of the Fatherland) on January 21, 1970, accused Shahnur of having a pathological relationship to his Armenian identity: "That article of yours articulates the diseased psychology of a man who has distanced himself from his own people and has disowned its language and letters."[42] Outside pathology, Davtian cannot conceive of a reasonable explanation for Shahnur's unfavorable and negative attitude toward Armenian culture. Moreover, he takes particular issue with Shahnur's rejection of Soviet Armenia. He continues, "How else can one explain that surprising impression you leave in your article (which is more about the fate of the Armenian people rather than Gomidas) by absolutely ignoring and renouncing the existence of today's Armenia: an existence that serves as the anchor, the rampart, that ensures the existence of all Armenians, an existence, where the Armenian people's new destiny is being written."[43] Davtian singles out Shahnur's failure to mention Soviet Armenia as a place where Armenian culture lives and flourishes and where Armenian society progresses, an idea that he hints at by attributing to the Soviet Republic the promise to carve out the Armenians' "new destiny." In fact, true to Davtian's observations, Shahnur does not acknowledge Soviet Armenia's existence anywhere in his article.[44] His critique addresses Armenians as "a group of wretched and miserable pariahs."[45] His remarks are targeted explicitly at Armenians in dispersion, but owing to his generalized tone, his disparagement seems to encompass the Armenian people as a whole. Without knowing the origin of the article, Davtian cannot account for Shahnur's hostile tone within the context of the heightened and bloody internal politics of the 1930s diaspora.

Indeed, the article was originally written in response to that decade's atmosphere. Therefore, its republication in 1969 immediately called attention to many dated comments. Even the author himself took note of them. On January 25, 1970, just a few days after the appearance of Davtian's open letter in *Hayrenik'i Dzayn*, Shahnur published a revised "Azadn Gomidas" in *Harach*. Shahnur later claimed to have been unaware of Davtian's letter, but he addressed many of the same issues Davtian had raised in his critical commentary. For instance, in the revised version, Shahnur qualified the group of "pariahs" as "slaves," changing the word *dzrug* (leech) to *sdrug* (slave). He describes Armenians as slaves "who are heroized in homicidal fraternal fights,"[46] referring to the clashes between members of the various political parties during the 1930s.[47] In addition to situating the article in its appropriately dated context, Shahnur revised the language with which he referred to the Armenian people. By adding the word *kaght'aganut'iwn* (a collective of immigrants), he narrowed the scope of his address and specified that diaspora Armenians had been the target of his earlier disappointment.[48]

Nevertheless, the discussion surrounding "Azadn Gomidas" echoed in all of the major newspapers and journals of the diaspora, from Beirut's *Pakin* to Paris's *Harach* and Boston's *Bayk'ar*. Aside from their private correspondence on this occasion, both Davtian and Shahnur continued to publish follow-up articles. This public exchange marked Shahnur as a figure of controversy.[49] Although many of the editors of the diaspora's journals expressed protective sentiments with respect to Shahnur when framing the debate, Shahnur's harsh critical regard (however old) of diasporan Armenians remained offensive to their sense of collectivity. To salvage their respect for his great talent, they attributed his low estimation of Armenians to the pressures of integration. Consequently, the concretization of the accepted reading of his emblematic *Nahanchĕ* as a defeatist novel about assimilation became the legacy of this controversy.

Indeed, following Shahnur's death, *Nahanchĕ* became synonymous with its author. Mourning the loss of one of the diaspora's most notable writers, the Beirut-based *Pakin* writes, "Shahnur wrote his masterpiece,

a work synonymous with and analogous to his name, *Nahanchĕ Aṙants'*
Erki. Some of its pages may pale under the pressures of their journalistic
identity. Others yet may drown in the waters of anachronistic sentiments.
What will remain indestructible is its truth, its design, its call, its supplica-
tion, its soul-sustaining spirit, 'that old melody, familiar to all.'"[50] In addition to the implied parallel between the author and his novel's protagonist
(we might think of it as Shahnur/Lubin = Bedros/Pierre), *Pakin*'s editorial designated an afterlife of responsibility for *Nahanchĕ*. Attributing to
it "indestructible" qualities that would withstand time, the editorial is one
of the many commemorative articles that archived *Nahanchĕ* as a novel
that forewarns its readers of the dangers of assimilation.

Thus recruited into a nationalist agenda of cultural preservation,
Nahanchĕ became the "exceptional" novel of the diaspora because of its
widespread circulation and readership. It gained representational authority for its warning against assimilation, which directly nurtured the concept of return inherent to the national narrative. As such, it fitted neatly
into the emergent post–World War II literacy apparatus that sought to cultivate a collective imagination of homeland. On the occasion of the fiftieth
anniversary of the novel's publication, Krikor Keoseian drastically contrasted this accepted perception by claiming that *"Nahanchĕ Aṙants' Erki*
has not yet been read."[51] He meant that it had not been read outside the
framework of its prescriptive interpretation of a "warning against assimilation." He elaborated, "Shahnur remains our most read and most talked
about 'diasporan Armenian' writer, but it is with bitterness that I repeat
the above statement, and to add that we have not yet understood anything
from it. Or rather, we have not wanted to understand, since nothing has
changed in our way of thinking or acting during this past half a century."[52]

Although Keoseian's concern might still hold true today within the
curriculum of the diaspora's Armenian high schools, *Nahanchĕ* has
enjoyed new and innovative readings by Armenian literary critics. Most
notable are the analytical works of Marc Nichanian and Krikor Beledian,
who emerged as critics, writers, and translators during the decade following Shahnur's death. Often regarded as the continuers of the interrupted
French Armenian tradition of the 1930s, Nichanian and Beledian have
offered compelling readings of the work of the Menk generation. In the

case of *Nahanchě*, they have provoked new critical readings by engaging the novel's theme of sexuality and desire as a way of addressing the national question that appeared exhausted in previous readings.[53] In particular, their contributions to developing the idea of the "internal estrangement of Armenians" or the "internal Othering" enable us to read in *Nahanchě* Shahnur's attempt at redefining the category of the "national" as *azkaynagan* rather than *azkayin*. Beledian limits Shahnur's understanding of the national question as developed in *Nahanchě* by using the term *azkaynagan*, and translates it as "l'esprit national." The discussion around *azkaynagan* echoes back to Nigoghos Sarafian's distinction of the term from *azkayin*, developed in his contribution to the debate "Azkayinn u Michazkayině Kraganutyan Mēch" (The National and International in Literature), published in *Zuart'nots'* in 1929.[54] *Azkaynagan* is meant to have a constructivist, cultural connotation rather than an essentialist, nationalist one.

Within Shahnur's novel, the realm of the *azkayin*, the unquestioned "national," is embodied by the Armenian Church. It is precisely this notion of *azkayin* that Shahnur wants to disrupt by opposing it with pornography and the realm of the French. *Azkaynagan*, or what Beledian refers to as "l'esprit national,"[55] is the spirit that results from the encounter between Armenian and French, church and pornography. *Azkaynagan*, for protagonist Bedros/Pierre, translates to a spirit of retreat and loss, whereas for Shahnur it becomes the foundational element for the creation of a novel. In the novel's prescriptive interpretation, the character of Suren, rather than Bedros, is emphasized as the exemplary "assimilator." Among the group of young Armenians that Bedros occasionally associates with, Suren is a vocal intellectual who takes a resentful stance against Armenian culture and embraces the French, in whose language he writes. He is best remembered for delivering a long, inflammatory speech defaming the *Book of Lamentations* by the tenth-century Armenian monk and poet Grigor Narekatsi. Interestingly, the denigration of this book of biblical and mystical poems, which Armenians regard as fundamental to the development of the Armenian language, occurs in the middle of a discussion of pornography.

The character of Suren has often been read, too hastily, as being the closest to Shahnur's own voice. In a piece that compares *Nahanchě*'s original publication with a later Soviet Armenian edition, *Pakin*'s editorial states, "The real issue is the 'affliction of the nationalist,' that common psychosis of our 1920s and 30s exiled youth, which each of their souls turned into a chaos of deep cries, painful deliriums, and violent curses and led each of them to 'unconditionally throw someone on the culprit's chair.' Shahnur grabbed Narekatsi's collar."[56] This *Pakin* article equates a fictional character's remarks about Narekatsi with the author's own point of view, without problematizing or presenting any awareness of the conflation. Rather, based on a misguided assumption, the article excuses Shahnur's accusation of Narekatsi by describing the need to blame as a condition of the postgenocide Armenian youth.

Moreover, with this justification, *Pakin* suggests that it is entitled to take a protective stance with respect to the passages in which Suren makes his anti-Narekatsi speech. In fact, the article is intended to criticize Soviet Armenia's publication of *Nahanchĕ* and its many omissions, especially of Suren's speech. In the original publication of *Nahanchĕ*, Suren launches his attack by claiming, "Armenians have a book. It is their worst, most annoying, most erroneous, most harmful, and above all, their most immoral book. I denounce Narek[57] as the greatest enemy of Armenians; I accuse the wretched person who spit out its lines."[58] The speech extends over the next few pages of the novel. Although Suren begins by accusing Grigor Narekatsi, he shifts the responsibility to Armenians in general for accepting the "poisonous" book's content as a foundational decree for their identity construction. According to Suren, this unquestioned acceptance has resulted in the Armenians' defeatist history and ideology by forcing multiple generations to ignore the development of their sense of individuality: "We didn't fight, we didn't bite, we didn't dispute. By accepting his faulty and imperfect interpretation of Christian dogma, we became unmindfully passive, accommodating, suppliant, and unconscious."[59] With no sign of objection or interruption from his listener, Bedros, Suren continues in his accusatory tone. He belittles Armenians throughout history as weak, destructive, and regressive, ultimately arriving at the present, which he declares the period of "retreat" (the title of the novel).

Whereas Suren's famous speech offended the sense of nationalism of many critics and readers, the editors and authors of *Pakin*, a literary journal associated with the ARF, the socialist party at the helm of the diaspora's cultural nationalism agenda, found Soviet Armenia's censorship politics even more offensive. Arguing that Suren/Shahnur's mentality marks a moment in the postgenocide psychology of Armenians in dispersion, the *Pakin* article condemns the Yerevan publication for violating the integrity of a diasporan work of art, especially since its diasporan readers have endowed the work with representative value. Thus, the article offers a comparative overview of the differences between the original publication and the Soviet Armenian publication: it lists the passages that have been reduced, revised, or cut, in both original and altered form. The list's final emphasis lies on the passage of Suren's speech. What *Pakin* counts as ninety-two lines in the original is reduced to ten lines in the Soviet publication. The ten lines make no mention of Narek or Narekatsi. Instead, they summarize Suren's speech as a "descending slope of reflections" and end his monologue with the declaration about the state of retreat.[60]

Pakin uses the example of this liberal omission as an opportunity to criticize Soviet Armenia and its censorship policies, as well as to express disappointment in Shahnur's failure to respond on the occasion of the Soviet publication in 1962. The article maintains its protectiveness toward Suren's speech, which it calls "a shocking, flavorful outcry." *Pakin*'s position was shared by few of Shahnur's readers and critics, who refused to defend or accept the defamation of Narekatsi. In an interesting parallel to the Soviet publication's omission, the English translation of the novel also leaves out the majority of Suren's speech. Mischa Kudian's 1982 translation *Retreat without Song* simply cuts out the beginning of the passage. Thus, skipping over the remarks about Narekatsi and the impact of his alleged defeatist legacy on Armenians, Kudian picks up the narrative with Suren's comments on the state of retreat.[61] Unlike the Soviet publication's attempt at neutral summary, Kudian's translation opts for a straightforward exclusion.[62] Up until the 2016 translation of Vorpuni's novel *The Candidate*, *Nahanchě* was the only novel of the Menk generation translated into English. Although its widespread circulation means that the novel is an exception among the French Armenian novels published between the wars, the exception lies not in the work itself, but in its mode of reception. Its acceptance into the canon of diaspora literature reveals a violent appropriation of the work, a series of forced alterations in the reading and reproduction of the text to make it fit the cultural narrative of the diaspora.

Shahnur's lasting popularity as both a figure of controversy and a representative of his generation presents him as a writer who "survived" the move of the diaspora's intellectual center from Paris to the Middle East following World War II. Yet it was not only later critics who contributed to his popularity by engaging with his work. Many of his contemporary colleagues during the first decade of his literary career also vocally opposed his provocative outcries and his views on "retreat" as an unavoidable yet artistically productive realm. Although Menk maintained a resolute stance in line with Shahnur's in favor of a literature of dispersion, polarities regarding the question of national literature and homeland existed from the group's conception. One who stands out as particularly vocal on the opposite end of the spectrum from Shahnur is Vazken Shushanian (1903–41), most of whose work has been published posthumously in Beirut and recently in Yerevan. Shushanian's popularity in posthumous publication suggests an interesting parallel to Shahnur, and, against the backdrop of their opposing political and literary ideologies, it raises questions about their exceptional reception by critics, journalists, and publishing institutions.

When he died at age thirty-eight, Shushanian left behind a considerable number of unpublished manuscripts. Although he had published poetry, prose, and journalistic writings in various community journals and newspapers, *Karnanayin, Siroy Hez Namagner* (Springtime: Gentle Love Letters) (Paris, 1928) and *Amran Kisherner* (Summer Nights) (Cairo, 1930) were his only two standalone publications prior to his death. The survival of his personal archives was ensured, for the most part, by his meticulous efforts to document the whereabouts of his manuscripts. Following his death, *Hayrenik' Monthly* published a list, prepared by Shushanian, that presents his writings by genre, title, form in which they were preserved, and number of pages and categorizes them according to location.[63] The list reveals that the majority of his manuscripts were saved at the Mkhitarian Monastery in Vienna, awaiting editing and publication. Over the next few decades, many of the novelistic writings on the list were published in Beirut.[64] Although the publication trend was concentrated in the 1950s, interest in Shushanian's work remained active, as many of his novels underwent second publications. Efforts to demystify Shushanian's politics, in contrast, were slow to develop, but reached fruition through the publication of his writings against Shahnur.

First published by *Pakin* in 1997 and then published as a book in 1998, Shushanian's *Mart Mĕ Or Ararat Ch'uni Ir Hokwoyn Khorĕ* (A Man Who Has No Ararat in the Depth of His Soul) accuses Shahnur of lacking all sense of national belonging. Written as an angry, unleashed rant, the 144-page criticism refuses to hide behind euphemisms and attacks Shahnur and his reputation as a prominent figure in Armenian national literature using specific references, dates, and publications. *Nahanchĕ*'s Suren's defamatory speech about Narekatsi lies at the heart of Shushanian's tirade. Referring to Shahnur as a "dirty, sucking louse," he devotes many pages of his narrative to setting Narekatsi on a pedestal and calls him a "king," "a roaring poet and son of the gods."[65] In fact, Shushanian devotes an entire chapter, "Our Gratefulness to Narekatsi," to rebuking Shahnur's attacks and reclaiming the contributions of Narekatsi to the creation of the Armenian spirit. Concurrently, he develops his argument that Shahnur's soul is devoid of that very spirit. Extending his disappointment further, he claims that many, like Shahnur, are unaware that they need to cast the light of their criticism with caution when it comes to certain domains that hold national value. For Shushanian, Shahnur exceeds them all: "It's not up to every Shahnur to hold up a crooked scale, like that of a Skiwdar[66] shop-keeper, to stand in front of history, and to place an entire living nation on one side and a common rascal's endless self-conceit on the other. To place in one of the scale's trays a nation's entire civilization, and in the other, a vulgar apostate's dark soul."[67] According to Shushanian, Shahnur's lack of sensitivity toward the figure of Narekatsi reflects a deeper abandonment of cultural and national values, and it derives from having a "dark soul." In other words, in the eyes of Shushanian, Shahnur has embraced a defeatist position that not only passively accepts retreat as the natural course, but also uses the process of retreat to actively denounce the culture he leaves behind.

The title of the work defines "dark soul" a bit more elaborately as a soul empty of "Ararat." Mount Ararat is an Armenian national symbol,

although it is now located in Turkey. Though it can be seen from the
Armenian Republic's capital, Yerevan, its image is all the more present
in the collective imagination of Armenians living in the diaspora. It has
come to represent a unified Armenia, since its incorporation would entail
the inclusion of historic Armenian lands into modern Armenia's borders.
Thus, the accusation that Shahnur lacks this symbolic referent succinctly
conveys Shushanian's understanding of Shahnur's politics. Rather than
connecting Shahnur's literary efforts with his proposal of a diaspora politics, Shushanian continuously reads Shahnur against his own nationalist
politics,[68] which invariably demand a politics of return. Hence, the homeland debate once again commands all discussion surrounding the potential of national literature in the diaspora. Subsequently, the generational
divide is implied through the discussion of Armenian literary tradition.
In *Mart Mĕ Or Ararat Ch'uni Ir Hokwoyn Khorĕ*, Shushanian positions
Shahnur against the surviving generation of writers, whose work he praises
as exemplary, and urges his colleagues to look to them as teachers. Shushanian, who edited the first two issues of *Menk'*, had clearly abandoned the
fundamental principles of the group by 1939, when he completed *Mart
Mĕ Or Ararat Ch'uni Ir Hokwoyn Khorĕ*. Rather than calling for a break
from the literary tradition of the past, he vehemently advocates following
the example of Oshagan, Levon Shant, Hamasdegh, and Zabel Yesayan.[69]
In this way, he fits neatly into the cultural narrative that emerged from
Beirut after World War II. Shushanian is generally seen not as a figure
who disrupts the chain of tradition, but rather as someone who links the
nationalist narrative of pre-1915 Constantinople to the post–World War II
diaspora. Shahnur, in contrast, is seen as a figure of controversy and used
as an example to warn against assimilation and retreat.

Literary Creation and the Building of a Nation in Exile

In Shahnur's *Nahanchĕ*, Bedros's friend Lokhum is the only character who
refuses to retreat into French culture. This refusal leads him to the verge of
delirium and drug use. Lokhum feels trapped in exile and attempts to leave
France, the site of his prison. Having left his parents behind in Istanbul, he
appeals to the Turkish embassy for a return visa, but his efforts are in vain.

He turns to the Russian embassy for permission to enter Soviet Armenia, but he is brutally rejected. In a moment of madness, he cries out to Bedros, "What ungodly, inhumane, barbaric law is this? Which cursed hand recorded it? Which withering brain forced it on our fate? I have a mother. I have a father. Why should I stay away from them? . . . Why should I not be allowed to go to Istanbul? Who am I? What am I? Which state will concern itself with me, with us?"[70] Lokhum's statelessness deprives him of choice and compels him to question his very existence. He feels imprisoned in France, knowing that this host country will eventually efface his ethnic and cultural heritage, and hence his identity. Although Lokhum's hauntingly expressed feelings of entrapment spoke to many Armenian refugees in dispersion, his response appears unproductive.

Menk proposed that exile might have the opposite effect on the artist and the intellectual. Urging his contemporaries to embrace the state of exile, Menk's Sarafian speaks with a liberating undertone: "Our homeland fled, it slipped away from underneath our feet, leaving us to the open sea. But this is the best opportunity to learn how to swim. It is up to us to dive in, without stopping to measure, without fear."[71] What Sarafian and the short-lived Menk group put forth is a case for exile as a productive experience. Within this framework, dispersion is seen as a realm that is constructive not only for occasioning confrontation with other cultures, but also for allowing a networked consciousness of Armenian communities. And while Sarafian claims that Yerevan will one day serve as the real opportunity to create something uncompromisingly Armenian, he sees opportunity and promise in carving out a new space of exiled community (*kaghut'ayin*)[72] literature.

By contrast, Costan Zarian, responding to Sarafian, dismisses Menk's celebration of exile. He argues that a language cannot exist outside state institutions that validate and standardize linguistic development. He writes, "Language exists where people live in assimilated masses, where there are schools, universities, and some semblance of state-sanctioned life. Language exists where there are streets, where they curse in Armenian, where there are factories filled with Armenian laborers, where the villager still cultivates his land and sings his song."[73] On this basis, he finds the notion of exilic literature improbable: it is an ambitious and immature objective that blocks recognition of the dire political circumstances of dispersion.[74]

In fact, Zarian's insistence that a nation-state is integral to the development of the literary arts ultimately became the dominant assumption that dictated literary production. The polarization of the homeland debate that followed World War II and the triumph of the idea of a unified homeland in the diaspora prevented Menk's proposed literary and artistic project from reaching its transnational potential. In the following decades, a more nationalist narrative defined dispersion as diaspora and imagined it as a temporary reality that had to prepare for an eventual return. The national model that guided literary production following World War II prioritized the linguistic homogenization of dispersed communities, believing, in the vein of Zarian's argument, that a standardized Western Armenian would be both the means of repairing the genocide's rupture and the key to safeguarding the potential of return.

5

Homogenous Time

The Making of Diaspora's Grand Narrative

In 1958, Simon Simonian, a public intellectual originally from Aleppo, established a weekly journal called *Sp'iwṙk'* (Diaspora) in Beirut. Seeking to represent cultural and literary life in the diaspora, the journal carried weight in its name that would later acquire historical significance. In bearing the name *Sp'iwṙk'*, a term that was gaining currency at the time, the journal also contributed to the process of naming the transnationally dispersed Armenian communities as a single collective body, inevitably centered in Beirut. The journal's appearance marked the end of the transition period that reshaped Armenian intellectual life in dispersion following World War II. During this period, those individuals who were once referred to during the years of postgenocide dispersion as *t'rk'ahayut'iwn* (Turkish Armenians), *ts'ruadzut'iwn* (dispersion), *kaghut'ahayut'iwn* (exiled community of Armenians), *kaght'ahayut'iwn* (migrant Armenians), and *ardasahmni hayut'iwn* (Armenians abroad) became solidified as *sp'iwṙk'* (diaspora),[1] owing to the formation of community institutions that cultivated a transnational network along with a corresponding grand narrative. As a result, the center of discourse shifted away from the longer-standing Armenian communities in places like Boston, New York, and Paris to the Middle East, where intellectuals young and old spearheaded the articulation of a narrative that refashioned diaspora as a homogenous entity and recognized its literature as a national literature in exile. They established this narrative by distinguishing the Western Armenian literary tradition from its Eastern Armenian counterpart and by critiquing the idea that diaspora literature should serve the Soviet project. While some intellectuals and writers whose political outlook aligned them with Soviet Armenia envisioned Armenian literature as unitary, many diaspora writers of this period imagined Western Armenian literature as a distinctly diasporic space, independent of any hierarchical relationship with Soviet Armenian literature. In other words, they saw Western Armenian literature as operating horizontally across other Armenian diaspora communities, and vertically, in a reflexive relationship with the past of its own tradition and not that of the Soviet Armenian nation-state.

Sp'iwṙk''s editor shared the same view regarding the Armenian diaspora's autonomy from Soviet Armenia. In one of its first editorial pieces, Simonian highlighted the diasporic nature of the Armenian experience and reminded his readers that most Armenians in the world live in diasporic communities, in what he divided as the "Soviet-Armenian Diaspora" and the "Non-Soviet Armenian Diaspora."[2] Underscoring this diasporicity as a permanent reality for Armenians, he argued that the task of culturally preserving the Soviet Armenian diaspora belongs to the homeland (that is, the Soviet Armenian Republic), whereas the cultural cultivation of the non-Soviet Armenian diaspora falls under the jurisdiction of diasporic institutions such as his journal.[3] In its initial years of publication, going beyond the mission of cultural preservation, *Sp'iwṙk'*'s editorials argued for lofty endeavors of diasporic governance like the foundation of a central Armenian bank in the diaspora and the establishment of an Armenian Supreme Council to oversee the affairs of the Armenian diaspora.[4] Just a few decades earlier, in one of the early uses of the term *sp'iwṙk'*, the editors of *Ergunk'* had published surveys that asked their readers for aid in collecting demographic information about community life in host countries. "In which cities of your host country do Armenians live?" asked one of the survey questions.[5] Within these early and later efforts of defining the dispersed communities, two parallel questions emerged that link the machinations of diasporic organization with the politics of naming. What was the driving force behind the need to organize the surviving generations of Armenians living outside Soviet Armenia as a distinct political entity? How, in tandem, did the language of communities in dispersion come to be replaced with the language of diaspora?[6]

Ideas of homeland and return guided the discursive refashioning of dispersion into diaspora. The language of dispersion that gave meaning to the postgenocide reality of Armenian life rightly envisioned a scattering of survivors across the world into a perpetually expanding network of communities. In the 1920s, discussions of return were concrete, bound to the specific sites of the survivors' expulsion (their homes and towns), and they were soon recognized as fruitless and abandoned. The notion of return gained currency once again in the 1940s, when upon the request of the new Armenian catholicos Gevorg VI, Stalin asked for the repatriation of diaspora Armenians to Soviet Armenia. From 1945 to 1948, about a hundred thousand refugees (less than 10 percent of Armenians in dispersion) emigrated to Soviet Armenia, as the result of an organized campaign that was supported by the Armenian Church and Armenian political parties throughout the world.[7] The refugees, who were originally from historic Armenia or Cilicia, complicated the notion of return through their emigration to Soviet Armenia. This return was not a literal one, but a symbolic one founded on a nationalist embrace of Soviet Armenia as home. For those persons who were left out of the repatriating caravans, the reality of dispersion gained permanence and gave birth to an all the more symbolic, and perhaps even mythical, idea of return. As dispersed communities imagined themselves more and more as a diaspora, they began to envision a delayed return to a unified homeland that would one day include the lands lost to Turkey and Soviet Armenia. Khachig Tölölyan describes this process of collective imagining as "exilic transnationalism," advanced by the efforts of communal elites and institutions who formed a diasporic civil society with the goal of preserving the nation in exile while awaiting return.[8]

I would like to propose that this shift toward fashioning a global Armenian diaspora, which was political in nature, was facilitated by a linguistic and literary debate concerning Western Armenian and a corresponding literary theory that produced competing models of national literature. It was precisely through these debates concerning language that the campaign of *azkabahbanum*, what Tölölyan calls "nation preservation," developed. The logic of this campaign called for the development of a transnational literacy apparatus meant to cultivate Western Armenian language in exile by repairing its severed link to the past and by preparing for its eventual return to the homeland. Part of what fueled the emphasis on language and literature as a marker of national identity was the growing rift between Western Armenian and its Eastern counterpart, owing to the progress the latter linguistic form was making in Soviet Armenia. As part of its program for a cultural revolution, Soviet Armenia officially proclaimed Armenian its state language and began to build its cultural infrastructure, which consisted of establishing a national library, museum, theater, university, and so on.[9] In a 1921 decree to eradicate illiteracy, orthography was also reformed. As a result, by 1940, the Armenian government was able to announce its adult population's attainment of full literacy. While the reformed orthography helped achieve the linguistic homogenization of Soviet Armenia's population (a desired outcome), it also widened the division between Soviet Armenians and the people in dispersion. With the exception of Iranian Armenians, Armenians living outside Soviet Armenia were speakers of Western Armenian, and this language's literature factions and publishing institutions continued to use the classical orthography. As Eastern Armenian benefited from state sponsorship and built a mechanism of production, publication, and circulation, anti-Soviet intellectuals in the diaspora began to question the motives of Soviet authorities and argued that the language reforms were part of an orchestrated campaign to further separate Soviet Armenians from those Armenians in dispersion. The politicization of the language debate reached a turning point immediately after World War II, when in the midst of the repatriation campaign, Middle Eastern Armenian intellectuals began to write explicitly against Soviet Armenia, criticizing its refusal to recognize the validity of Western Armenian as part of the greater Armenian culture.

In this chapter, I examine the literary debates produced by two competing conferences that served as catalysts for solidifying the dispersion as diaspora and for shifting its intellectual center from Paris to the Middle East. Whereas the post–World War I group of writers in Paris, predominantly the ones gathered around the literary group Menk, had sought to lay the foundations for a new literature outside of tradition and rooted in their experience of displacement in the French locale, the post–World

War II writers in Lebanon and Syria attempted to connect to the pre-1915 tradition and to develop a national literature in Western Armenian against the backdrop of an imagined unified homeland of the future. I argue that the Second Congress of the Soviet Armenian Writers' Union, held in Yerevan in 1946 with the participation of a select group of diaspora writers, and a reactionary conference organized by the Writers' Association of Syria and Lebanon, held in Shtora, Lebanon, in 1948, served to launch a new body of literature that now explicitly called itself literature of the Armenian diaspora. These rival conferences caused diaspora intellectuals to realize the threat facing the Western Armenian language in exile and incidentally to position Beirut, and more broadly the Middle East, as the hub for the centralization and standardization efforts of Western Armenian language and literature. By following the debates that these rival conferences inspired, we can trace not only the emergence of a new intellectual and cultural center, but also the making of a more political grand narrative of the diaspora.

Diaspora's Contested Presence at the 1946 Congress of Soviet Armenian Writers' Union

In September 1946, nine diaspora writers—Garabed Sidal (1891–1972) from the United States; Levon Mesrob (1880–1960), Zareh Vorpuni (1902–80), and Aram Charek (1874–1947) from France; Vahé Vahian (1907–98) and Hovhannes Aghbashian (1910–87) from Lebanon; Smpad Derounian (1923–2016) from Cyprus; and Hayk Garagash (1893–1960) and Aram Yeremian (1898–1972) from Iran—journeyed to the emergent capital of Soviet Armenia to participate in the Second Congress of the Soviet Armenian Writers' Union as invited guests. These select writers, who participated in the Congress with no official representative authority, savored the invitation mostly on a personal level, as a rare opportunity to rest their exiled feet on their people's soil and to validate their contribution to a national literary tradition. In his travel log, Vorpuni went as far as to claim that it was at the Yerevan airport that his childhood loss and the subsequent experience of orphanhood found closure and his process of becoming a mature subject began. "I was finally a man among men," he wrote.[10]

Following a 1932 decree by the Communist Party's Central Committee, the various existing writers' associations and organizations were dissolved in Soviet Armenia.[11] This move was prelude to the establishment of
a single union, the Union of Soviet Writers of Armenia, which was established in 1934.[12] In many ways, it functioned as the mechanism by which
publications were monitored and guaranteed to serve the party line.[13] By
extension, the union also dictated the terms of Soviet Armenian writers'
relationship with diaspora writers and the literature they produced. For
some in the diaspora, the centralization of literary output in Soviet Armenia was seen as an effort to create oppositional hierarchy between Soviet
and diasporic production of language and literature. In the initial year
of the union's formation, diaspora publications followed Soviet Armenia's
reorganization of writers' circles intently,[14] while, on the other hand, the
emergent Writers' Union curated a narrative of diaspora literature that
fit the Soviet Union's ideological demands. For example, at the Writers'
Union's first congress, Zabel Yesayan, who had settled down in Armenia
at that point and was one of the first twenty-five members accepted into
the union, addressed the politics of literature produced by Armenians
"abroad" and grouped diaspora intellectuals as either fascist-nationalists
or as being sympathetic to the revolutionary Soviet literature.[15]

Consequently, since no diaspora writers had been invited to the first
congress in 1934, the 1946 announcement of Avetik Isahakian (then president of the Writers' Union) that extended an invitation to diaspora writers
elicited mixed voices and uproar, especially among uninvited intellectuals from various diaspora communities.[16] Pro-Soviet publications immediately applauded the unprecedented inclusion of diaspora writers in the
momentous gathering that was to discuss the state and future of Armenian
literature at large.[17] Further, they viewed the invitation as an initial step in
the establishment of open relations between Soviet Armenia and the diaspora, directly coinciding with the greater plans for repatriation already
under way during those years.[18] Anti-Soviet publications, predominantly
affiliated directly or indirectly with the ARF, harshly criticized the invitation for imposing strictly ideological preconditions.[19] They claimed that
the invited writers had been chosen simply for their post-Soviet attitudes
and branded them as second rate,[20] even though the group of invitees

included established novelists like Zareh Vorpuni and Levon Mesrob and periodical editors like Hovhannes Aghbashian (*Zhoghovurti Tsayn*), Vahé Vahian (*Ani*), and Hayk Garagash (*Veradznunt*). Most important, they argued that Soviet Armenia's gesture constituted a political formality with false pretenses, ultimately designed to deny a representative voice to the diaspora and to exclude the Western Armenian language and culture from processes of nation building.

Amid the polarized debate, others still, such as Arshag Chobanian[21] of the Parisian review *Anahid*, were reluctant to either applaud or criticize. While agreeing with and commending the Writers' Union's gesture on principle, Chobanian remained skeptical of productive results and awaited the long-term outcome of diaspora-homeland relations by directing his anticipatory breath toward Soviet Armenia.[22] Indeed, the historical moment surrounding the Second Congress was ripe with possibilities that could shape or reshape the collective identities of Armenians living both in Soviet Armenia and in diaspora communities. The Second World War and the Soviet Union's triumph over the Nazi invasion had renewed Armenia's belief in the Soviet order—a patriotic sentiment that was shared by many nationalist Armenians abroad, who now embraced Soviet Armenia as a permanent homeland and thus as a place for desired return. Furthermore, the Soviet claims to Kars and Ardahan and the ensuing process of repatriation, launched in 1945 and welcomed across political party lines in diaspora communities, infused Soviet Armenia with a new sense of nationalism that, on the one hand, highlighted and affirmed the quality of salvation attributed to the Soviet project and, on the other hand, explicitly bound a defined plot of Armenian land to the concept of homeland. Simultaneously, in offering some diaspora Armenians a release from exilic life, the repatriation helped to consolidate the remaining dispersed communities into a single entity that self-reflexively began referring to itself as the diaspora, in direct relation to either Soviet Armenia or an imagined greater Armenia.

The consolidation of diasporic Armenian populations following World War II also had a literary counterpart. Although Armenian intellectuals continued to gather around publications in various cities of the world, the dominant post–World War I intellectual scene shifted from

Paris to the Middle East, where Cairo, Aleppo, and especially Beirut began to take center stage in the diaspora's intellectual discourse and literary production. After a few decades of community building in dispersion, the threat of assimilation had become a daunting reality for Armenian communities in Western countries. In 1948, an article in Boston's *Hayrenik'* *Monthly* referred to the Armenian community in the United States as the most *annbasd* (disadvantageous) community, arguing that in the absence of Armenian day schools, there were no prospects for language mainte-nance.[23] Assessing the Middle East communities as more favorable spaces, political parties there worked toward constructing cultural and educa-tional structures that sought to preserve the language.[24] These newfound educational institutions made a concerted effort to standardize and reviv-ify the Western Armenian linguistic form. In addition to standardization efforts in Armenian day schools, a political campaign designed to prohibit the use of Turkish in colloquial speech within the refugee population was adopted by community organizations.[25] Ultimately, both endeavors forged a linguistically homogenous group out of a culturally diverse population. Within a few decades, regional dialects and Turkish colloquial speech had given way to a standard Western Armenian that was based on the pre-1915 Constantinople or "Bolis" variant.[26] In due course, Beirut and Aleppo, with their publishing houses, emerged as centers of production for textbooks, journals, and literature that cultivated the new standard.

Thus, it should come as no surprise that the debate over affiliation and belonging instigated by the 1946 Congress of the Soviet Armenian Writ-ers' Union revolved around the issue of language. While the controversy might appear simply to mirror political alignments and ideological argu-ments,[27] the central debate that emerged from the Second Congress was about the fate of the Western Armenian linguistic form. The debate that developed in the diaspora's journals was inspired by the congress's treat-ment of diaspora literature as subsidiary to Soviet Armenian literature. Avetik Isahakian's opening remarks promptly claimed that the congress's most valuable outcome would be the strengthening of relations between literature of the homeland and literature of the diaspora. To explain how this projected goal should translate to tangible action by writers of the diaspora, he pronounced a phrase, "Mi kraganut'iwn mi zhoghovurt ē"

(One literature is one people),[28] which subsequently became the dictum of his speech, to be used, reproduced, translated, and mistranslated by diaspora journals as "one literature, one nation," "one literature, one language", and so on. In fact, Isahakian's phrase was meant to explain the cultural and historical significance of literature's representational value. In other words, it implies that literature is the representation of its people. With this meaning, the phrase serves as the preamble to his overview of the history of Armenian literature, in which Isahakian links the Eastern Armenian literary tradition to Soviet Armenian literature, which in turn he fundamentally subordinates to what he calls "the greatest and most progressive literature of the world," that of the Soviet Union. In calling for the perpetuation of socialist realism, a literary approach in which works propagate Soviet ideology, Isahakian turns to military language and identifies Soviet Armenian literature as a *chogad*, or a "detachment," of Soviet literature, and names diaspora writers as *zinagits*, "comrades in arms," of that unit. He tasks the diaspora writer with "a holy obligation" to sing the praise of Soviet Armenia as the only homeland for Armenians and to ensure the success of repatriation through his or her written word. He says, "They shall serve as a bridge in order to spread the cultural, artistic, and literary wealth of Soviet Armenia and to create a unified literature around Soviet Armenian literature."[29]

In many respects, the hierarchy outlined by Isahakian in his opening remarks provided the overall structure for the first series of reports presented at the congress. The overarching direction of literary production was dictated by the report on Soviet literature, presented earlier that month at the meeting of the Soviet Writers' Union in Leningrad and prepared by Andrei Zhdanov, who had just been appointed by Stalin to direct the Soviet Union's cultural policy and was also present at the congress in Yerevan.[30] The outgoing secretary of the Soviet Armenian Writers' Union, Hrachia Krikorian, presented the report "Soviet Armenian Literature and Its Paths for Future Development."[31] And Eduard Topchian, a Yerevan native, presented the report "Contemporary Armenian Literature Abroad."

While the diaspora invitees were allocated fifteen minutes each to present their views on Armenian literature of their regions, Topchian's report served as the official stance of the Writers' Union on diaspora literature. Denying the diaspora any possibility for artistic creation in exile, the report says, "Over the last thirty years, the Armenian people, who were uprooted from their fatherland, passed through the roads of suffering and bore countless grievances and deprivation. Artistic literature shared the people's fate, bearing the deadly stamp of alienation."[32] It then presents a number of French Armenian and American Armenian writers within the framework of assimilation's threat and criticizes others such as Levon Shant, Hagop Oshagan, and Hamasdegh for their nationalistic approach of looking backward at history rather than forward to the future as inspiration for their writing.[33] Topchian concludes his report by recommending that diaspora literature consider nurturing the concept of return and the building of a socialist homeland as its sole trajectory. Otherwise, he sees only decline and death in its future, a verdict that he is not reluctant to express openly: "This literature, which is detached from its homeland and its people, has no prospect for development. True art can flourish only if it is intimately fused with its motherland and its people."[34] Implicit in Topchian's dismissal of art in exile is the narrow limitation of the Armenian people to those individuals living on Armenian lands. But more important, similar to Isahakian's call to build a literature around Soviet Armenian literature, it completely omits the Western Armenian literary tradition from the establishment of this unified Armenian literature.

The invited diaspora writers at the congress were not quick to raise the issue of the Western Armenian language and literature. Overwhelmed by feelings of homecoming, they embraced the ideal of unity. At the conference, Hovhannes Aghbashian took the stage and on behalf of Syrian and Lebanese Armenians thanked comrade Stalin for initiating the repatriation efforts and saving Western Armenians from perpetual exile. He added, "This is a historically unique conference, because in tandem with the unification of the Armenian people already under way, it seeks to unify the Armenian literature of the mother fatherland and of the Diaspora."[35] For Aghbashian, this particular conference objective was both timely and historically significant, since no such endeavor had been attempted during the many centuries that divided the two cultural components of the Armenian people. In a similar vein, Vahé Vahian's articles in his journal

Ani, penned upon his return to Beirut, reiterate Isahakian's dictum and affirm Topchian's dismissal of art in exile.[36] Vahian writes: "Until the complete realization of the ideal, one people and one literature, joined together on the fatherland, the only force of existence for our literature that has been imbued with the fate of exile, can sprout from our mother country, our people, and a deep, unconditional, and holy communication with its culture. There you have it! This is the faith and direction for those who believe in the Armenian spirit."[37] His travel log, *Haralēzneru Hashdut'iwnĕ* (The Reconciliation of the Aralez),[38] first published serially in *Ani* in 1947 and then in book form in 1953, offers an expanded development of the same conviction. Avoiding the question of linguistic form altogether, Vahian's *Haralēzneru Hashdut'iwnĕ* performs precisely what Isahakian and Topchian demand of literature produced in the diaspora: it praises Soviet Armenia and encourages the repatriation campaign.[39] In fact, Vahé Vahian's and Hovhannes Aghbashian's journey to Soviet Armenia began on the fifth ship of repatriates to leave the port of Beirut on September 12, 1946, a coincidence that offers a convenient narrative parallel to Vahian's memoir of return, which is filled with emotional language about homecoming, belonging, and the economic, educational, and cultural progress of Soviet Armenia. Content with the univocal alignment of language, literature, people, and land, he ends his travel memoir with a slogan that once again hints at Isahakian's dictum, exclaiming, "One people, one culture."

One of the French invitees, novelist Zareh Vorpuni, also published his travel logs, in this case as a book called *Tēbi Ergir* (Toward Homeland) in 1948. Both in his articles published in periodicals such as *Arewmudk'* and in his travel memoir, Vorpuni is more critical than Vahian of Topchian's report. While claiming that it does not paint an accurate picture of diaspora literature, he excuses Topchian's faulty conclusions by blaming the lack of resources at hand, a condition he feels resulted from diaspora writers' refusal to send copies of their books to Soviet Armenia. In general, although Vorpuni's travel memoir is more cognizant of the language issue at stake and the emphasis on a single unified literature, it buries the greater related questions of literary affiliation and belonging once again under a narrative of homecoming.

Other diaspora writers, however, responded in an uproar following the release and publication of Isahakian's speech and Topchian's report presented at the Second Congress. As expected, the political party affiliations of the intellectuals and journals dictated the general nature of their responses. Yet, interestingly, the arguments presented had less to do with political ideology in the form of praising or criticizing the Soviet order than with language and literary tradition. The articles published in *Hayrenik' Monthly* treat Topchian's report as a direct attack on Western Armenian, which they more frequently refer to as *t'rk'ahayerēn* (Turkish Armenian). Minas Teoleolian, an Armenian educator and journalist originally from Istanbul, then residing in Aleppo, was among the most outspoken critics of the 1946 congress.[40] In an article titled "The Soviet Armenian Writers' Congress and Us," written under the pen name Armen Amadian, Teoleolian introduces a new term, *mayrenik'* (motherland), which he claims signifies language, in opposition to *hayrenik'* (fatherland), signifying soil.[41] Whereas in Armenian, "language," often referred to as mother tongue, is always used as a feminine concept, here it is rendered as equivalent to the masculine "land." Furthermore, Teoleolian belittles Soviet Armenia's appreciation of language as a repository of the national spirit and argues that unlike Soviet Armenians, diaspora Armenians have understood and embraced the limits of language as a direct result of the threat of assimilation.

In fact, the idea that language (and more specifically Western Armenian) could serve as a "homeland in exile" was not new. In the early 1930s, it had been celebrated by the writers of Menk, who used it to cultivate the concept of "little Armenias."[42] The Menk writers had sought to rethink exile as a productive space and to testify to their experience of the aftermath of genocide, rather than narrating the events of the past. In doing so, they believed themselves to be launching Armenian literature anew in exile and thus symbolically regrouping the dispersed through language. However, when intellectuals from the Middle East revisited the idea of "language as home," the concept was fashioned as a building block for the diaspora's nationalist narrative of return that emerged in the years following World War II. Within this new paradigm, Western Armenian language was celebrated not as the dynamic offspring of diasporic life, but rather as a golden emblem of the past to be guarded and preserved for an eventual return.

Similarly, the pages of the Aleppo-based journal *Nayiri* are filled with criticism of the congress in the form of a defense of the Western Armenian linguistic form and literary tradition. Alongside editor Antranig Dzarugian, who was affiliated with the ARF Party at the time, it is once again Minas Teoleolian who delivers the harshest analysis of Topchian.[43] In an effort to equate Topchian's report with an attack on Western Armenian, and not satisfied to cite the implicit language used in his report, Teoleolian offers a quote that Topchian had published in the Paris-based *Zhoghovurt* earlier that year. It reads: "Prior to 1915, the Western Armenian language was a language of collective high culture. Since then, the language of contemporary diaspora literature has significantly dropped from its previous status, and under the heavy influence of foreign languages, it has lost the vitality and the appeal of a national language, and often times, it has become incomprehensible to a common reader."[44] In Teoleolian's framing, Topchian's comments about Western Armenian's decline seem to be part of his greater effort to strip the linguistic form of any claim to being considered a national language. In addition to refuting the claim regarding the language's demise, Teoleolian responds by critiquing the state of Eastern Armenian within the Soviet sphere and examines the infusion of Russian words into the literary language.[45]

Although diaspora periodicals sympathetic to the ARF generally shared Teoleolian's outrage about the 1946 congress's stamping of Western Armenian literature with an expiration date, diaspora communities' awakening to the need for language revitalization spread across party lines. Arshag Chobanian, for instance, raises alarm about discussions of assimilating Western Armenian into the Eastern standard and offers a striking defense of maintaining and cultivating both linguistic forms (which he refers to as "cultural treasures") and the classical orthography.[46] Subsequently, the enormity of the language-maintenance task highlighted the need for organizations that networked across diaspora communities. Under this rubric, *Nayiri*'s editorial team initiated an effort to form an organized collective of diaspora intellectuals by proposing the establishment of a writers' association centered in the Middle East. Although the outcome fell short of the desired grand vision, the initiative produced a discourse that enabled the imagining of a transnationally networked Armenian diaspora, an image that resolutely survived for some decades to come.

In the Name of Linguistic and Literary Autonomy: The 1948 Conference of Middle Eastern Armenian Writers

Aram Charek, from France, was the only one of the 1946 congress invitees to be granted permission to stay on in Soviet Armenia. The following year, news of his death emerged abruptly in the Soviet-leaning press of diaspora communities, raising conspiratorial alarm. The announcement of his death, signed by twenty-five prominent Soviet Armenian writers, offered condolences and cited a serious and long-term illness as the cause of death, which occurred en route from Yerevan to Paris. *Nayiri*'s editorial immediately responded by questioning the nature of the announcement and by framing Charek's death as a possible murder: an attempt to silence a former Armenian nationalist revolutionary.[47] *Nayiri*'s response captures the general skepticism that most anti-Soviet Armenians shared in a divided diaspora. The Soviet project's longevity had begun to give Soviet Armenia historical validity, and its state-sponsored cultural institutions were often seen as a threat to the production of culture outside Armenia.

By the mid-1940s, the ARF had emerged as the anti-Soviet camp. And even prior to the 1946 conference, tensions highlighting ideological differences between the party and Soviet Armenia had already spilled over to literary discussions.[48] In 1944, Soviet Armenian writer Gevork Abov published a short poem called "Menk' chenk' moṙats'el" (We Have Not Forgotten), accusing past revolutionaries, former leaders of the short-lived republic, and current members affiliated with the ARF of being the biggest traitors and criminals of the Armenian nation. In response, the Aleppo-based Antranig Dzarugian published a long verse called *T'ught' aṙ Erevan* (Letter to Yerevan). In inviting Gevork Abov and Soviet Armenian thinkers to look beyond Soviet doctrine and propaganda, Dzarugian's letter (composed, interestingly, in Eastern Armenian) defended the work of cultural preservation initiated by intellectuals and political leaders in dispersion. Hagop Oshagan's public support for Dzarugian, particularly developed in his 1946 publication of *Vgayu'iwn mě* (A Testimony) elicited an uproar from pro-Soviet periodicals, which personally targeted the Western Armenian literary critic. The pro-Soviet newspaper *Zhoghovurti Tsayn* went as far as to call him "the sworn enemy of Eastern Armenians."[49]

In this atmosphere, the recent 1946 congress's dismissal and critique of the Western Armenian linguistic form was translated as an attempt to silence the diaspora and thus incited discussions about the need to create a forum that would allow diasporan voices to speak. Most notably developing in the pages of *Nayiri*, the argument that diaspora intellectuals began to raise was founded on the principle that they had the right to protect their literary autonomy. A series of articles, including Eduard Boyajian's "Let's Start Thinking," focused on the 1946 congress's mandate that diaspora literature serve the Soviet project and claimed that artistic expression could not and should not be used for propaganda.[50] Soon Antranig Dzarugian began to publish editorials calling for a conference of writers in dispersion. The two main goals of the conference were outlined as the creation of "1. A writer's union that links together writers of the diaspora, from various communities; 2. A well-established publishing house, in a luminous center."[51]

Nayiri's editorials are accompanied by excerpts of letters from various diaspora writers stating their enthusiasm for the idea of a conference. This list of supporters includes Costan Zarian, Hamasdegh, Aram Haigaz, and Simon Vratsian from the United States; Shavarsh Misakian and Nigoghos Sarafian from France; and Vahan Navasartian, Kourken Mkhitarian, and Benjamin Tashjian from Egypt. Most of the letter writers see a diaspora gathering as a necessary response to the Soviet Armenian Writers' Union's Congress and its attempt to "speak for" the diaspora. The writer Seza is quoted as saying: "After the Soviet Armenian Writers' Congress, a conference for Armenian community writers is a reasonable consequence but not necessarily a rival event. The ignored Armenian intellectuals living abroad are obliged to speak for themselves, and more importantly, to showcase their work."[52] While she echoes sentiments similar to those comments of the other supporters mentioned, she warns against framing the gathering as a rival conference, for such a framing could undermine the diaspora's aim of speaking and acting autonomously.

Although it hosted the forum where the momentum for a diaspora conference was gathering, *Nayiri* did not seek to organize the event and instead called on the Mekhitarist Congregation of Venice or the Armenian Educational and Cultural Society, known as Hamazkayin, to take the reins in the organizational efforts.[53] *Nayiri*'s announcements were met with an uproar in the press from various communities. While Paris's *Haṙach*, Boston's *Hayrenik'*, Cairo's *Husaper*, and Beirut's *Aztarar* and *Aztag* encouraged the idea, other newspapers more loyal to Soviet Armenia (such as Beirut's *Zhoghovurti Tsayn* and *Ararat* and Cairo's *Arew*) harshly critiqued *Nayiri*'s efforts as anti-Armenian propaganda organized by ARF leaders. Amid this polarized response, no existing diaspora institution volunteered to take on the organizational efforts, resulting in the establishment of a new association tasked solely with organizing a Diaspora[54] Armenian Writers' Conference. Meeting in Shtora,[55] Lebanon, on August 10, 1947, a group of Armenian writers and intellectuals from Syria and Lebanon laid the foundations for the Writers' Association of Syria and Lebanon (WASL) and elected as their executive body Nigol Aghpalian, Antranig Dzarugian, Garo Sasuni, Mushegh Ishkhan, Armen Anush, and Eduard Boyajian. Owing to the lack of resources and the regional turmoil caused by the 1948 war in Palestine, the association fell short of organizing a Diaspora Armenian Writers' Conference. Instead, it organized a Middle Eastern Armenian Writers' Conference to serve as a stepping-stone for the still desired pan-community gathering.

Following an open invitation, the Middle Eastern Writers' Conference took place on September 18–20, 1948, in Shtora, Lebanon, with attendees mostly from Syria and Lebanon. Vahé Oshagan was present from Palestine, Armen Garoné arrived late from Tehran, and the two scheduled delegates from Egypt were unable to make it at all. Despite the intention of reaching diaspora writers across party lines, the 1948 conference ended up principally gathering writers affiliated with the ARF. While Garo Sasuni was elected the acting president of the meeting, the attendees unanimously elected Levon Shant, who had recently left for the United States, its honorary president. Minas Teoleolian was elected the meeting's recording secretary, a position that allowed him to subsequently publish the conference proceedings and minutes in *Hayrenik' Monthly* under one of his pen names, Vazken Vanantian.[56] Similarly, *Nayiri*'s August–September 1948 joint issue published most of the papers delivered. The conference's three-day agenda consisted of the following seven presentation topics:[57]

- "Armenian Prose in the Diaspora," by Eduard Boyajian
- "Armenian Drama in the Diaspora," by Vahé Oshagan
- "Diaspora's Armenian Press," by Minas Teoleolian
- "Issues Concerning the Armenian Language," by Eduard Daronian
- "Poetry in the Diaspora," by Mushegh Ishkhan
- "Diasporan Armenian Literature's Trajectory," by Garo Sasuni
- "Soviet Armenian Literature," by Antranig Dzarugian

In his opening remarks, Garo Sasuni described the conference's aim of being "in service to the protection of Armenian language and literature," implying the recognition of an impending threat to these two realms as the impetus for the gathering.[58] Although he spoke of safeguarding Armenian language and literature in general terms, the subsequent conference papers attempted to define the parameters of cultural production spread across Armenian communities. While Sasuni's address uses the term *kaght'ashkharh* (migrant world) to refer to the transnational, exilic realm of Armenian life burgeoning outside Soviet Armenia, most of the presentation titles use the term *sp'iwṙk'* (diaspora), with a few exceptions such as *ardasahman* (abroad).

Moreover, during the course of the conference, several discussions explicitly addressed the question of terminology and definition with respect to the word "diaspora," finally reaching the consensus that "that which we term diaspora literature is the continuation of Western Armenian literature. We call 'diaspora literature' works that have been informed by our dispersion."[59] The participants drew a clear thread connecting the pre-1915 Western Armenian literary tradition, which was centered in Constantinople, to the scattered collection of works published in the years following the genocide, across Armenian communities. Furthermore, they excluded the works of the surviving generation, such as ones by Costan Zarian and Hagop Oshagan, from "diaspora literature" and claimed that only works informed and formed by the experience of dispersion constituted this new category. The process of arriving at this definition consisted of in-depth discussions regarding the possibilities available to literatures in exilic or stateless languages. Over the three days, the presenters and attendees examined questions of stylistic orientation with regard to the influence of Western literary trends; questions of what constitutes the category of "national" when referring to national themes; the question of whether diaspora writers, owing to their position as immigrants, have social and political responsibility beyond aesthetic expression; and, in general, questions that negotiated between the diasporic, the national, the international, and the universal in the production of literature.

Standing in the wake of World War II, the conference participants enjoyed a unique vantage point from which to evaluate the preceding decades. Using the two world wars as markers, they reconceptualized the Western Armenian literary tradition within a measurable framework. In surveying three decades of post-1915 literary and linguistic progress, they realized the potential to produce literature in dispersion, on the one hand, and turned toward a rhetoric of self-preservation, on the other. The realization of potential coupled with the recognition of the threat of linguistic assimilation prompted the initiation of projects aimed at safeguarding tradition. In these efforts, the threat of linguistic assimilation was recognized as coming from multiple directions. The United States and Europe were frequently brought up as examples of spaces that hindered the linguistic development of immigrant communities and validated the shift of the intellectual center from Paris to the Middle East. Furthermore, Soviet Armenia's orthography reforms[60] and the Writers' Union's position in the 1946 congress were seen as similarly viable threats that endangered the continuity of the Western Armenian literary tradition. Teoleolian, once again as Vanantian, went as far as to claim that the Soviet Armenian Writers' Congress was nothing more than "an assassination effort targeted toward the literature of exiled communities."[61]

Not all Armenian intellectuals of the Middle East agreed with the conference's assessment of Western Armenian literature. Writing in the

Ramgavar Party's Beirut-based newspaper, *Bayk'ar*, Puzant Yeghiayan offered a divergent perspective on diaspora literature, which he did not characterize as an extension of the pre-1915 Constantinople brand. Using the two world wars as markers, Yeghiayan in this article envisions diaspora literature as a category of its own, consisting of sparse attempts that never achieve literary greatness, but nevertheless represent the experience of the catastrophe's aftermath. For Yeghiayan, post-1915 Western Armenian literature fails to produce works that are relevant to the aesthetic movements of the time, suffers from lack of an intellectual center (though he gives credit to Paris for trying to be one), and strays from "Armenian values" within its content. He writes, "Living far from the fatherland, the diaspora was forced to set root on foreign soil, and its literature successively began to echo those foreign environments."[62] Believing that a literary tradition cannot flourish beyond a certain point without being grounded in its own land, he highlights the need to look toward Soviet Armenia as Western Armenian literature's only salvation. In other words, he recognizes the literary ventures made between the wars, but cannot see a future for them in the post–World War II era.

Whereas the 1948 conference participants were much more optimistic about the possibility for literary production in a diaspora that was independent of its Soviet counterpart, they shared a concern similar to the one Yeghiayan raises in his essay regarding content that takes the Armenian world or its system of values as its "locale." The conference participants rendered these already nebulous concepts with the equally broad term *hayets'i* to refer to things that are Armenian-oriented or all-around Armenian. Both Sasuni in his opening remarks and Eduard Boyajian in his discussion of prose emphasized the need to cultivate *hayets'i kraganut'iwn, hayets'i vēb* ("Armenian-oriented" literature and the "Armenian-oriented" novel).[63] Since the idea of *hayets'i* is hard to define in specific terms, it is usually understood dialectically, in relation to all things non-Armenian. As a result, it becomes understood in exclusionary terms and leads to discussions of cultural purity.

By extension, discussions about language preservation at the conference fell within this rubric, for their emphasis lay on language purification and cleansing, rather than development and dynamism. Many of the conference participants stressed the importance of keeping the literary language clean, free of regional or foreign influence. Teoleolian's conference presentation expands the argument to the Armenian used in the press, which he sees as a particularly vulnerable site for Western Armenian's deterioration. He exclaims, "We need to fight against linguistic barbarity with extreme meticulousness and to the point of being condemned." Teoleolian's case for ensuring Western Armenian's longevity serves a broader political agenda, which he is quick to relate: "One day, if we gather in our fatherland, perhaps our languages will become one. The unrecognizable state of Soviet Armenian language forces us to care for our language, so that one day we may offer the necessary antidote."[64] Here, Teoleolian reverses the critique of Western Armenian as a language incapable of sustaining itself in exile that was delivered at the 1946 Soviet Armenian Writers' Union conference. In fact, he presents the Eastern Armenian of Soviet Armenia as endangered, substantiating the need for language preservation in the diaspora as a principled, pan-national cause, albeit centered in the Middle East.[65]

Indeed, all the presenters saw the need to centralize the diaspora in order to ensure the survival and cultivation of their respective artistic genres, and Syria and Lebanon indirectly emerged as the possible centers. Vahé Oshagan, for instance, proposed the formation of a central committee to organize a traveling theater troupe, to prepare an annual list of productions, to guarantee financial resources, and to reward talent.[66] Boyajian stressed the importance of creating a network for exchange among diaspora writers by establishing a writers' association.[67] Teoleolian emphasized the need for larger publishing houses that could secure a broader diasporic circulation of works.[68] Daronian called for the preparation of Armenian-language textbooks that could be used across communities and could allow for the standardization of the Western Armenian language.[69] At the core of all their presentations lay a concern regarding the public. Many presentations explicitly addressed the need to cultivate a reading and viewing public. In other words, the writers believed the fundamental task at hand to be the building of a diasporic society that would support the arts and that, in turn, the arts would represent. Their proposed projects that sought to organize and institutionalize literary, linguistic, and artistic production aimed to construct an environment where art could be produced and subsequently received by a strong base of consumers. In many ways, these formative discussions conceived of Armenian diaspora literature and art similarly to the way a national literature is conceptualized, even though this literature and art were not produced in a territorially bound nation-state. In his presentation, poet and educator Mushegh Ishkhan recognized the absurdity in conceiving of the transnationally spread Armenian communities uniformly yet called for a clear articulation of what "diaspora" constitutes. He writes, "It is necessary to clearly envision the immense and unique borders of Diaspora's expanse. With the exception of the main fatherland, the entire globe can be considered Diaspora. Such an extraordinary fate and in particular, such an unnatural sight to comprehend and categorize all of that as a harmonious, unified page in a people's history."[70] This paradoxical need to "contain" diaspora within clearly defined terms while recognizing the impossibility of such an endeavor when considering the diversity of the communities can be understood simply as a need to "center" diaspora.

In fact, the Middle East in general came forth as the diaspora's cultural and literary center, thanks to the rival conferences of 1946 and 1948 and the public debates that they produced. More specifically, Syria and particularly Lebanon were spaces where language, literary production, and a grand narrative became institutionalized in the years and decades following World War II.[71] In 1951, Antranig Dzarugian moved his literary monthly, *Nayiri*, to Beirut, sharing the floor with Vahé Vahian's *Ani*. By the 1960s, Hamazkayin began to publish *Pakin* and Simon Simonian had already established his *Sp'iwṙk'*, adding to the list of Beirut-based publications that shaped new forums for discussions about literature and culture in the diaspora.[72] Simonian published his weekly journal in his own publishing house called Sevan, which was in the company of many other Armenian publishing houses in Beirut, including Atlas, Mshag, Ara, Huys, Donigian, Rotos, Onebar, and Edvan.[73] The Armenian newspapers *Aztag, Zart'onk'*, and *Ararat*, as well the catholicosate of Cilicia in Antelias and the Hamazkayin Cultural Association, also had printing facilities. The educational policy of Lebanon allowed the Armenian community to develop an autonomous educational system, and Armenian day schools totaled sixty-three by 1958.[74] These schools not only provided the mechanism for linguistic preservation in the Middle East, but also produced the educators, editors, and writers necessary to sustain Armenian cultural production in the diaspora at large. Indeed, the Armenian day-school movement initiated in the United States during the 1960s modeled itself on the Armenian educational institutions of the Middle East and to this day continues to rely on Armenian-language teachers trained in Lebanon and Syria for language instruction.[75] Furthermore, by the end of the 1960s, higher-education institutions in Lebanon like Haigazian College, the Hamazkayin-organized Palandjian College, and an established chair at Saint-Joseph University began to offer specialized programs and degrees in Armenology. These frameworks of Armenian-language training, alongside cultural organizations, publishing houses, and periodicals that allowed for intellectual exchange, created a climate that encouraged increased activity in the literary arts, establishing Beirut as the nucleus for the production and circulation of Western Armenian literature.[76]

More important, these diaspora institutions signaled the making of a full-fledged literacy and *literary* apparatus that ultimately shaped Western Armenian's vitality within a national framework, against Soviet Armenian and with the aim of an eventual adoption by a homeland state. In his final article before his death, Hagop Oshagan contemplates diaspora literature's future in face of pessimism about Western Armenian's literary potential in exile. He urges his readers not to focus on land or homeland as a precondition for literary production by reminding them of the tradition's pre-1915 activity centered in Venice, Paris, Izmir, and Istanbul. "Diaspora literature will live until the Armenian people's complete assembly on ancestral lands. After that coveted day, Diaspora's literature will be placed in a museum, just like the Armenian literatures of Venetians, the Romantics, the teachers, and the aesthetes. Until then, let them leave us at peace. We cannot *not* produce our literature!"[77] As Oshagan's arc shows, Western Armenian literature will bear the diaspora label only temporarily, for it is diasporic insofar as it is produced within a particular historical experience. And that historical experience is called diasporic insofar as it is understood as an interim state of being until an eventual return.

The WASL's 1948 conference claimed not to be a reaction to the 1946 congress, but its attempts to preserve the autonomy of Western Armenian artistic expression in the face of threatened servitude to the Soviet Project relegated artistic expression to a position of servitude to the Diaspora Project.[78] The 1948 conference was not followed by additional gatherings, nor was the future ideal of a Diaspora Armenian Writers' Association ever realized. Its legacy, however, was the forging of a homogenous diasporan cultural identity that became centralized in the Middle East, particularly in Beirut. While these attempts to fashion diaspora as a homogenous entity contributed to the flourishing of intellectual and cultural activity in the decades following World War II, they produced problematic forms of cultural essentialism that proved detrimental to literary expression and production in the years to come.

6

Symbolic Territory

Language and the Myth of Homeland

In a lecture delivered in Brussels in February 1955, Nigoghos Sarafian addressed the Belgian Armenian Student Association by meditating on dispersed Armenians' search for identity and belonging in foreign lands and on the importance of cultural vitality to that quest. In trying to define culture, Sarafian critically examined various modes of cultural production and engagement in dispersion and noted the emergence of a new concept in diaspora institutions. He said, "Recently, a demand for *hayets'i* literature has taken shape. That is to say, a need to produce literature that pours out of the Armenian heart and speaks to fellow Armenians. It's a fine thought, of course. But this national mandate forces literature into stagnation, it limits our culture, it negates all innovation. Through this type of nationalization, literature and the arts can rarely transcend mediocrity. We often see this cheap and plentiful nationalism, for those who exploit their nation's emotions are the ones most visible on public platforms."[1]

What these remarks allude to is the umbrella term for "Armenian-oriented," adopted at the 1948 Middle Eastern Armenian Writers' Association Conference as a mode of literary practice that was to maintain the autonomy of cultural production in the diaspora. Shaped in opposition to Soviet Armenia's amalgamating project, the *hayets'i* mode of production had quickly become the guiding logic of Beirut-based institutions' publishing and educational endeavors. It meant that the emergent literary scene needed to serve as the connecting link to the pre-1915 tradition, that literary works needed to address Armenianness through unifying categories of national identity such as language or victimhood, and that schools needed to prepare a new generation through a standardized curriculum. In his lecture, Sarafian—a former member of Menk—criticized the new intellectual center's insistence on fashioning literature within a centralized national model that disregarded the particularities of dispersed Armenian communities by universalizing their differences under the cloak of a standardized language, curriculum, and publishing program. While Sarafian had survived the center's geographic transition by actively contributing to Armenian publications in Lebanon, he continued to live in France and, as we see in the quotation above, found the drive to nationalize Western Armenian literature restrictive and detrimental to creativity.

Armenian intellectuals of the Middle East fashioned Western Armenian literature against the literary cosmopolitanism of the Soviet project, in which each republic was encouraged to simultaneously cultivate its vernacular and serve the greater party line of the union. In reaction to the threat that the diaspora's literature would be recruited to participate in the union's "democratizing" cultural policy, Beirut-based intellectuals sought to nationalize the diaspora's cultural production. Doing so meant developing an alternative to the transnational model of the Paris scene. Rather than cultivating representations that emphasized the vernacular and the particular, educators, editors, and writers in Beirut forged a literary cosmopolitanism intended to universalize Armenian language and literary tradition in the diaspora. Ultimately, what they produced was a national literature in exile rather than transnational literature in dispersion.

While it was framed as a form of resistance to the universalizing Soviet cultural project, the nationalization of Western Armenian in fact replicated the hegemonizing structure of a state, regardless of the cultural diversity of its dispersed communities. In constructing its symbolic territory, this nationalization nurtured a myth of the homeland as a place to which diaspora Armenians could eventually return. Within this model, language and literature served as placeholders, offering the Armenian diaspora something similar to what Joanne Nucho has called a "permanently temporary" dwelling. Looking at two "permanently temporary" informal Armenian settlements in what later became the municipality of Bourj Hammoud in Beirut, Nucho examines the Armenian refugees' collective desire for permanence in the host country of Lebanon during the years immediately following the genocide and the role of popular histories that authenticated spaces of belonging.[2] While Nucho is mainly interested in informal property regimes, the Armenian refugees' quest for permanence (even as they simultaneously harbored a desire to return to lands lost) found a similar articulation in the politics of cultural production in the Middle East. The two-pronged approach to nationalizing Western Armenian literature (language standardization and *hayets'i* production) served the aim of developing a sustainable model for a long-term-temporary culture. As noted at the 1948 conference, the task of the diaspora's writers was to preserve Western Armenian for its eventual return to a unified homeland that encompassed not only the lands lost to Turkey, but Soviet Armenia as well.

The mandate for *hayets'i*, as an antiassimilationist tool, was largely perpetuated by the literacy apparatus of institutions affiliated with the ARF. As we saw in chapter 5, many of the 1948 conference participants were either members of the party or sympathetic to its views. In some ways, *hayets'i* literature could be seen as synonymous to what others have called *tashnagts'agan kraganut'iwn* (literature abiding by ARF ideology), often defined as diaspora literature preoccupied with the pre-1915 past.[3] I would like to propose that in both its scope and its practice, *hayets'i* literature reached beyond the party. Yet, more broadly speaking, the move toward *hayets'i* education had precedence in the party's efforts to organize the Lebanese Armenian community through national education. According to Nicola Schahgaldian, in the 1920s, the ARF launched an effort to educate the refugee population with the objective of infusing "subjective and symbolic meaning into merely objective distinctions which separated most local Armenians from the native Arab population of Lebanon."[4] For Schahgaldian, this approach was carried out through the purging of Islamic Turkish cultural influences in the refugee population's lifestyles. In the decades following World War II, more and more institutions and publications affiliated with pro-Soviet parties adopted similar frameworks for cultural preservation. The campaign for language "cleansing" and standardization, for instance, was embraced across party lines. Whereas in the 1930s *Aztag* of the ARF was the newspaper that published the most extensive series of articles against the use of Turkish by the refugee population, in 1946, it was *Ararat* of the Hnchagian Party that warned its readers not to forget the community-wide campaign launched by the political parties in the 1930s. The article criticized the wide circulation of Turkish in the Armenian neighborhoods of Beirut and called for the resurrection of the old campaign's posters, which reprimanded its readers with "tʻrkʻerēn mi khosir" (Don't Speak Turkish!).[5] In other words, pro-Soviet publications shared the concern with standardizing Western Armenian. And while they participated in the making of diasporic culture, they upheld the centrality of Soviet Armenia as the nucleus of the Armenian literary world.

Regardless of their allegiance to Soviet Armenian literature, Beirut-based intellectuals contributed to the development of Armenian cultural life in Lebanon, rapidly establishing Beirut as what Nicola Migliorino calls "a flourishing cultural hub, a safe haven for Armenian media, literature, theatre, music and plastic arts." Migliorino attributes the emergence of Lebanon as an Armenian diasporic center to the state's liberal governance of cultural production. He argues that lenient policies concerning expression and education granted autonomy to educational and publishing institutions. Thanks also to Syrian intellectuals' move from Aleppo to Beirut owing to the growing constrictions on freedom of opinion there, Lebanon became the center of Armenian literary and culture life in the diaspora, with its Armenian periodical titles tallying forty-four by 1965.[6]

Taking educational and publishing institutions as potent indicators of the "centering" of the diaspora, chapter 6 examines how the expansion of Lebanon's Armenian literacy apparatus contributed to the narrative construction of the diaspora. By looking at canon formation within the broader process of developing a standardized curriculum for the schools, at the turn toward poetry within the *hayetsʻi* mode of literary production developed by publishing programs, and at efforts to create cultural memory linked to the pre-1915 tradition, I argue that art in the diaspora came to be framed as national literature in exile rather than transnational literature in dispersion. In poetry, anthologies, textbooks, and memoirs, writers like Mushegh Ishkhan, Garo Sasuni, Minas Teoleolian, and Antranig Dzarugian—many of whom were educators in the burgeoning Armenian day-school scene of Beirut—celebrated the Armenian language as a symbolic territory. Their work perpetuated the myth of a unified homeland

and the myth of return and formed the canon of Western Armenian literature that educated generations of diaspora Armenians in the decades to come. As we shall see, while these efforts to nationalize diaspora culture, initially launched at the 1948 conference, were successful in forging "a critical mass of readers and writers"[7] in Western Armenian language, their turn away from cultivating literature informed by multilocal transnational belonging ultimately placed an expiration date on the diaspora's literary output.

The Literary Canon and Nation Building in the Diaspora

By the 1950s, efforts to standardize Western Armenian were encompassed within a much more ambitious goal: to standardize education in the Armenian schools of Lebanon and, by extension, of the Middle East. To this end, the intellectual elite focused on the curatorial work necessary to build a literary canon that preserved the literary legitimacy of works published prior to the 1915 rupture and developed a collection that connected the national identity of Armenians of the diaspora to the literary tradition of the past. Two of the active members of the Writers' Association of Syria and Lebanon, Garo Sasuni and Minas Teoleolian, published anthologies intended mainly for classroom use. In his introduction to *Badmut'iwn Arewmdahay Arti Kraganut'ean* (The History of Modern Western Armenian Literature) (1953), Sasuni claims that "a classical canon is the foundation of a scholastic education," as he reflects on the current disorderly state of Armenian classrooms across Lebanon, where teachers were left to curate curricula individually.[8]

First introduced at the 1948 conference, canon formation was seen as a necessary process for forging the diaspora into a separate entity, distinct from Soviet Armenia, or a process of "image building," as Sarah Corse would call it. For Corse, "national literatures, like nations, are created by the cultural work of specific people engaged in an identifiable set of activities," such as canon formation. In this vein, the case of Armenians in Lebanon indicates that canon formation was not only a literary process, but a political one as well, as it put literature in the service of nation building. Remarking on the difficulty of defining "the canon," Nel Van Dijk describes it as "a metaphorical notion that refers to a collection of highly regarded literary works that can assume a different appearance at different moments, in different situations, and for different groups of people." The sociological approach to understanding the canon underscores that literary value is not an intrinsic quality, but rather something that is attributed to a work. Along the same line, French sociologist Pierre Bourdieu has argued that the status of cultural objects is determined by the relative positions of the persons and institutions that produce, consume, and evaluate them.[9] In the case of Armenians in dispersion bound by language rather than territory, literary works produced in Western Armenian served as the "cultural objects" in need of rebranding for the solidification of diasporic identity. Following World War II, the leading intellectuals of Lebanon partook in an orchestrated effort to reproduce and evaluate literary works for a new group of consumers: the diaspora-born generation of students being trained in the restandardized Western Armenian language.[10]

The anthology *The History of Modern Western Armenian Literature* not only reflects on the history of Western Armenian literature, but actively shapes this history through its compilation. Its marked focus on nineteenth-century literary production is framed by two dates: 1840 (the modernization of Western Armenian) and 1915 (the date when many of the showcased authors were killed). Sasuni regards literature developed from the 1920s onward as "contemporary" and does not include it in the anthology, with the exception of surviving writers like Levon Shant, A. Chobanian, V. Tekeyan, Z. Yesayan, H. Oshagan, A. Andonian, C. Zarian, and Hamasdegh. Hamasdegh, who is more aptly characterized as belonging to the orphaned generation, is the youngest author in the collection. His first novella, *Kiwghě* (The Village), was published in 1924 in Boston. Sasuni claims to have singled him out of the contemporary generation because he serves as the connecting thread to the pre-1915 generation. Hamasdegh's exceptional treatment may be explained by the author's commitment to narrating the Ottoman past, unlike the Menk generation's rejection of this past as a topic of literary exploration. For Sasuni, the "*hayets'i* characters" grant Hamasdegh's works literary value, a judgment that hints at the political undertones of his curatorial project.[11] Otherwise, writers active beyond 1920, including many Menk writers, are merely listed on the final two pages of the anthology as "contemporary authors," grouped according to three geographic regions: Europe, the United States, and the Middle East. While the decision to end Western Armenian literary history's trajectory in 1915 casts doubt on Sasuni's claim that the book covers the "modern" period, it had a long-lasting effect. This framing influenced future textbooks, which similarly ended the history of Western Armenian with the genocide.[12]

Sasuni's history-making project organizes Western Armenian literary production into four main periods: Renaissance Writers in two phases (1840–70, 1870–85), Realist Writers (1885–95), Revolutionary Writers ("The Artist Generation") (1895–1915), and Freedom Writers (1908–14). While the realist designation signals the European literary and artistic movement's influence on Armenian literature, the other three groupings are grounded in the local and refer to works shaped by the Armenian Ottoman historical context. "Renaissance," for instance, refers to the Ottoman Armenians' period of national awakening, facilitated by efforts to modernize the language by distancing it from classical Armenian and moving it toward the spoken vernacular. Sasuni's collection lists the authors in each of these four periods and introduces each one with a brief biography and an overview of their publications. The anthology does not include excerpts of the works themselves, which confirms that the main intent was to produce a literary history.

Sasuni's *The History of Modern Western Armenian Literature* ends with an invitation. After listing the names of contemporary authors on the final pages of the volume, he writes, "This period of Armenian literature awaits its historian."[13] A few years later, Minas Teoleolian answered the call with his 1956 publication of the two-volume *Tar mě Kraganut'iwn (1850–1950)* (A Century of Literature [1850–1950]). Teoleolian's first volume covers the period 1850–1922, with divisions along similar lines as in Sasuni's book: Period of Awakening (1850–85), Realist Movement (1884–1900), and Aesthetic Movement (1900–1922). But the second volume (1920–50) picks up where Sasuni left off. In contrast to Sasuni's historicizing endeavor, Teoleolian's project showcases excerpts from the works of selected authors, chosen based on their thematic and stylistic suitability for middle school readers. While the anthology won institutional legitimacy as a textbook and gained currency as a cultural product, it otherwise eluded the identity of being an economic commodity. Teoleolian presents it as a national resource, labeling the anthology a "service."[14] In other words, he downplays the authoritativeness of his authorship and instead highlights the community as the true proprietor of the work. In time, this two-volume anthology not only introduced literary works to new generations, but also gave shape to a new structural organization to diaspora's national narrative.

Period designations do not form the organizing logic of Teoleolian's anthology. Instead, the second volume is divided according to a political distinction: diaspora and Soviet. In this way, the space of diaspora is mapped in opposition to or in the company of Soviet Armenia, and not in any hierarchical relationship to it. In other words, the "diaspora" in question is not Soviet Armenia's diaspora, but rather a stateless entity with just as much claim to national legitimacy as Soviet Armenia. Teoleolian writes, "We present our literature of the last three decades with the epithet 'diasporic,' because we find characterizations like 'post-war,' 'recent,' 'contemporary,' or 'desert generation' insufficient in expressing the complete experiences and yearnings of the surviving generation, as well as the two generations that established their worth after 1915 or attempted to gaze at our life with the same spiritual, national, and intellectual commitment."[15] Teoleolian's curatorial project moves beyond the creation of a literary canon to participate in the process of naming the boundaries of the "national." Through its literary canon, the diaspora emerges as a unified, homogeneous zone capable of producing a uniform response to the shared experience of loss and dispersion. Further, by connecting the two most recent generations with the surviving writers, Teoleolian suggests that continuity is integral to the nation-building imperative of the project, whose aim is to standardize the education of Armenian students in diaspora communities.

The ubiquitous *hayets'i* comes up once again in Teoleolian's introduction as a defining marker and a connecting thread among the geographically disparate works highlighted in the anthology. He uses a similar iteration to frame the inclusion of Soviet Armenian texts in the anthology. In contrast to the sharply critical and exclusionary tone that marks Teoleolian's journalistic writings about Soviet Armenian literature during the 1946 Congress of Soviet Armenian Writers, Teoleolian's framing of Soviet Armenian literature is softer and more inclusive here. He claims to showcase works that have maintained their "Armenian essence" regardless of the pressures of the state. Writing from the vantage point of Soviet Armenia's renationalization process following Stalin's death, he writes, "The oppression weighing heavy on our country for thirty years was not enough to hamper the glow of the Armenian soul. Not even the most loyal Bolshevik has been able to drown out the voice of this race in its essence, and obstruct the immaterial gates of passage to its past, its blood, its authentic constitution."[16] Rather than criticizing the Armenian writers, Teoleolian targets the Soviet state and highlights its foreignness. He also attempts to salvage the Armenian writers by expressing sympathy for their lack of choice under the Communist Party's mandate.

Teoleolian makes his critique of the Soviet state in the name of literary autonomy, and in a similar vein, he emphasizes his project's aspiration to form a truly representative canon. He thereby extends his defense of creative freedom, initially aimed at Soviet Armenian literature, to diaspora literature as well. By acknowledging the negative impact that the calamity of 1915 and the subsequent dispersion into foreign environments have had on literary production in Western Armenian, Teoleolian exposes the vulnerabilities of diaspora literature, which faces the challenge of linguistic and cultural assimilation. Moreover, he questions the possibility of artistic creation in the aftermath of mass violence and exile: "What kind of literary appetite or work can we anticipate from a people who neither had a social life nor the warmth of a familial nest?"[17] For Teoleolian, the postgenocide literary output is nothing short of miraculous given the conditions under which it was produced. This triumphant framing borders on the patriotic, as he insists on the unwavering Armenianness of the collected works at hand.

In Teoleolian's formulation, Soviet Armenia's literature, particularly that featured in the anthology, has maintained its Armenian essence, the Western diaspora's literature has reinvented Armenianness by representing the new Armenian reality's confrontation with foreign environments, and the Middle East's Armenian communities have produced the revered *hayets'i* literature. For Teoleolian, *hayets'i* is defined as literature written in a literary style reminiscent of the pre-1915 tradition: "Over the last three decades, the poetry produced within the Middle Eastern belt maintains its *hayets'i* character most and stays close to the Western Armenian literary tradition." The literature produced by Middle Eastern writers thus gains centrality through its alignment with the national literature of the pregenocide era. As a project intended to aid community-building efforts, Teoleolian's anthology seeks to gather works that together can represent the Armenian nation, in both its stateless and its Soviet iterations. In the introduction to the first volume of the anthology, Teoleolian clearly positions himself against essentialist, racist literary aspirations, arguing that literature must instead seek to find and represent the universally "human."[18] For him, literature that expresses the revolutionary ideals of cultural nationalism, which are conditions of the "human," can be classified as humanist literature. It is within this latter rubric that Teoleolian grants representational authority to the contemporary Armenian literature of the Middle East. Unlike French Armenian literature, he argues, the literature of the Middle East uses the Armenian to access the human.

Thus, Teoleolian's anthology positions the Middle East at the center of the diaspora's literary network, arguing that the literature produced there is a connecting link, or "bridge," to the pre-1915 generation. In the decades that follow, this dual claim reappears in literary criticism as an unquestioned assumption. When the Armenian-studies chair at Beirut's Haigazian University organizes a "Week of Armenian Diaspora Literature" in 1969, *Sp'iwŕk'*'s editor Simon Simonian reports on the event, claiming, "Diaspora's Armenian Literature is existentially Western Armenian Literature, It is its continuation."[19] This seamless connection to the pregenocide literary tradition buries the literary outlook of the Menk generation, who saw rupture as the defining element of literature of dispersion. Soviet Armenian criticism shares a similar framing of diaspora literature, centering it in the Middle East and linking it with the pre-1915 Western Armenian tradition. Discussing the poetry of Vahian, Dzarugian, Ishkhan, and Hagopian (all from the Middle East), Vazken Kaprielian writes, "In continuing the tradition of classical Western Armenian poetry, under the direct influence of Tekian, they bring us the diaspora's (and especially its patriotic intellectuals'), sentiments, borne out of the conditions forced upon all diaspora Armenians."[20] Thus, over time, "Western Armenian–Middle East–diaspora" became the neatly tethered definition of diaspora literature, in large part as a result of the canon-making endeavor set out by the 1948 conference.

In Teoleolian's anthology, while the emphasis of centering diaspora is on the literature's *hayets'i* character, the author also acknowledges the importance of the population's size in creating this center, because it provided a consumer base for Armenian-language cultural products. "The catastrophe dictated the centrality of the Middle East for Armenians," he writes, referring to the high concentration of the genocide's refugee population.[21] The genocide's deportation routes led the survivors to Syria and Lebanon. While many moved farther westward because they had the financial means or familial connections to do so, or because they lived in orphanages that moved west, the majority of the refugees stayed and formed the foundation of the diasporic community of the Middle East. According to historian Sisag Varjabedian, between 1918 and 1923, 31,400 Armenian survivors ended up in Lebanon. The majority of them settled in Beirut, where nine major refugee camps were available to receive them. In fact, an estimated 19,380 Armenians entered the camps of Beirut. Per Varjabedian's estimates, following decades of community-building efforts by Armenian organizations, the number of Armenians residing in Lebanon reached 200,000 by 1975.[22]

Interestingly, in Teoleolian's configuration, Iran is included in the diaspora's literary center. He writes, "Within the geographic formulation of 'the Middle East,' we include Syria and Lebanon, Palestine, Egypt, Iraq and Iran. This latter community, while loyal to the Eastern Armenian language, in its literary legacy, exhibits no fundamental difference in depth of perspective. It's the same creative climate, therefore, the same experiences, and same spiritual form."[23] In the anthology, Iran's community, which is Eastern Armenian–speaking and precedes the 1915 genocide, is considered a node in the production of diaspora literature, suggesting that diasporic experience and the use of the Western Armenian language are not the sole criteria that define the *hayets'i* category. And to understand what is meant by *hayets'i*'s uniformity in "depth of perspective" and "spiritual form," we will now turn to the poetry of some of the canonical authors discussed in the next section.

Hayets'i Literature: The Search for Homeland in Poetry

Most critics see prose as the privileged literary form that constructs the narrative authority of a nation. In *Poems of Nation, Anthems of Empire*, Suvir Kaul instead makes a case for the significance of poetic form in criticizing nationalist projects. Focusing on eighteenth-century English poetry, Kaul examines structures of power and exclusion within the British imperial framework to ask: "Why should poetry become so manifestly the literary and imaginative space for such cultural and ideological work?"[24] For Kaul, it was the poets who equipped the nation with the literary and cultural capital necessary to substantiate Great Britain's branding as a global power. Armenian writers in post–World War II Beirut similarly turned to poetry in their effort to participate in the diaspora's nation-building project. It was because of poetry's lyrical potential that the writers were able to develop the *hayets'i* mandate that celebrated language as a symbolic territory necessary for the collectivization of dispersed Armenians. On a more practical level, poetry circulates easily: it fits well within textbooks and anthologies, and it is easy to memorize and recite publicly. Poetry, therefore, was integral to the canon-making process with which Middle Eastern Armenians attempted to standardize education and to produce a new generation of homogenously trained diaspora Armenians.

The marked shift from prose to poetry was defined by the *hayets'i* character of the Middle Eastern Armenian writers' poetics. While the debate that forged the concept of *hayets'i* was politically motivated, the poetic articulation of *hayets'i* is nonpartisan and politically vague. The underlying patriotism of *hayets'i* poetry renders it ambiguous enough to signal multiple referents, particularly when it comes to the notion of homeland. This new wave of poetry develops its patriotic tone by highlighting the grandeur and resilience of the Armenian nation, lamenting the traumatic break caused by the genocide, and carving an imagined homeland on the symbolic territory of the Armenian language. Ultimately, in these poems, language emerges as an identity marker necessary to the experience of collective belonging in exile.

While Mushegh Ishkhan was a playwright and a prose writer, it was his poetry that established him as one of the most prominent literary voices of the post–World War II generation. Born in Ankara in 1913, Ishkhan spent his early years in Damascus, Beirut, and Cyprus, jumping from one Armenian educational institution to another. After his higher education in Brussels was cut short by World War II, he settled in Beirut, where he taught at and eventually served as a supervisor of Hamazkayin's Jemaran Academy. A prolific writer, he published poetry collections, novels, anthologies, and plays until his death in 1990. His poems occupied a central place in the new literary canon taught in Armenian-language schools in the diaspora. In them, laments of exile and homelessness are coupled with celebrations of ancestral inheritance and language, which are presented as sites for perseverance. In this section, I will examine Ishkhan's poetry as a model of poetic intervention in the debates about *hayets'i* and as a literary tool used in the process of forging a diaspora identity. While I focus on Ishkhan's poetry, I supplement my discussion of each theme by mentioning similar attempts by his contemporaries.

Over the few decades following the 1948 conference, Mushegh Ishkhan produced poems that represented his generation's need to reclaim their Armenianness by asserting ownership of the Armenian cultural legacy of the recent and distant past.[25] "I Am the Child of Armenia" is the title of a poem published in *Gyank' ew Eraz* (Life and Dream) (1949), in which Ishkhan claims belonging to the Armenian people by singing the praises of past glory, by acknowledging present suffering, and by asserting the potential for rebirth. While the language oscillates between images of triumph and struggle, the repetition of the line "I am the child of Armenia" spotlights the poem's message, which functions as an announcement of national belonging. Much of Ishkhan's work is devoted to forging a transnational Armenian space through the language of poetry. Another poem written in a similar vein begins with "O, miraculous, marvelous Armenian soul." The poem, "The Armenian Soul," is a lyrical ode to the indefatigability of the Armenian spirit. It invokes images from the history of the

Armenian nation, from its mythical origins and pagan gods like Vahagn and Asdghig to the saint Gregory of Narek, the tenth-century poet and monk, and Gomidas, the twentieth-century Armenian priest and musicologist. The soul moves through the centuries, inheriting the nation's cultural and spiritual wealth along the way, strengthened by attacks from outside: "Many swords pierced it / Many chains struck its proud flight / But it remained vibrant as ever."[26] The soul, first presented as ethereal ("glistening like an eternal light / it descended from the heights of Ararat / and it conquered the darkness of countless centuries"), gains materiality as the Armenian language. Ishkhan writes, "It is its [the soul's] authentic image, our sacred language."[27] Thus, the Armenian language becomes the corporeal site that preserves the Armenian spirit and, by extension, the Armenian spirituality.

Boston-based writer Hamasdegh echoes similar sentiments in his similarly titled poem "The Armenian Spirit," published in *Pakin* in 1962. The poem begins by forbidding questions about the Armenian spirit's origins: "Don't ask: what is it? Where is it? / Where does the Armenian spirit come from?" Nevertheless, the remaining stanzas function as an attempt at definition. They are an attempt to locate the Armenian spirit on a recognizable trajectory of national history that begins with mythical figures of Hayk and David of Sasun, glosses over the fifth-century battle of Avarayr against Sassanid Persia, and ends with Gregory of Narek's poetic reinvention of the Armenian language. Ultimately, the lyrical quest for meaning situates the Armenian spirit in the Armenian language and, more specifically, the Armenian alphabet:

It is of Mesrob's grave and dream
the alphabet
the Armenian spirit.
Our brilliant language is both body and soul.[28]

Hamasdegh's claim to the Armenian cultural legacy of his predecessors, like that of Mushegh Ishkhan, rests on the Armenian language, as the only surviving site—however symbolic—of continuity.

The carving out of a figurative territory gains urgency through lamentations about the loss of land. Whereas exile was salvaged by the Menk generation as a force conducive to creation, for the post–World War II generation, exile is stripped of its imaginative potential. Exile is presented as an experience of loss, only to be mourned through poems elegizing homelessness. Mushegh Ishkhan's series of poems on homelessness, though, express hope without glorifying displacement and exile. His poem "An Army of Orphans," for instance, pays tribute to the orphaned generation without undermining the severity of the experience of displacement. There is nothing salvageable in exile; rather, it is the orphans who are celebrated for enduring the extremely demoralizing conditions of survival after the genocide and for anchoring the generation that came immediately after them. Ishkhan writes, "When feebly we stood in the midst of the storm / we searched only for a simple raft / Under our feet, you became the magical boat that rocked us over the abyss."[29] Even though Mushegh Ishkhan was born two years before the genocide, the poem's speaker identifies with the generation that was born after the catastrophic years and looks on the orphaned generation with gratitude for grounding his experience of dispersion.

In Mushegh Ishkhan's poems, dispersion and exile do not include encounters with foreign Others. Even though the lack of such confrontations may be attributed to the Middle Eastern Armenian community's relatively insular and autonomous character, the poems seem to deliberately emphasize the wandering nature of the displaced Armenian rather than acculturation into a host society, developing the dual themes of loss and return. In the poem called "Our House,"[30] a father struggles to explain the exilic condition of Armenians to his small child, to whom the temporary house of refuge seems like a palace. "How do I tell you that we don't have a home?" ponders the father in response to the naive sense of security that his child experiences with regard to the shack they call home.[31] Similarly, in "Where Do You Go?" the poet speaks to his fellow displaced countrymen, saying, "Country to country, shore to shore, / Always wandering, always on the go, / Always more pale, / Compatriot, where do you go?" Tucked away in the question ("where do you go?") is an implied imperative: "stay!"[32] The compatriot, like a vagabond, is forced into a life of wandering. The poet's appeal is for community. The question "where do you go?" also implies a lack of possible destinations. In other words, the poem suggests that home, once lost, cannot be regained elsewhere.

Elsewhere, loss is not as irrevocable. The poem titled "Ancient Land" addresses the lost ancestral lands through an apostrophe: "Yearning and longing sprouted from your spirit / What am I without you? A mere vagabond."[33] Here, the figure of the vagabond is contrasted with the condition of living in exile while harboring sentiments of return. The ancestral land gives the poet a longing for return that a vagabond does not experience. The possibility of return, therefore, not only sustains but defines the exile. In "The Armenian Grandmother's Prayer," Ishkhan writes, "Enough, dear God, return our land, our home to us."[34] In this poem, the Armenian mother is synonymous with the diasporic mother, who has reached the limit of her suffering in exile. Her appeal to God is desperate: she does not wish her fate on anyone, not even her enemies. Her request lacks a nationalist frame. Rather, it is driven by a human need to find refuge for her young. She does not invoke the fate of other nationalities for comparison. Instead, she cites the dens of wild animals and the nests of birds to underscore the urgency of her appeal.

Vahé Vahian's poems in the collection *Osgi Gamurch* (Golden Bridge) echo Mushegh Ishkhan's theme of displacement. While the latter calls for a return to lands lost, Vahian references Soviet Armenia as the site of return. The poems frame exile as a degrading experience. In "Song of the Migrant Child," the young Armenian of the diaspora says, "I am a shrub, thrown to a foreign land . . . ," claiming a position of insignificance and invisibility. In "Longing for Land," the poet says, "Our songs were mournful like the howling of the wind, / Fear of loss, cries of longing, the pain of a life in ruins . . . ," hinting at the impossibility of art and creation in the diaspora. But for Vahian, while exile and dispersion have no redeeming qualities, salvation is promised by Soviet Armenia, which occupies a central position in the poems. "Longing for Land," for instance, is specifically dedicated to Soviet Armenia. Unlike in Mushegh Ishkhan's poetry, "land" and "Armenian" are not all-encompassing terms with fluid referents. Vahian makes a clear distinction between the dispersed collective of Western Armenians and Armenians living in the emergent Soviet project.

In his poem "Diaspora," the exiled masses are referred to collectively as "My nation, turned pitiful Diaspora, a faded and colorless fragment." They are a fragment, a torn-off morsel of the whole, which, as in "Paternal Love," is the "Perpetual, sacred alarm calling us back." Published in 1945, at the beginning of the repatriation campaign, this collection of poems serves a political agenda that differs from Ishkhan's. Whereas in Mushegh Ishkhan's poetry the aim is to cultivate a space for *hayets'i* in exile by linking the dispersed masses to a mythical notion of return, in Vahian's poetry, the aim is to claim Soviet Armenia as a substitute for lost lands and to link the diasporic experience to a concrete plot of land. "As though it is the palace of your ancestors, that opens its arms wide, / to greet you, not as a migrant but as a valiant, native heir / of thirty fertile centuries," he writes, in "Diaspora."[35]

Unlike the writers of Menk, for whom dispersion meant the collapse of patriarchy, the poetic explorations of the Middle Eastern writers advance a clear discourse of patriotism that relies on the resurrection of patriarchy as a precondition for the transnation. In addition to invoking ancestors, as they often do in their nationalist poetics, the Middle Eastern Armenian writers highlight themes of transference, particularly from father to son. Mushegh Ishkhan's "Lullaby," which is part of a larger collection dedicated to his son, reconfigures the lyrics of a traditional Armenian lullaby, *ōrōr*, into a poem that serves the larger ideological narrative of return. The first stanza addresses the son with images of slumber, dreams, and kisses, common to the lullaby genre. But the second stanza immediately places the child within the world of the Armenian diaspora. Ishkhan writes, "You are the only luminous column of our house, / Heir to my countless dead martyrs."[36] The son is both a source of light and the supporting structure of the home. In carrying the memory of the dead, he embodies survival, continuity, and hope for the future. In "Legacy," a poem in the same collection, Ishkhan reclaims the son more explicitly as the inheritor, saying, "I want you to be the torch bearer / of a bright paternal tradition." Here, the paternal tradition is the legacy passed down through the generations. The tradition, in the form of inheritance, is also more precisely named in this poem:

> It's yours, my son, this splendid grand vision of ours,
> Which, against the sea of tears and blood,
> Beamed as the rainbow of renewed life,
> And in whose gaze, my father forever closed his eyes.[37]

Three generations are named in this stanza. The poet speaks to his son about the legacy of his ancestors by invoking his father, specifically his father in the moment of his death. We learn that the legacy that the son must inherit is a vision of survival and return. It is a vision of home, taken by force, but revived as a dream guiding the survivors in dispersion. The genocide is referred to as a sea of tears and blood, signifying the loss of life and the subsequent process of mourning and underscoring the importance of the legacy of an eventual triumph. In other words, hope for the promise of a new life is secured through continuity, through legacy. What the poem suggests, therefore, is that the child's inheritance is patrimony.

Vahé Vahian's "To a Newborn Child," dedicated to his son Vahram, offers his child a similar dream of homeland as inheritance. While the poet's child is the direct addressee of the poem, the opening of the following stanza expands the address to encompass an entire generation. Vahian writes:

> Know this, my child, and let all the children of tomorrow know:
> The dream that created you scent by scent, dew by dew,
> So many times, plunged into a sea of ashes, of blood,
> But it rose once again and it shone with new light.[38]

The dream that is being handed down to the new generation does not arrive unchallenged. Echoing the "sea of tears and ashes" of Ishkhan's poetry, the dream of homeland in Vahian's poem has been through a "sea of ashes, of blood," once again referring to the genocide. But while in Ishkhan's poem the dream survives only as a vision, here the dream rises as a concrete reality. In the following stanza, the resurrected dream is referred to as the "newly freed fatherland," signaling Soviet Armenia. In the poem Vahian explicitly positions Soviet Armenia as the son's bequest:

The free master of those lands, the gardener of that garden,
In the beating of your forearm, hear your legacy. Countless
Forearms that were reaped like fiery spikes of wheat,
Having not yet laid a bed or planted a single tree.[39]

Here, Vahian makes a direct link between victims of the genocide, the surviving generation, and Soviet Armenia as the site of salvation for the former. Homeland is not a mythical vision or dream. Nor it is a substitute for lands lost. It is a garden accessible to Armenians of the diaspora. It is a space of irrevocable belonging, of legacy, and of ownership. It is the patrimonial inheritance of all Armenians. For historian Sisag Varjabedian, Vahian's limitation of his imagined homeland to Soviet Armenia testifies to his relevance. He argues against the idealistic imaginations of homeland, constructed on notions of past glory, that were cultivated by the trio of Hagop Oshagan, Antranig Dzarugian, and Mushegh Ishkhan. Citing Ishkhan most specifically, he criticizes this school: "Ishkhan tried to walk the path of past-worship and represent everything in a heroic light, beneath the weight of which lay buried Armenia, clad in the frock coat of grief and sorrow. As an image containing an Armenia in its depths, perhaps that past was a beautiful one to envision. But it was one that did not correspond with the current reality and did not correlate with the authority of an existing homeland, which was a palpable and true reality above all else."[40] Vahé Vahian, Varjabedian argues, delivers an "opposition song" to the poets stuck in the past.

In Ishkhan's school of poetry, the site of return remains implicit. But in time, the concept of homeland in poetry is supplanted with something slightly more tangible than a mythical vision: the Armenian language becomes a substitute home in exile. Finding home in language was not a conceptualization unique to Armenians at the time. Beginning in the 1960s, Palestinian literature similarly turned to language as a site for refuge and creation. Following the mandate for Israel and the 1948 Nakba, the catastrophe that permanently displaced more than seven hundred thousand Palestinians from their homeland, Palestinian writers began to reflect on the historical experience of their people by combining their personal narratives of exile with the politics of displacement that caused it, in what Edward Said has referred to as the uneasy relationship between the personal and the public.[41] The literature Palestinian writers produced emphasized land to capture sentiments of loss and longing that it evokes. As a body of works that collectively played a role in Palestine's national liberation movement, the first wave of literature that demonstrated political engagement is referred to by scholars as "poetry of resistance," coined by author and activist Ghassan Kanafani.[42]

Mahmoud Darwish, the poet who became the icon of this resistance, explored the relationship between private and public not only in the content of his poems, but also in their delivery. As a performing poet, Darwish was well recognized for his ability to pack stadiums for his recitals. This form of public engagement, which marked the author as Palestine's national poet, repurposes poetry to the type of nationalist project the Middle East's Armenian writers were cultivating around the same time. Writing his earlier works in Israel, Darwish's choice of the Arabic language itself was seen as a form of resistance. This form of linguistic defiance, coupled with the perpetual search for home that characterized his poetry, makes it difficult not to draw parallels between Darwish's brand of Palestinian literature and the Armenian *hayets'i* literature produced in neighboring Lebanon. Like the ambivalent feelings about diasporic belonging, its irrevocability, and its gravitation toward a myth of return expressed in Ishkhan's poetry, Darwish's poems capture the irreconcilable nature of longing in exile. In "Who Am I, without Exile?" Darwish writes:

> There's nothing left of me but you, and nothing left of you
> but me, a stranger massaging his stranger's thigh: O
> stranger! what will we do with what is left to us
> of calm . . . and of a snooze between two myths?
> And nothing carries us: not the road and not the house.[43]

In personifying exile as a stranger who is nevertheless inextricably tied to the narrator, Darwish highlights the feelings of familiarity and strangeness that define the experience of long-term displacement. No dwelling place, be it the road or a house, can have the desired "homing" effect that the exiled person nevertheless continues to search for.

The symbolic realm of language, through the dual acts of creation and utterance, comes closest to providing a "homing" effect, however transitory, for exiled or diasporic people like Darwish.[44] It is in the fleeting moments of writing, listening, or reading that author, reader, and auditor alike find a sense of home. While we see this cultivation of symbolic territory in both Armenian and Palestinian diaspora literature, in its scope, Palestinian writers' relationship with Arabic drives forward a different politics of language than what the Middle East's Armenian writers had with Western Armenian. In the case of many Palestinian writers, the Arabic language served to develop not just regional collective identity, but wider Arab unity. The Palestinian Druze poet Samih al-Qasim, for instance, in discussing Arabic poetry's revolutionary work in constructing the Arab nation, has said that it "should be united by the Arabic language. One Nation, one culture, one language, one history."[45] Echoing similar reverberations to Avetik Isahakian's "One literature, one people" dictum discussed in chapter 5, al-Qasim's designation of Arabic as a unifying force differs from the model of *hayets'i* literature, which emphasized literary production in Western Armenian as a mode of distinguishing between diaspora and Soviet Armenian identities.

For the writers affiliated with the Writers' Association of Syria and Lebanon, *hayets'i* literary production functioned as a mode of preserving the integrity of Western Armenian from its linguistic counterpart, Eastern Armenian of Soviet Armenia. While developed because of Soviet-diaspora relations, *hayets'i* literature's attention to the uniqueness of Western Armenian also fell in line with its impetus toward the past. The call to maintain the Western and Eastern literary forms separate was initially generated by the pre-1915 generation of writers. Taniel Varujan, for example, when asked about the fate of Western Armenian (referred to as "Turkish Armenian") in 1911 replied, "The two dialects are not an obstacle to the impassioned, idealistic, and psychologically harmonious co-existence of the two segments of the Armenian world. And indeed, is it not in distinction that the most beautiful harmony is found?"[46] The writers of the WASL made a concerted effort to link the pre-1915 tradition with their present production and adopting the platform of their predecessors further endowed Western Armenian with symbolic value.

One of Mushegh Ishkhan's most celebrated poems, "The Armenian Language Is the Home of the Armenian," presents the Armenian language as the only place in the world where diaspora Armenians can be sovereign. The poem opens with the following declaration:

The Armenian language is the home of Armenians from around the world
It's where every Armenian enters as a true proprietor.
There, he receives love and nourishment, proud exultation of the heart.
And from wild beasts and snowstorms, he remains always free.[47]

The poem suggests that within the world constructed by the Armenian language, exiled Armenians can keep the integrity of their identity intact. Proprietorship in a symbolic universe means claiming ownership of life's meaning-making apparatus and controlling the narrative of self or, in this case, of the collective. The world constructed through Armenian also offers protection for the cultivation of this identity. In this safe space, Armenian identity is nourished and loved. These conditions are conducive to the growth and necessary for the practice of culture, now ensured by the freedom and autonomy provided by the linguistic realm. Ishkhan concludes the poem by saying: "It is only there that every Armenian can once again find / Lost in the masses of foreign crowds, his soul, / The infinite past and present, even the obscure future."[48] Language is home insofar as it is a sanctuary. It is a place of refuge that safeguards the Armenian "soul" from getting lost in "foreign crowds." In other words, the Armenian language is the only means of resisting cultural assimilation. The metaphor of language as home, therefore, presents a model for the development of national destiny within an international space. Indeed, the last line of the poem draws a continuum of time (past, present, and future), now mapped onto this new symbolic territory.

In his poem "We," Egypt-based poet Jacques Hagopian offers a mélange of referents in the form of meditations on Armenian identity, configuring language as its central component. The poem begins with "We, a small plot of land in this world," referring to the Soviet Republic as the only claim Armenians have left to statehood. Later, it defines Armenians by saying, "We, foreign passports, cranes with no nests," now referring to the exiled masses dispersed across the world. And it closes with "We, triumphant, independent Ararat," referring to lands lost during the genocide. While Mount Ararat is a national symbol for Armenians and dominates the skyline of Armenia's capital, Yerevan, it falls within the borders of Turkey. The poem ends with the poet's desire for victory in the form of returned lands, but a more poetic definition of Armenian identity can be found nestled between these references to homeland and exiled bodies. In one of the middle stanzas, Hagopian writes, "We, Mesrob's invention, we, language of lyre/ Where the Armenian soul vibrates."[49] Language is presented as the dwelling place for the Armenian soul. As a home, language is evoked with all the depth of its history. The musical characteristic of the language's phonetic values is paired with the centuries-old history of its script, as Armenian is referred to as "Mesrob's language." Mesrob Mashdots is the early medieval priest and linguist credited with inventing the Armenian alphabet in AD 405. Ultimately, the poem celebrates the glory of the Armenian nation by offering a comprehensive vocabulary of homeland, which includes the linguistic realm as a symbolic territory of belonging.

In his poem "Ancient Parchments," Syria-based writer Armen Anush writes an ode to medieval Armenian manuscripts, where "the slumbrous meditation of centuries" lives along with "the deep tempestuous song of our exquisite language." While on the surface the poem reads like an inspired celebration of tradition, resilience, and hope, it also partakes in the project of building the image of language as home. Anush writes, "These manuscripts, animated like their tenacious lives, / Where their wild hearts still churn and simmer / It's in those inflamed hearts that lives the Armenian world."[50] Through a series of interpolations, Anush links the Armenian written tradition of the past to the lived world of Armenians in his present day. In other words, the poem suggests that language serves as a place of residence or a repository for all Armenian creation. The manuscripts, which are illuminated in the Armenian tradition, are likened to the animated lives of the ancestors. They are also presented as the dwelling place for the ancestors' memory: the ancestors' hearts still churn there, within the pages of the manuscript. The "inflamed heart" symbolizing the ancestral spirit is the metaphorical landscape that forms the parameters of the Armenian world in perpetuity.

All three poems present the Armenian language as the figurative home for Armenians physically dispersed across the world. The cultural power that the poets grant to the Armenian language lies in its ability to cut across time and space. The poems describe language as the nexus of past traditions, present imagined communities, and the future's creative potential. As such, the symbolic realm transcends the politics of borders that produce problematic notions of home for the displaced Armenians in the postgenocide era. Language, as an evolving system of meaning, carries within it both the history and the geography of its usage over time and forms an appealing metaphor that compensates for the physical loss of land.

Conclusion

In 1979, four years into the Lebanese Civil War, Armenian parliament member Suren Khanamirian was provoked by an interviewer from a francophone magazine who remarked that there were some who opposed the presence of Armenians in Lebanon. Khanamirian answered: "Who opposes our presence? To them I say that we are here to stay. And we have just as many rights as all other communities." By then, Lebanon had ceased to be the temporary place of refuge that it had been for so many survivors following the genocide. Lebanon had become the home of Armenians in exile, and its integrity as the center of the diaspora needed to be guarded at all costs. In fact, in a follow-up question about the future of Armenians in Lebanon, Khanamirian said, "We are going to try to bring all migrant Armenians back to Lebanon. When the situation turns to normal, the children of our community will return. We will do our best in this regard and we will succeed."[51] Hinting at the mass migration out of Lebanon as a result of the war, Khanamirian adopted the language of return, so familiar to the Armenian diasporic experience, but took Lebanon as its referent instead of an Armenian homeland. In other words, his words suggest a refashioning of Lebanon as an Armenian home, to which Armenians have just as much claim as any other community living there.[52]

Indeed, the weakening of the Lebanese stronghold in the Armenian diaspora was a major concern for political party leaders and intellectuals during the civil war. Lebanon was seen as the only bastion of survival for Western Armenian culture, the only place capable of producing Armenian-language teachers, writers, and newspaper editors who could supply what was needed in other diaspora communities. After all, the country boasted a high concentration of Armenian day schools, teacher-training colleges, university-level Armenian-studies departments, countless printing and publishing houses, newspapers and magazines, active political parties, athletic and cultural clubs, and a large population of consumers and participants. These diaspora institutions were evidence of the full-fledged literacy apparatus that, following World War II, had shaped Western Armenian's vitality within a national framework, against Soviet Armenian, and with the aim of an eventual adoption by a homeland state.

Hagop Oshagan's contemplation of diaspora literature's future in the face of pessimism about Western Armenian's literary potential in exile came at the beginning of this language revitalization trajectory. As mentioned before, it was on the eve of his death in 1948 that he urged his readers not to focus on land or homeland as a precondition for literary production by reminding them of the tradition's pre-1915 activity in "diasporic" centers: "Diaspora literature will live until the Armenian people's complete assembly on ancestral lands. After that coveted day, Diaspora's literature will be placed in a museum, just like the Armenian literatures of Venetians, the Romantics, the teachers, and the aesthetes."[53] In Oshagan's formulation, Western Armenian literature bears the diaspora label only temporarily, for it is diasporic insofar as it is produced within that particular historical experience. And that historical experience is called diasporic insofar as it is understood as an interim state of being that precedes an eventual assembly in ancestral lands. Directed at Soviet Armenian critics of Western Armenian literature, Oshagan's words at once advocate for literary production in an exilic language and place an expiration date on exilic experience.

The nationalized *hayets'i* mode of literary production that members of the Writers' Association of Syria and Lebanon launched in 1948 developed a new understanding of diaspora that, unlike Oshagan's claim, recognized the 1915 dispersion as its precondition. In this way, rather than imagining an eventual assembly as Oshagan did, it propagated a narrative of return. In doing so, it conflated historical facts such as the loss of land to Turkey and the Sovietization of Eastern Armenian lands with concepts like homeland and nation, creating a powerful myth of diaspora that ultimately could not survive the establishment of a state. The 1991 independence of Armenia, enabled by the collapse of the Soviet Union, marked the end of the diaspora project, which was fashioned through the revitalization of Western Armenian. As Eastern Armenian was consecrated as the state language, Western Armenian remained bound to a dated diaspora identity that, lacking its Soviet Armenian counterpart, no longer carried potency.

As new diasporas have formed following the westward migration of Armenians from the Middle East and the mass exodus from the former Soviet Armenia, and subsequently from the Armenia Republic, the existing institutions and the hermetically sealed narratives of the traditional diaspora are proving unable to support the dynamic, pluralistic version of a new, diverse diaspora. The depletion of Armenian communities in the Middle East, particularly following the Syrian Civil War, has contributed to endangering Western Armenians' vitality, especially because sustainable models for linguistic and literary production do not exist in diaspora communities in the West. Several decades ago, in her seminal work on Armenian Americans, sociologist Anny Bakalian argued that within the American context, where ethnic languages "fare poorly," "the language is the component of culture that is the least likely to be retained after the second generation."[54] Her study found that in a monolingual society like the United States, in order to achieve economic integration, Armenians traded their language for English and instead explored other sources of identity like cuisine and family. While Armenian American communities at the time of Bakalian's study consisted predominantly of Western Armenian descendants, the communities' demographics have drastically evolved over the past four decades, further complicating language transference. In large cities like Los Angeles, the majority of first- and second-generation Armenians are speakers of an Eastern Armenian dialect. For

Los Angeles–based linguist Shushan Karapetian, this scenario forces us to increasingly think of Eastern Armenian speakers as potential Western Armenian learners. She writes, "The emerging picture is the following—for many Armenian day schools or Western Armenian courses at the college level, up to half of the student population comes to the classroom with some kind of an Eastern Armenian background, speaking a home variety that does not match standard Western Armenian . . . and is either a colloquial or dialectal variant, often in contact with English and potentially other Armenian varieties."[55] Karapetian's observation suggests Western Armenian's inextricability from Eastern Armenian. In other words, rather than Western Armenian developing competitively against Eastern Armenian, as was the case of the Middle East's revitalization project, today, in diaspora communities of the West, Western Armenian develops through a model of hybridization with, and eventually assimilation into, Eastern Armenian.

Western communities like that of Los Angeles, each with complex and intricate language dynamics, will continue to burgeon alongside the emergent republic. Within this process, Western Armenian can no longer be regarded as the facilitator of diasporic identity. This transformative moment foregrounds the imperative to rethink the notion of a center for the diaspora's intellectual and literary production and ask: Which model of literary production is most conducive to Western Armenian's prolonged linguistic vitality? Menk's archive may hold the key to envisioning a model of literary production that is at once decentered and specific. With the term "specific," I refer to an alignment of the local that informs both content and form, which in our case are diasporic communities and the Western Armenian language, respectively. This model suggests that rather than producing literature in Armenian that expresses all things Armenian in a universal, nebulous fashion (the *hayets'i* model), literature should interpret local experience (however multiple and diverse) through Western Armenian. Consequently, this model positions Western Armenian as a system through which life's experiences can be represented and understood, and so ensures the language's vitality.

Within the pages of Lebanon's *Ahegan*, a literary journal published in the late 1960s, we find early efforts to sync Armenian literature's link between language, form, and content, through a rubric referred to as *integré* (integrated) literature. In a literary debate that sought to reflect on the idea of "diaspora" literature, first introduced at the WASL's 1948 conference, the next generation of literary critics such as Haroutiun Kurkjian and Krikor Chahinian discussed the limits of the "diaspora" brand. "Where is the literature borne out of Bourj Hamoud's realities?" they asked.[56] In other words, the participants of this debate, now from the vantage point of an aged, organized diaspora, sought to examine post-1915 production to see if any of the literary schools in dispersion were able to represent their diasporic realities by narrating their present and thus demonstrating a diasporic consciousness (*integré*) that was truly transnational rather than national. While they could not agree on any exemplary authors, they suggested that the Parisian writers of Menk and their contemporary Krikor Beledian came closest to presenting an integrated form of literature: the former in their commitment to present their Parisian present and the latter in his ability to push the boundaries of language's formal qualities. Ultimately, for *Ahegan*'s critics, diaspora literature needed to be informed by its contemporaneous moment and place of production rather than a grander national narrative, something they saw lacking in the canonical literature of diaspora's institutions.[57]

Today, Western Armenian's literary activity is sporadic and spans cities across the world. One of its most prolific writers, Krikor Beledian is from Beirut, resides in Paris, writes about past diasporic memories lost in his family's fading Western dialect, and publishes in Yerevan. Other authors like Vehanush Tekian (originally from Beirut), Maroush Yeramian (originally from Aleppo), and Christian Batikian (originally from Istanbul) write from New Jersey, Yerevan, and Paris, and publish through various presses or online journals. Marc Nichanian produces literary criticism in Armenian and organizes initiatives to translate philosophical texts into Western Armenian. These books, published in Yerevan, circulate beyond diaspora communities and find an audience in Eastern Armenian readers of Armenia. Hamazkayin's literary journal, *Pakin*, based in Beirut but led by Beirut-born and Montreal-based Sonia Kiledjian and an international editorial team, continues to provide space for emergent Western Armenian writers. Aras Publishing in Istanbul remains committed to printing previously unpublished Western Armenian texts, republishes titles that have been left out of the Middle East's canon, and translates into Armenian children's literature published in other languages. The Lisbon-based Calouste Gulbenkian Foundation's Armenian Communities department, among its many language-revitalization initiatives, funds publications aimed at generating young Western Armenian readers. While these examples do not paint a complete picture, they give us a sense of Western Armenian's literary potential outside of a centered, national framework. Many of diaspora's classical institutions still cultivate a canon wherein Armenian literature is valued through its treatment of national symbols and all things Armenian. Yet for prolonged vitality that accommodates the Armenian world's shifting language dynamics, Western Armenian needs to be nurtured as a system through which local realities and specific experiences are processed. In other words, if time, place, experience, author, and narrator are aligned and gain meaning through the Western Armenian linguistic system, the literary text will regain its authority as a form of representation and reposition the vitality of its source language: Western Armenian.

Western Armenian, in its relationship with national belonging, does not present a unique phenomenon among languages of the world. Gayatri Spivak, contemplating the disciplinary problem of comparative literature in American academia in 2003, meditated on the fate of indigenous languages that fell outside national literatures when Europe drew new maps of its colonized territories. She wrote, "Yet the languages that were historically prevented from having a constituted readership or are now losing readership might be allowed to prosper as well. . . . We do not need to map them. Together we can offer them the solidarity of borders that are easily crossed, again and again, as a permanent from-below interruption of a Comparative Literature to come, the irony of globalization."[58] Writing at a time when literary studies in North America was seeking to move away from the language of nation and toward the language of world, Spivak critiqued the mapping impetus embedded in literary criticism, arguing that it directly affects the politics of production and circulation in borderless languages. Similarly, I would like to conclude my discussion of Western Armenian's postgenocide literary history with an invitation to resist mapping, understood as the need to either center diaspora or subordinate it to the framework of a nation. Instead, in its statelessness, Western Armenian may find a renewed vitality that befits the global sociocultural refashioning of our times.

NOTES

BIBLIOGRAPHY

INDEX

Notes

Introduction

1. For a detailed breakdown of deportation numbers and routes per Armenian populated regions of the empire, see Raymond Kévorkian's *The Armenian Genocide: A Complete History*, 349–816. Based on numbers collected by the Armenian Patriarchate in 1878, Kévorkian estimates the number of Armenians living across the Ottoman Empire to have been 3 million (352). According to Richard Hovannisian, the Armenian population of the empire had decreased to 2.1 million by 1912, owing to the Hamidian massacres of 1894–96, the 1909 Adana massacre, and the ongoing exodus to the Caucasus, Europe, and the United States. Richard G. Hovannisian, "The Armenian Question in the Ottoman Empire, 1876–1914," 234.

2. UNESCO's Atlas of the World's Languages in Danger designated Western Armenian as "definitely endangered," which falls in the middle of a six-point scale ranging from "safe," "vulnerable," and "definitely endangered" to "severely endangered," "critically endangered," and "extinct." http://www.unesco.org/new/en/culture/themes/endangered-languages/atlas-of-languages-in-danger/.

3. Vartan Matiossian, "In Lieu of a Conclusion," 147.

4. Vehanush Tekian, "Arewmdahayerēni Verchin Jknazhamĕ [Western Armenian's Final Crisis]," in *Dohmadzaṙ* [Family Tree], 38.

5. Ishkhan Jinbashian, "Keriragan Hayerēn: Lezun Hamaynagerdumi Sharzhĕntʻatsʻkʻin Mēch [Surreal Armenian: Language amid the Process of Community Construction]," 94.

6. George Bournoutian, "Eastern Armenia from the Seventeenth Century to the Russian Annexation," 81.

7. Ronald Grigor Suny, "Eastern Armenians under Tsarist Rule," 112.

8. Houri Berberian, *Roving Revolutionaries: Armenians and the Connected Revolutions in the Russian, Iranian, and Ottoman Worlds*, 4.

9. Hrachia Ajarian, *Hayotsʻ Lezvi Patmutʻyun*, 471.

10. Vahé Oshagan, "Modern Armenian Literature and Intellectual History from 1700 to 1915," 155.

11. Oshagan, "Modern Armenian Literature," 155.

12. The Mekhitarist monks are members of a monastic order of the Armenian Catholic Church, based in Venice with a second branch in Vienna. The order was established in 1701 by Father Mekhitar of Sebastia (Sivas). They played a central role in the development and dissemination of Armenian's modern standard. In recent years, historian Sebouh Aslanian has traced the Mekhitarist and the Armenian mercantile class's establishment of printing presses and cultivation of circulation networks during the early modern period. For example, see "Reader Response and the Circulation of Mkhit'arist Books across the Armenian Communities of the Early Modern Indian Ocean."

13. V. Oshagan, "Modern Armenian Literature," 139–74.

14. Kevork Bardakjian, *A Reference Guide to Modern Armenian Literature, 1500–1920*, 102.

15. Boghos Levon Zekiyan sees secularization as a feature of the *zart'onk'* movement, arguing that it was in this period that the cultural domination of the church and the clergy ended within Armenian life. He thus frames this period in history in an emancipatory light, highlighting the rapid establishment of school networks, the development of the press, and women's emancipation as some of the movement's main achievements. Zekiyan, *The Armenian Way to Modernity*, 67–82.

16. Bardakjian, *Reference Guide*, 102.

17. Vahé Oshagan, "Modernization in Western Armenian Literature," 67.

18. V. Oshagan, "Modernization in Western Armenian Literature," 63.

19. Beginning with the 1880s, several revolutionary parties were formed, both within and outside the Ottoman Empire, each with distinct objectives that ranged from the liberation to the autonomy and the civil rights protections of western Armenians. Most notable among them were the Armenakan Organization, founded in Van; the Social Democratic Hunchakian Party, founded in Geneva; and the Armenian Revolutionary Federation (ARF, initially known as the Federation of Armenian Revolutionaries), founded in Tbilisi. For comparative discussions of the Armenian revolutionary movement within the greater Ottoman constitutional revolutions or within the context of revolutions in neighboring empires, see Bedross Der Matossian's *Shattered Dreams of Revolution: From Liberty to Violence in the Late Ottoman Empire*; and Houri Berberian's *Roving Revolutionaries*.

20. In discussing the dynamics of the Armenian genocide's denial, historian Richard G. Hovannisian describes how revisionist historians try to justify the deportations by claiming that Ottoman Armenian citizens had provoked the measures by organizing uprisings during the late Ottoman period. Hovannisian, "Denial of the Armenian Genocide in Comparison with Holocaust Denial." Genocide scholar Taner Akçam similarly discusses how the Ottoman authorities used the Armenian uprisings as a pretext for the deportations by claiming that the Armenian revolutionaries were collaborating with Russia, the enemy of the state. Akçam, *A Shameful Act: The Armenian Genocide*

and the Question of Turkish Responsibility, 196–204. In studying testimonies of genocide survivors, Donald E. Miller and Lorna Touryan Miller also claim that "the possibility of genocide is always increased when a modernizing minority is linked politically to an enemy of the state in which they reside." Miller and Miller, *Survivors: An Oral History of the Armenian Genocide*, 49. They even find this rationale internalized in the group of survivor interviewees who demonstrate the type of response they categorize as "explanation and rationalization" (159–60).

21. Christopher J. Walker, "World War I and the Armenian Genocide," 252.

22. The arrest and killing of Constantinople's intellectual class is seen as the end mark for the modern Western Armenian literary tradition that was launched in the nineteenth century, during the period known as the Armenian renaissance. One of the last prominent literary activities prior to this break was an aesthetic movement that celebrated the "Armenian soul" and called for the cultivation of autonomous literary expression in the Armenian language. "Mer Hankanagě [Our Manifesto]," *Mehean*, no. 1 (1914): 1–3. Formed in Constantinople in 1914, *Mehean* is often referred to as the final chapter of Western Armenian's modernization period, especially since many surviving writers like Hagop Oshagan and Costan Zarian had been involved with it.

23. *Harach*, Apr. 21, 1929, 4.

24. In *The Politics of Naming the Armenian Genocide: Language, History and "Medz Yeghern,"* Vartan Matiossian examines the evolution of the genocide's naming politics in the Armenian language to suggest that *Medz Yeghern* was in fact the proper name that Armenians used to designate the same meaning as Lemkin's later definition to the events of 1915.

25. Razmik Panossian, *The Armenians: From Kings and Priests to Merchants and Commissars*, 320, 358, 322.

26. Hovannisian, "Denial of the Armenian Genocide."

27. Taner Akçam, *From Empire to Republic: Turkish Nationalism and the Armenian Genocide*, 180–207.

28. Examining a Turkish property law that was passed while the Treaty of Lausanne was still in session, Levon Marashlian claims, "There is a clear continuity between the old Ottoman government's policy of deportation, extermination, and property confiscation set into motion in 1915, and the new Turkish government's policy in the 1920s." The law granted all properties of non-Muslims who had left for any reason prior to the signing of the treaty to the Turkish government. Marashlian, "Finishing the Genocide: Cleansing Turkey of Armenian Survivors, 1920–1923," 139.

29. Akçam, *From Empire to Republic*, 208–25.

30. Cathy Caruth, *Unclaimed Experience: Trauma, Narrative, and History*, 11.

31. Shoshana Felman and Dori Laub, MD, *Testimony: Crisis of Witnessing in Literature, Psychoanalysis, and History*, 81.

32. Giorgio Agamben, *Remnants of Auschwitz: The Witness and the Archive*, 33–34.

33. Not all discourse within trauma studies takes the inherent "unspeakability" of trauma as its focal point. More recently, scholars have argued for a more versatile and pluralistic understanding of trauma. Within this model, trauma's latent haunting is but one potential response to a catastrophic event. These scholars have claimed that multiple factors, ranging from an individual's character to external cultural situations, can determine the varied responses of survivors to extreme events. Moreover, they have warned against the conflation of the victim's subjective experience, historical memory, and artistic representation. For example, see Naomi Mandel's *Against the Unspeakable: Complicity, the Holocaust, and Slavery in America*. Beyond arguing for the possibility of healing and "working through," these later-wave scholars have also emphasized the generative possibilities that traumatic experiences open up by giving rise to new creative practices of representation. In addition, there are questions of ethics raised within discussions of trauma's representation. In this regard, Theodor Adorno's famous dictum is frequently quoted: "To write poetry after Auschwitz is barbaric." Adorno, *Prisms*, 34. Often approached within the framework of poetic representation's impossibility, the quote is better understood as hinting at the new forms of aesthetics that catastrophe inevitably brings about. See Antony Rowland, "Rethinking 'Impossibility' and 'Barbarism': Adorno and Post-Holocaust Poetics."

34. Hagop Oshagan quoted in Marc Nichanian, "The Style of Violence," 1. Prior to the 1915 genocide, the term "catastrophe" was used in the literary response to the earlier, localized, massacres. Most notably, Zabel Yesayan's testimonial work, *Aweragnerun Mēch* (Among the Ruins), refers to the 1909 massacre of Adana as *aghēd*. In this quotation, Oshagan remains a bit ambiguous regarding the precise referent of *aghēd*, seemingly referring to the collection of atrocities that consecutively befell Ottoman Armenians from 1895 to 1915.

35. Marc Nichanian, *Writers of Disaster: Armenian Literature in the Twentieth Century*, 12.

36. David Kazanjian, "Between Genocide and Catastrophe," 129.

37. Nichanian's most extended work to date, on the discussion of Genocide and Catastrophe, is *The Historiographic Perversion* (first published in French in 2006), where he offers a critique of genocide historiography in relation to denial and political recognition campaigns. He argues that the 1915 event was catastrophic insofar as it destroyed its own archive—he criticizes the historicization of testimony and the adoption of its function as proof for producing surviving generations that are locked in a compulsion to prove their own destruction. For Nichanian, "The monument has always already been corrupted by the document." Nichanian, *The Historiographic Perversion*, 123.

38. Robin Cohen, "Diasporas and the Nation-State: From Victims to Challengers."

39. Simon Vratsian, "Ur ē P'rgut'iwnĕ [Where Is the Salvation?]," *Haṛach*, Aug. 29, 1926, 2.

40. The root of the compound word *kaghut'ahayut'iwn* is *kaghut'*, which literally translates to "colony." Khachig Tölölyan has often written about the links between the

Armenian *kaghut'* and Hebrew *galut*, similarly meaning settlement outside the home-land. Initially referring to the exile of Jerusalem elite to Babylon from 586 to 530 BC, *galut* encompasses the Jewish concept of communal exile, closely resembling *kaghut'*, the Armenian iteration of exiled community. See Tölölyan, "Rethinking Diaspora(s)."

41. William Safran, "Diasporas in Modern Societies: Myths of Homeland and Return," 83.

42. Roger Brubaker, "The 'Diaspora' Diaspora."

43. Khachig Tölölyan, "Rethinking Diaspora(s): Stateless Power in the Transnational Moment," 28.

44. Tölölyan, "Rethinking Diaspora(s)," 7–8.

45. While the myth of homeland was an ideal shared by all of the factions in the Armenian diaspora, it was propagated most explicitly by the Armenian Revolutionary Federation. The political party, which vehemently opposed the Sovietization of Armenia, consisted of many ex-parliament members of Armenia's short-lived republic (1918–20). As the dominant political party in dispersion, the ARF played a key role in organizing the diaspora. Best exemplified in the party slogan "Free, Independent, United Armenia," the myth of homeland was central to defining diaspora through a narrative of deferred return. The majority of writers in the WASL and many members of the group Menk were affiliated with the ARF. Although a longer discussion would be beyond the scope of this book, the Western Armenian literary center's move from Paris to Beirut can be linked to the move from Europe to the Middle East of ARF's highest administrative body, its bureau.

46. In discussing the discursive turn from exile to diaspora in the Armenian context, Khachig Tölölyan writes, "Today, diasporic elites have begun to view the totality of diasporic communities as the *permanent Armenian transnation*." Tölölyan, "Elites and Institutions in the Armenian Transnation," 115.

47. Levon Chormisian, "Darakrut'iwne ew Hayrenik' [Exile and Homeland]," *Harach*, Apr. 24, 1926, 2.

48. Sossie Kasbarian, "The Myth and Reality of 'Return': Diaspora in the Homeland," 359.

49. While Eastern Armenian is the de facto official language of the Republic of Armenia, some scholars contend that legally, the state does not exclude Western Armenian from its constitution, which, based on a 1993 language law, uses the umbrella term "Armenian language," without mentioning its Eastern or Western standards. Article 1 of the Language Law calls for the preservation of the Armenian language both in the Republic and within Armenian populations outside of its borders, and for unification of orthography. Anahid Donabédian sees the extension of language-unification efforts outside of the Republic as an attempt to consolidate its Eastern-speaking diaspora through the production of material resources. See "La politique linguistique en Arménie: De l'Union Soviétique à la République indépendante." Recognizing Western Armenian as "factually"

stateless, Hagop Gulludjian argues that our insistence on using the separate Eastern and Western designations creates a hierarchy that, enabled by the ambiguity of Armenia's constitution, leads to the demotion of the Western standard. See "Language Vitality through 'Creative Literacy.'"

50. Since the Western Armenian language is my focus of inquiry, I have not engaged with the body of non-Armenian works that is sometimes referred to as Armenian diaspora literature. Lorne Shirinian argues for the "Armenian diaspora" designation to be used for English-language works written by Armenians living in North America. Reading them through the framework of minor literature as proposed by Deleuze and Guattari and referring to literature that a minority constructs in a majority language, Shirinian argues that many North American Armenian writers represent Armenian diasporic life using a mode of defamiliarization that deterritorializes the English language, allowing them to be read as part of the Armenian diaspora's literary canon. See Shirinian, *Armenian–North American Literature, a Critical Introduction: Genocide, Diaspora, and Symbols.*

51. Mads Rosendahl Thomsen, *Mapping World Literature: International Canonization and Transnational Literatures*, 2.

52. See Aamir R. Mufti, *Forget English! Orientalisms and World Literatures*; and Gayatri Ch. Spivak, *Death of a Discipline.*

53. Mufti, *Forget English!*, 52.

54. Hagop Gulludjian, "Language Vitality through 'Creative Literacy.'"

1. Generative Orphanhood

1. Zareh Vorpuni, "Husher [Recollections]," 6.

2. Krikor Beledian, "Menk'-i aṙt'iw [On Menk]," 1.

3. For a more complete discussion of the immediate prehistory of Armenian literature in the diaspora, see Nichanian's *Writers of Disaster.*

4. Levon Chormisian, *Hamabadger Arewmdahay Mēg Taru Badmut'ean: Hay Sp'iwṙk'ě, Fransahayeru Badmut'iwně* [Overview of Western Armenian Centennial History: Armenian Diaspora, French Armenian History], 165.

5. The announcement deliberately rejects the label of "manifesto" and presents the forging of a manifesto as one of the group's primary aims.

6. Krikor Beledian also refers to them as the Paris School, the "Ecole de Paris," in "L'expérience de la catastrophe dans la literature arménienne," 171.

7. In arguing for a relocation of modern Western culture from a postcolonial perspective, Bhabha writes, "The borderline work of culture demands an encounter with 'newness' that is not part of the continuum of past and present. It creates a sense of the new as an insurgent act of cultural translation. Such art does not merely recall the past as social cause or aesthetic precedent; it renews the past, refiguring it as a contingent

'in-between' space, that innovates and interrupts the performance of the present." Homi Bhabha, *The Location of Culture*, 7.

8. I use the formulation "Menk generation" to refer to the young writers who were members of Menk or adjacent to its activities. This generation has also been referred to as "Menkists" (V. Oshagan, "Modernization in Western Armenian Literature," 72), as "the Menk circle" (K. Bardakjian, *Reference Guide*, 235), and as "Paris Boys" or "Paris School," as mentioned earlier.

9. Jeremy Stubbs, "Surrealist Literature and Urban Crime," 168.

10. In his unfinished work, *The Arcades Project*, cultural theorist Walter Benjamin situates Paris as the central cultural milieu of the nineteenth century.

11. In *Paris Noir: African Americans in the City of Lights*, Tyler Stovall traces ebb and flow of migration to France during and following World War I and warns us that contrary to the general belief that France did not have a race problem during this time owing to its favorable treatment of black troops fighting for the Allied powers, its treatment of colonial laborers tells a different story. He says, "Almost without exception, like their African American brothers, these nonwhite laborers performed the worst jobs and received the lowest pay of anyone in France during the war" (20).

12. In his seminal book, *Imagined Communities: Reflections on the Origins and Spread of Nationalism*, Benedict Anderson links national consciousness to print capitalism, which he claims allowed people to situate themselves within an imagined community, that is, the nation. Anderson traces how print capitalism, in the form of book publishing, contributed to the demise of Latin and to the standardization of vernaculars. He claims that this process contributed to the decline of the imagined community of Christendom and gave rise to the imagined community of the nation-state. Reflecting on the print medium's celebrated genres of the book and the newspaper, he develops a theory of simultaneity central to the process of "imagining" cultivated through print: "The idea of a sociological organism moving calendrically through homogeneous, empty time is a precise analogue of the idea of the nation, which is also conceived as a solid community moving steadily down (or up) history. An American will never meet, or even know the names of more than a handful of his 240,000-odd fellow-Americans. He has no idea of what they are up to at any one time. But he has complete confidence in their steady, anonymous, simultaneous activity" (26).

13. Brent Hayes Edwards, *The Practice of Diaspora: Literature, Translation, and the Rise of Black Internationalism*, 118.

14. Lilyan Kesteloot, *Black Writers in French: A Literary History of Negritude*, 60.

15. Kesteloot, *Black Writers in French*, 102.

16. Reiland Rabaka, *The Negritude Movement*, xi.

17. Kesteloot, *Black Writers in French*, 83.

18. Edmond Khayadjian, *Archag Chobanian et le movement armenophile en France*, 167.

19. Levon Chormisian, *Hamabadger*, 23.

20. The Armenian Question refers to the Armenian community's calls for protection of their freedoms within the Ottoman Empire from Russian and European powers. The plight of the Armenians first reached the international stage as Article 16 of the Russo-Turkish Peace Treaty of San Stefano, signed in 1878. It called for Armenian self-administration as a condition for Russian withdrawal. Later that year at the Berlin Congress, Armenian demands were demoted to Article 61, which tabled the discussion of Armenian self-administration and left the supervision of reforms to European powers collectively. With the lack of accountability, the Armenian Question was tabled for fifteen years and became a topic of international discussion again following the Armenian massacres of 1895–96 under the reign of Sultan Abdul Hamid II.

21. Maud S. Mandel, *In the Aftermath of Genocide: Armenians and Jews in Twentieth-Century France*, 26.

22. Arshag Chobanian, "Hay Azkin Paregamnerĕ [Friends of the Armenian Nation]," 120.

23. *Ergunkʻ* differs from the other party periodicals in that it presents itself as a "revue littéraire." Shavarsh Nartuni, who would also become a founding member of *Menkʻ*, edited the journal. In a similar parallel, *Ergunkʻ*'s efforts to draw distinctions between the orphan generation and the surviving generation of Armenians were echoed in *Menkʻ*. In an announcement called "Our Position," *Ergunkʻ*'s editorial claims, "It is not for ourselves that we will write these lines. We, the orphans, are familiar with our position. Rather, these lines are for those who have aged and faded, who no longer understand the soul of the new boys. . . . Long live the new generation! Especially the multitude called orphans! . . . It is our duty to show you the soul of the post-war generation" ("Mer Tirkʻĕ [Our Position]," 1).

24. *Haṛach*'s success lies in the extraordinary efforts of the newspaper's founder and editor Shavarsh Misakian, whose legacy continued for many decades through the editorship of his daughter, Arpik Misakian. He was instrumental in providing a free forum for literary debates and a stage for upcoming writers, even if he was critical of their writings. It was he who introduced Shahan Shahnur to the Armenian public, by publishing his controversial novel *The Retreat without Song* in serial form. The first segment appeared in the newspaper on May 28, 1929. For a nicely compiled collection of Shavarsh Misakian's journalistic and literary writings, see *Ōrer ew Zhamer* (Days and Hours).

25. Krikor Beledian, *Cinquante ans de littérature arménienne en France*, 31.

26. Editorial, "Miutʻiwn [Unity]," *Abakay*, Feb. 5, 1921, 1.

27. "Nor Hawadkʻĕ [The New Faith]," 1.

28. "Mēg Janabarh Miayn [One Path Only]," 1.

29. "Mer Tirkʻĕ [Our Position]," 1.

30. Kevork Bardakjian refers to this group of writers as the "desert generation." Bardakjian, *Reference Guide*, 234.

31. For more on the connection between *Hart'kogh* and *Zuart'nots'*, see Krikor Beledian's "Hart'koghēn Zuart'nots' [From Hart'kogh to Zuart'nots']," *Harach: Midk' ew Aruesd*, May 9, 2004, 2.

32. "Jagadin Vray [On the Front]," 1.

33. In his November 20, 1928, letter to Hrant Palouyan, Shavarsh Nartuni, one of the key members of the still forthcoming Menk group, reveals that he is the author of the *Zuart'nots'*'s inaugural editorial, calling it the journal's "front" and admitting to having given it the tone of a "manifesto" (*Harach: Midk' ew Aruesd*, May 9, 2004, 4).

34. A. Hagopian, reviews.

35. The English translation lessens the idea of newness. In Armenian, it reads *norakuyn*, hinting at "newer" or "newest," "latest," or "cutting edge," and not simply "new."

36. In a 1952 interview with Garo Poladian, Nartuni remarks that he and a number of the group's signatories contributed fifty francs each toward the cost of publication. *Zruyts'* [Conversation], 164. I should also note that the third issue of the journal switches to Navarre Press, and the final joint issue is printed by Bezezian Press.

37. It is important to note a few exclusions and additions here. Hrach Zartarian, one of the active writers of the time and one whose work this book will examine, is absent from the list, although his brother's name appears. The reasons for the absence of his name are not known. He is often listed as one of the Menk-generation boys. For instance, see Poladian, *Zruyts'*, 169; and Bardakjian, *Reference Guide*, 235. In the final few issues of the journal, while the list of contributors significantly drops, two new names appear: H. Kosdantian and B. Zaroyan. In his interview with Poladian, Shavarsh Nartuni claims that he had also asked Araxi Torossian to join the group many times, but the writer refused (she would have been the only female writer in the group). He also claims that Hrant Palouyan had changed his mind about joining the group because of Vazken Shushanian's participation. Poladian, *Zruyts'*, 163–64.

38. *Menk: Revue littéraire armenienne*, no. 1 (1931): 3.

39. *Menk: Revue littéraire armenienne*, no. 1 (1931): 4.

40. A few examples of previously published texts that are associated with the Menk group are Shahan Shahnur's *Nahanchĕ Arants' Erki* (The Retreat without Song) (1929), Zareh Vorpuni's *P'ortsĕ* (The Attempt) (1929), Nigoghos Sarafian's *Anchrbedi mĕ Krawumĕ* (An Outerspace Conquest) (1929), Vazken Shushanian's *Amran Kisherner* (Summer Nights) (1930), and Meloyan's *Erek' Ĕngernerĕ* (The Three Friends) (1931). Advertisements showcasing these titles adorn the inside back covers of *Menk*'s issues.

41. Arshag Chobanian is one of the earliest critics to point to the absence of genocide's explicit representation in the first novels of Shahnur and Vorpuni. He writes, "One critique that we can make is that in both Vorpuni's and Shahnur's novels, the great catastrophe (or to be more precise the series of catastrophes), while they inform the theme's backdrop, are not centrally treated in either novel." Chobanian, "Agnarg mĕ Ayzhmean

Hay Mdawor Geank'in Vray: Ardasahmani Mêch [A Look at Contemporary Armenian Intellectual Life: Abroad]," 113.

42. Caruth, *Unclaimed Experience*, 4.

43. Cathy Caruth, introduction to *Trauma: Explorations in Memory*, 8.

44. Following the Holocaust, Jewish intellectuals explored the question of aesthetics in many ways, factoring in both the postcatastrophe failure of language and the survivors' fear of betraying the dead. In one approach, as argued by Elie Wiesel, the uniqueness of the Holocaust required the cultivation of its own aesthetic approach. In looking at the literature of the surviving generation of Armenian writers in comparison with Jewish literature, Rubina Peroomian similarly argues that the act of fictionalizing the genocide required the creation of an "imaginative truth that is the world of the artist of genocide." Peroomian, *Literary Reponses to Catastrophe*, 5. For Theodor Adorno, on the other hand, rendering the horror of the Holocaust in beautiful forms was unethical, as expressed by his famous 1949 statement "To write poetry after Auschwitz is barbaric," a claim he modified later in life.

45. Many of the contributors showcased in *Hayrenik' Monthly* were ex-political leaders and ex-parliamentary members of the short-lived Armenian Republic, such as Simon Vratsian, Alexander Khadisian, Hovhannes Kachaznuni, Armen Garo, and Avedis Aharonian. In fact, the journal's inaugural issue opens with an editorial announcement that positions the journal as a project that aims to serve the greater goal of establishing an "Armenian independent state." *Hayrenik' Monthly* 1, no. 1 (1922): 2.

46. Shavarsh Nartuni, "Reviews," 61.

47. V. Oshagan, "Modernization in Western Armenian Literature," 71.

48. Shahan Shahnur, "Menk', Part II," *Harach*, Jan. 26, 1932, 2.

49. Shavarsh Nartuni, "Menk', Menk', Menk'," 39.

50. For a more extensive discussion of responses to genocide, see Donald E. Miller and Lorna Touryan Miller's analysis of survivor accounts in *Survivors: An Oral History of the Armenian Genocide* (1993). One of the emergent themes in survivor responses is the questioning of the victims' compliant behavior during the marches (88).

51. See Der Matossian's *Shattered Dreams of Revolution*.

52. Zabel Yesayan later settled in Yerevan, Armenia, in 1933, believing that an Armenian writer should create only on their native soil. Although at first she was celebrated in the ranks of Soviet Armenian writers, in 1937, she was arrested and sent to Siberia during the Stalinist Purges owing to the "nostalgic" nature of her novel *The Gardens of Sihlidar*. She died somewhere en route to Siberia in 1943, at the age of sixty-five.

53. Yesayan quoted in Shahan Shahnur, "Menk', Part I," *Harach*, Jan. 24, 1932, 2.

54. Nigoghos Sarafian, "Menk'," 70.

55. Shahan Shahnur, "Menk', Part III," *Harach*, Jan. 27, 1932, 2.

56. Nartuni, "Menk', Menk', Menk'," 40.

57. Shahnur, "Menk', Part II," 2.

58. Costan Zarian, "Azkayinn u Michazkayinĕ Kraganut'ean Mĕch [The National and International in Literature]," 108.

59. Zarian's condescension about Armenian exiles' ability to produce transnational literature can both be attributed to and seen as a stark contrast to his background as a truly transnational figure. Born in Shemakha, Azerbaijan, he was educated in a Russian school in Baku and later pursued higher education in Paris. He learned Armenian only at the age of twenty-five, in Venice, after which he moved to Constantinople and published the journal *Mehean* in 1914. After escaping the slaughter of intellectuals, he spent the rest of his life living in Italy, France, the United States, the Middle East, and finally Soviet Armenia. Bardakjian, *Reference Guide*, 577.

60. Zarian, "Azkayinn u Michazkayinĕ," 107.

61. Hagop Oshagan, *Mayrenineru Shuk'in Dag* [Under the Shade of Cedar Trees], 96.

62. Announcement by Signatories, *Menk: Revue littéraire armenienne*, no. 1 (1931): 3.

63. Shahnur, "Menk', Part II," 2.

64. The former prime minister of the short-lived Armenian Republic, Simon Vratsian, conflates Shahnur's call of "All eyes toward Armenians" with the revolutionary slogan of the prewar generation, "Tĕbi ergir" (Toward country), coined by activist Eduard Agnuni. "Tĕbi ergir" was a call for eastern Armenians, urging them to turn their attention to the plight of western Armenians living under Ottoman rule. For Vratsian, Shahnur's call invokes a similarly nationalist sentiment, leading him to claim that the Menk generation's platform is nothing but a regurgitation of the previous generation's ideology. Simon Vratsian, "'Menk' ew 'Duk'' ['We' and 'You']," 148.

65. Shavarsh Nartuni, "Garōd Hay Lezui [Longing for the Armenian Language]," *Haṙach*, Oct. 28, 1928, 2.

66. Nigoghos Sarafian, "Haigazian Paṙaran [Haigazian Dictionary]."

67. Nigoghos Sarafian, "Azkayinn u Michazkayinĕ Kraganutean Mĕch [The National and International in Literature]," 70.

68. Nigoghos Sarafian, "Azkayinn u Michazkayinĕ Kraganut'ean Mĕch [The National and International in Literature]," 70, 71.

69. Over the course of the past few decades, similar efforts have been seen in the academic fields of postcolonial studies and trauma studies. For instance, Edward Said's collection of essays titled *Reflections on Exile* presents exile as a productive space. Similarly, in the 2003 publication *Loss: The Politics of Mourning*, David L. Eng and David Kazanjian present a number of essays that seek to reformulate loss. Ali Behdad, though, in his essay "Global Disjunctures, Diaspora Differences, and the New World (Dis-)Order," critiques postcolonial critics' valorization of "deterritorialization's redemptive power," arguing that such a perception of displacement fails to historicize the particular predicaments of racial "othering" in various cosmopolitan contexts.

70. Françoise Lionnet and Shu-mei Shish, eds., *Minor Transnationalism*, 7.

71. See Avtar's *Cartographies of Diaspora*.

72. Nigoghos Sarafian, untitled, 42.

73. Since these borders were drawn and presented by President Woodrow Wilson at the Treaty of Sèvres, claims to lands in historic Armenia are often referred to as Wilsonian Armenia, which forms an all-inclusive vision of homeland in the general Armenian imaginary even today.

74. The terms of the circular were published in translation in Haṙach on Aug. 5, 1925.

75. Shavarsh Misakian, "Menkʻ Tʻurkʻ Chʻenkʻ [We Are Not Turks]," Haṙach, Nov. 1, 1925, 1.

76. "Haygagan Hbadagutʻean Khntirě [The Issue of Armenian Nationality]," Haṙach, Aug. 9, 1925, 1.

77. Levon Chormisian, "Darakrutʻiwně ew Hayrenikʻ [Exile and Homeland]," Haṙach, Apr. 24, 1926, 2.

78. Movses Bchakjian, "Interview with Zareh Vorpuni, Part B," 57.

79. Poladian, Zruytsʻ, 163–66.

80. Krikor Chahinian, Gensakrutʻiwn ew Madenakidutʻiwn Shahan Shahnuri [Biography and Bibliography of Shahan Shahnur], 33.

81. Vorpuni, "Husher [Recollections]," 6.

82. Bebo Simonian, "Pʻarizi Menkʻin Deghě Spʻiwrkʻahay Kragan Mamuli Badmutʻean Mēch [The Place of Paris's Menk in the History of the Armenian Diaspora's Literary Press]," 226.

83. See Krikor Beledian, "In the Language of Catastrophe."

2. Interrupted Time

1. Shahan Shahnur, "Menkʻ, Part III," Haṙach, Jan. 27, 1932, 2.

2. In This Thing Called the World: The Contemporary Novel as Global Form, Debjani Ganguly calls sympathy and sovereignty the "narrative grammar of the human," which, she claims, like Ian Watt and Micheal McKeon before her, "shaped the evolution of the novel as a genre manifesting a capacity to respond sympathetically to distant suffering due to the emergence of new conventions of moral responsibility and a new sense of self generated by the rise of a new commercial society in the wake of technological advancements of early capitalism" (27–28).

3. See Marc Nichanian, "Zareh Orpuni: Zhamanag ew Hayrutʻiwn (Zareh Orpuni: Time and Fatherhood)," 100.

4. See Nichanian, Writers of Disaster, vol. 1, The National Revolution.

5. This is not to say that the group did not occasionally publish poetry in its journal. N. Sarafian, K. Kegharkuni, Osdanig, P. Mikaelian, A. Dadrian, and R. Zartarian each published one or two pieces of poetry in the Menkʻ journal. At the same time, around the group's active years, most members produced their first novels. In addition to the ones discussed in this book, some notable novels are Shushanian's Amran Kisherner (Summer

Nights) (1930), Sarafian's *Khariskhēn Heṙu* (Far from Anchor) (1932), Beshigtashlian's *Sitonna* (Sedona) (1928), P. Mikayelian's *Arew, Arew* (Sun, Sun) (1933), Meloyan's *Erek Ĕngernerĕ* (The Three Friends) (1931), and Nartuni's *Erusaghem, Erusaghem* (Jerusalem, Jerusalem) (1938).

6. See Krikor Beledian, "Ergtimin Eṙangiwnin Mēch [The Ambiguous in the Triangle]," 331.

7. Vratsian, "'Menk'' ew 'Duk'' ['We' and 'You']," 151.

8. In *Loss*, a collection of essays, David L. Eng and David Kazanjian similarly make a case for the creative quality of loss. They write, "Indeed, the politics of mourning may be described as that creative process mediating a hopeful or hopeless relationship between loss and history" (2).

9. The imperative to fill the father's position within the surviving familial structure is a male preoccupation, of course. Because of the gendered nature of the genocidal crime, the majority of the "fathers" are literally missing, for they were rounded up and massacred around their Anatolian towns of origin. The refugee population that survived the deportation marches through the Syrian deserts consisted mostly of women and children. Although many of the Menk writers were survivors of the Syria–Greece–Marseille–Paris refugee trail, others arrived from Constantinople during the early 1920s. This latter group consisted mostly of young men who had left both parents behind in what is now Istanbul. Anxieties around procreation are common among groups who have undergone a genocide, an act aimed precisely at terminating a collective's progenitive lifeline. As Sevan Beukian has discussed, among Armenians, the 1915 genocide and regional instabilities like the first Karabakh war have produced a discourse of "the need to reproduce the next generations." She argues that reproductive anxieties stemming from the genocide have transgenerational consequences that in today's Armenia Republic lead to the discriminatory othering of LGBTQ people, who are presumed nonreproductive. "'National Anxiety' and Homosexuality in Post-Soviet Armenia: National Identity through Trauma and the Memory of Genocide and War," 161.

10. The meaning I intend to convey with the phrase "replace the father" is twofold. First, it implies the son's taking the place or assuming the role of the absent father within the family structure. Second, it refers to succeeding the father in the sense of continuing the paternal lineage. As a literary trope, the imperative to replace the father is never fulfilled, hinting at the Menk generation's invitation to reimagine the patriarchal construct of the Armenian family in dispersion.

11. Hrach Zartarian had a particularly overwhelming shadow to live under, one that might have influenced his dedication. His father, Rupen Zartarian (1874–1915), was a renowned writer and teacher in Constantinople. Although he produced folktales, prose poems, and short stories, beginning in 1908, he devoted himself mostly to editorial work and political activity, running the publication of the daily *Azadamard*. Bardakjian, *Reference Guide*, 166. Along with the Armenian intelligentsia of Constantinople, he was

arrested on the night of April 24, 1915, and killed later in that year. Hrach Zartarian's reluctance to claim his father's memory and present himself as his father's successor may be attributed to the idea that his father belonged to the community first and only secondarily to him and his family.

12. The figure of the absent father does not appear only in Armenian literature that came out of France. Lorne Shirinian similarly presents the problematic of thinking oneself or creating oneself as a son in the new situation of the diaspora as a recurring concern in North American literature by Armenian writers. He concludes, "The absence of a father indicated the absence of a model upon which to build the family and by extension the nation." Shirinian, "Lost Fathers and Abandoned Sons: The Silence of Generations in Armenian Diaspora Literature," 14.

13. The narrator is named Minas Yerazian in subsequent novels in the series. There is a large gap between the series' first installment, P'ortsĕ (1929), and the next, Tegnadzun (The Candidate), published in 1967.

14. Vorpuni, P'ortsĕ [The Attempt], 9.

15. Current scholarship relies on the language of "intention" to define shame in opposition to guilt. At its core, the notion of survivor guilt consists of feelings of culpability at the idea of having survived while so many others perished. For the survivor, the concern is less about whether having done things differently would have saved lives than about the question of being singled out: Why was I spared? In *From Guilt to Shame: Auschwitz and After*, Ruth Leys traces the post-1960s development of the discourse of shame theory, from Tomkins to Sedgwick to Agamben, to argue that conceptualizations of survivor guilt have been displaced by a new theory of shame that is anti-intentionalist and materialist and considers personal difference as the only issue of importance. For Leys, this privileging of shame disallows disagreements about intentions and meaning and instead favors personal identity. Whereas Leys's critique of the current trends in shame theory concerns larger questions of ethics and responsibility, her more specific attempt to reclaim and reposition guilt is important to my understanding of shame theory's overlap with trauma theory. A definition of intention-free guilt is crucial to my close readings of trauma's indexical representation in the French Armenian novel, where I see guilt as a form of internalized responsibility distinct from the notion of intentionality. In the case of these novels, it is not an unfulfilled responsibility toward the fallen victims that produces guilt, but rather an unfulfilled responsibility toward the survivors, particularly the family.

16. Vorpuni, P'ortsĕ [The Attempt], 9.

17. What I discuss as these gaps of memory in the narrator's narrative, Giorgio Agamben identifies as a testimony's inherent "lacuna," produced as a result of the survivors' relationship between their "subjecthood" and the language of testimony. He writes, "*Testimony takes place in the non-place of articulation. In the non-place of the Voice stands not writing, but the witness. And it is precisely because the relation (or, rather, non-relation) between the living being and the speaking being has the form of shame,*

of being reciprocally consigned to something that cannot be assumed by a subject, that the *ēthos* of this disjunction can only be testimony—that is, something that cannot be assigned to a subject but that nevertheless constitutes the subject's only dwelling place, its only possible consistency." Agamben, *Remnants of Auschwitz*, 130.

18. Vorpuni, *P'ortsĕ* [The Attempt], 12–13.

19. *Odarut'iwn* is difficult to translate. The root word *odar* is the Armenian word for "foreign" used to refer to foreigners (non-Armenians). *Odarut'iwn* refers to the state or abstract realm of "foreignness," and more specifically to diasporic, immigrant life. Whereas the English word "alienation" implies also the *process* of becoming estranged, *odarut'iwn* refers simply to the *state* of "alienness."

20. Vorpuni, *P'ortsĕ* [The Attempt], 9.

21. This latter emphasis on the survivors' response can be understood through the antimimetic theory of trauma, which imagines healing as possible by claiming that the victim's psychical integrity remains intact in traumatic situations. In contrast, mimetic theory of trauma does not see traumatic experience as an external event and recognizes the victim's inability to gain specular distance as the basis of the event's violence. In the language of Freudian psychoanalysis, the foundation of mimetic theory, "acting out," as a victim's response to trauma is on the opposite end of "working through." It is seen as a form of pathological mourning, a symptom of melancholia, characterized by an inability to remember and effectively mourn for a lost object. What the victim "acts out" in the present is a repressed memory of a traumatic past.

22. Vorpuni, *P'ortsĕ* [The Attempt], 14.

23. Here, my use of the term "right to mourn" as opposed to the psychological understanding of ability to mourn, which I use elsewhere, is linked to the philosophical language of trauma, the law of mourning, and the subsequent "interdiction of mourning," as discussed by Marc Nichanian. See Marc Nichanian, "Catastrophic Mourning," in *Loss*, ed. Eng and Kazanjian, 99–124. Within philosophical discourse, the interdiction of mourning as tied to the irrepresentability of trauma has also been critiqued. Gillian Rose, for instance, by arguing that democracy relies on representation, links the claim that the Holocaust or such genocidal violence is beyond reason to fascist thought. She argues that by prohibiting the study of tyranny's connection to justice through the framework of reason, we also eliminate the need for restorative political action. See Gillian Rose, *Mourning Becomes the Law: Philosophy and Representation*.

24. Vorpuni, *P'ortsĕ* [The Attempt], 70.

25. See Beledian, "Ergtimin Erangiwnin Mēch [The Ambiguous in the Triangle]," 348.

26. Vorpuni, *P'ortsĕ* [The Attempt], 91, 105.

27. Vorpuni, *P'ortsĕ* [The Attempt], 106.

28. Vorpuni, *P'ortsĕ* [The Attempt], 108.

29. A. Hagopian, "Nor Kirk'er [New Books]," 67; K. Fenerjian, "Nor Kirk'er [New Books]," 301.

30. Hrach Zartarian, *Mer Geank'ĕ* [Our Life], 62.

31. Zartarian, *Mer Geank'ĕ* [Our Life], 34.

32. Zartarian, *Mer Geank'ĕ* [Our Life], 35.

33. Zartarian, *Mer Geank'ĕ* [Our Life], 150. I should also note that Arsen's itinerary resembles that of his author. Hrach Zartarian had a similarly itinerant life, both before and after the genocide. As the son of well-known writer and educator Rupen Zartarian, he traveled from Kharpert to Izmir to Bulgaria and to Istanbul prior to the 1915 arrest and assassination of his father. For more on the author's biography, see Hrach Zartarian's letter to Alexander Topchian published in the introduction of the 1982 Soviet publication of *Mer Geank'ĕ*.

34. Zartarian, *Mer Geank'ĕ* [Our Life], 150.

35. Robert Eaglestone, "Knowledge, 'Afterwardness,' and the Future of Trauma Theory," 14; Caruth, *Unclaimed Experience*, 4.

36. Zartarian, *Mer Geank'ĕ* [Our Life], 81, 59, 60.

37. Zartarian, *Mer Geank'ĕ* [Our Life], 73.

38. What I refer to as the collapse of witnessing is similar to what Dori Laub calls the *crisis of witnessing* in his essay "An Event without a Witness: Truth Testimony and Survival." He argues that the Holocaust is an event without a witness since, owing to the catastrophic nature of the event, those individuals who experienced it cannot comply with the historical imperative to bear witness. Rather, for the survivor, the event begins to make sense and gain historical meaning only belatedly, through the experience of giving testimony. For a complete discussion, see Laub, "An Event without a Witness: Truth Testimony and Survival," in *Testimony*, ed. Felman and Laub, 57–74.

39. Felman and Laub, *Testimony*, 81.

40. Zartarian, *Mer Geank'ĕ* [Our Life], 162.

41. Zartarian, *Mer Geank'ĕ* [Our Life], 161.

42. While the distinction I'm making here between witnessing from the inside and witnessing from the outside is intended to draw attention to the complicated nature of belated testimony, the act of bearing witness is seen as an impossibility, regardless of its place of articulation or audience. Agamben identifies the cause of impossibility as the "lacuna" of testimony, arguing that the survivor is simply a pseudowitness, for the complete witness is the dead victim. In bearing witness to the missing testimony of the dead, the pseudowitnesses (the survivors) lose their sense of self: "To speak, to bear witness, is thus to enter into a vertiginous movement in which something sinks to the bottom, wholly desubjectified and silenced, and something subjectified speaks without truly having anything to say of its own." Agamben, *Remnants of Auschwitz*, 120.

43. Zartarian, *Mer Geank'ĕ* [Our Life], 242.

44. Nichanian, "Zareh Orpuni," 99.

45. Marianne Hirsch, *The Generation of Postmemory: Writing and Visual Culture after the Holocaust.*

46. Brett Ashley Kaplan, *Unwanted Beauty: Aesthetic Pleasure in Holocaust Representation*.

47. In *The Era of the Witness*, Annette Wiekiorka argues that the explosion of testimony following the Holocaust has created a competitive field between the witness and the scholarly historian. She writes, "For how can a coherent historical discourse be constructed if it is constantly countered by another truth, the truth of individual memory? How can the historian incite reflection, thought, and rigor when feelings and emotions invade the public?" (144).

48. See "Le témoignange: Du document au monument," chap. 4 in *La perversion historiographique: Une réflexion arménienne*, by Marc Nichanian, 91–116; and Nichanian's discussion with David Kazanjian in "Between Genocide and Catastrophe."

3. Lost Bodies

1. "*Gě khntrui ardasahmani t'ert'erēn ardadbel.*" During the 1920s, since the term "diaspora," *sp'iwřk'* in Armenian, was not in widespread usage, the "Search" announcements' final request indicates *ardasahman* to refer to Armenians and institutions in dispersion. Literally, the word means "outside the border."

2. Beledian, *Cinquante ans*, 228.

3. I capitalize "Other" to suggest a parallel between the marginalizing processes of Othering, as coined by Gayatri Spivak and understood in postcolonial studies, and the social exclusion experienced by Armenian refugees in France during the interwar years. Building on Lacan's distinctions of self and other, discussions within postcolonial studies use "Other" to refer to the group who holds the concentration of power, whereas "other" is used to refer to the colonized subject, who is "othered" in order to validate and consolidate the former's identity. As ethnic minorities and refugees living in imperial France, post–World War I Armenians were aware of the power of the French, in whose gaze they constructed their new sense of self. It was in this context, then, that the French were seen as objects of desire.

4. Shahnur's title takes the Turkish word *huynuzlě* and "Armenianizes" it by adding to it a definite, plural-ending -*nerě*. *Buynuzlě* literally signifies "the horned," but generally refers to a person who has been deceived.

5. Sigmund Freud, "The Horror of Incest," in *Totem and Taboo*, trans. James Strachey.

6. Otto Rank, *The Incest Theme in Literature and Legend: Fundamentals of a Psychology of Literary Creation*.

7. Kal F. Zender, *Faulkner and the Politics of Reading*, 1.

8. In "Blutschande: From the Incest Taboo to the Nuremberg Racial Laws," Christina von Braun traces the shift in meaning of the word *blutschande* (blood shame), which, while originally referring to the sin of intercourse with one's own blood relatives, began

to designate the sin of intercourse with alien bloodlines in nineteenth-century racist German literature.

9. Efraín Kristal, "The Incest Motif in Narratives of the United States and Spanish America," 390–403.

10. While conservative critics grouped incest and homosexuality together as topics offensive to the integrity of the Armenian "essence," the Menk writers approached them quite distinctly in their literature. While they saw incest as a form of sexual perversion that could serve as an apt allegory for the genocide's aftermath, they wanted to write openly about homosexuality as a mode of embracing the avant-garde of their cultural milieu. Addressing the surviving generation, Shahnur boasts, "Now that we live in the heart of Paris, we are fully aware of the new movements that you were ignorant to back in Istanbul or elsewhere. . . . If you want, we can give you Freudism, Valéry, Gide or homosexuality, the absurd or surrealism." Shahan Shahnur, "Menk', Part II," Haṙach, Jan. 26, 1932, 2.

In their body of work, Ghevont Meloyan's 1931 novel Erek' Ĕngernerĕ (The Three Friends) is the most developed narrative on this topic; it centers on a homosexual love affair that causes a major crisis among three young Armenian men living in Paris in the genocide's aftermath. The novel is a frame tale that interestingly distances the author from its first-person narrator.

11. The word that Oshagan uses is ts'egh, which literally translates as "race." In its widespread usage up until the mid-twentieth century, ts'egh was used to denote nation, not in its modern sense, but rather in the sense of a demarcated ethnic belonging. We will later see Costan Zarian use the word in the same sense. Both Oshagan and Zarian were part of the Constantinople-based literary group Mehean. The group's 1914 manifesto uses the term ts'egh to build a case for the creation of art reflective of the "Armenian soul."

12. H. Oshagan, Mayrenineru Shuk'in Dag [Under the Shade of Cedar Trees], 96.

13. For a more elaborate discussion of aspects of genocide in the twentieth century that distinguish the modern century from previous periods of human destructiveness, see Roger W. Smith, "State Power and Genocidal Intent: On the Uses of Genocide in the Twentieth Century," 3–14. See also Samuel Totten and William S. Parsons, eds., Century of Genocide: Essays and Eyewitness Accounts.

14. In The Regime of the Brother: After the Patriarchy, Juliet Flower MacCannell outlines the law of the brother's regime, saying, "It ought to be a law of liberation, one recognizing that, with the death of the father, everyone is in the same condition: without the despotic authority of the father, we are literally all equals. Instead, a new 'No!' rises to the lips of the leader in imitation of the father: the brother utters a prohibition, or rather acts it out silently. Like the primary Oedipal intergenerational incest taboos which are the basis of family, it is still directed against familial relations: but its focus is changed, widened, to work at the level of the group or society" (13).

15. "Vartsu Seneag" (Room for Rent), the title of this short story, which was written in Paris in 1929, gives its name to the collection in which it is found. The collection was published by Atmajian Publishing and printed at Arax Printing House in 1939. An unedited manuscript of a novel with the same title also exists in the author's personal archives. An edited excerpt from this novel was published and introduced by Krikor Beledian in the third issue of the *Gayk'*, the literary yearbook of the French Armenian Writers' Association. In his introduction, Beledian notes that Vorpuni spent six years developing the 1929 short story into a novel, completing it in 1975. Krikor Beledian, "Nshum," 42. The unpublished novel was to be the fifth in the author's series of novels titled *Haladzuadznerě* (The Persecuted), the first of which is called *P'ortsě* (The Attempt) and is discussed in chapter 2 of this book.

16. Zareh Vorpuni, *Vartsu Seneag* [Room for Rent], 11–12.

17. In *Camera Lucida: Reflections on Photography*, Roland Barthes uses the Latin term *punctum* to describe the striking element in a photograph that is purely personal and dependent upon the individual and that "pierces the viewer." Barthes presents this term in relation to what he calls the "studium," which denotes a photograph's obvious symbolic meaning or its general field. In this story, the image of a smile seems to have "pierced" Dikran in all three frames of his vision: the smile of a stranger walking in front in his present frame and the smile of his sister in the frames of at least two distinct photographs from the past. (Although the recently received photograph has a tangible existence, the family photograph that portrays the sister as a small child may be a memory, articulated in the language of photography.)

18. Vorpuni, *Vartsu Seneag* [Room for Rent], 12.

19. Vorpuni, *Vartsu Seneag* [Room for Rent], 13.

20. Vorpuni, *Vartsu Seneag* [Room for Rent], 19.

21. Vorpuni, *Vartsu Seneag* [Room for Rent], 20.

22. Bibliothèque Nubar in Paris holds some of Zareh Orpuni's correspondence. The letters are archived in boxes, in the form originally donated by the author. There is an interesting parallel between Dikran's positioning of the Frenchwoman and the Armenian woman side by side and the organization of Vorpuni's letters. In the box that contains his correspondence from the 1930s, the envelopes are neatly organized and tied in two separate stacks. One of them assembles the letters received from French lovers, and the other contains Armenian letters received from the author's sisters and mother.

23. Vorpuni, *Vartsu Seneag* [Room for Rent], 28.

24. Vorpuni, *Vartsu Seneag* [Room for Rent], 28, 32.

25. Along with Shavarsh Nartuni, Sarafian appeared most frequently among the Menk writers in the various daily and weekly periodicals of the time, especially in *Harach* and *Hayrenik' Monthly*. His contributions vary from poetry to commentary on social, cultural, and literary issues.

26. According to Beledian, Sarafian's *Ishkhanuhin* was first published as a serial novel in the short-lived periodical *Amrots'* (Fortress) in 1934, right before being published as an edited volume. Beledian, *Cinquante ans*, 223.

27. As discussed in chapter 2, Shahan Shahnur's *Nahanchĕ Aṙants' Erki* (The Retreat without Song, 1929), Zareh Orpuni's *P'ortsĕ* (The Attempt, 1929), and Hrach' Zartarian's *Mer Geank'ĕ* (Our Life, 1934) are often read together as the postgenocide diaspora's first wave of novels.

28. Both Beledian and Bardakjian criticize the structural weakness of *Ishkhanuhin* in their brief introductions of the novel. Beledian, *Cinquante ans*, 223; Bardakjian, *Reference Guide*, 247. In a book review published in *Hayrenik' Monthly*, one of Sarafian's contemporaries, P. Sanasar, attributes the novel's hurried pace to the "nervous and hasty rhythm" of the times and praises the novel for being "a faithful portrayal of the Armenian fate." *Hayrenik' Monthly* 13, no. 6 (1935): 150–51.

29. See scholarly studies of the topic in Rubina Peroomian's *And Those Who Continued Living in Turkey after 1915* (2008), Fethiye Çetin's *The Grandchildren: The Hidden Legacy of "Lost" Armenians in Turkey* (2014), and Avedis Hadjian's *Secret Nation: The Hidden Armenians of Turkey* (2018). The memoir trend includes Fethiye Çetin's *Anneannem* (My Grandmother) (2004), İrfan Palalı's *Tehcir Çocukları: Nenem bir Ermeni'ymiş* (The Children of Expulsion: My Grandmother Was Armenian) (2005), and Yusuf Bağı's *Ermeni Kızı Ağçik* (Armenian Girl: Aghcik) (2007).

30. Sarafian uses the Ottoman Turkish equivalent of Aisha (the name of the prophet Muhammad's wife), which is used frequently as a stereotypical Islamic name. Therefore, we might assume a correlation between Aïshé and the title of the book *Ishkhanuhin*, which marks her position as princess in the Armenian realm.

31. In their discussions of the incest motif in literature, both Otto Rank and Efraín Kristal identify the "recognition plot" as a recurring theme. According to Rank, though, the lovers more frequently recognize each other as siblings "before the longed-for but rejected union can occur." Rank, *Incest Theme in Literature and Legend*, 429.

32. Nigoghos Sarafian, *Ishkhanuhin* [The Princess], 3.

33. Pierre Loti (1850–1923) and Claude Farrère (1876–1957) were prolific French novelists who wrote stories set in "exotic" eastern locations. In his commentary on the contribution of imaginative and travel literature to the official genealogy of Orientalism, Edward Said includes Loti in the list of writers who "give a bolder outline to Disraeli's 'great Asiatic mystery.'" Edward Said, *Orientalism*, 99.

34. Sarafian, *Ishkhanuhin* [The Princess], 33.

35. For a more elaborate discussion of the creation of the Turkish Republic, see Akçam, *From Empire to Republic*. In tracing the passage of the multinational Ottoman Empire to the national Turkish state, Akçam presents five taboos that formed the foundational principles of the new republic, established on the French model. He identifies them as follows: "1) Turkish society has no classes. We are a classless, unified society.

2) There are no ethnic-cultural differences. All citizens are Turks. 3) Turkey is a secular state. Islam and Islamic culture have been declared enemies. 4) No massacre whatsoever was carried out and directed at the Armenians. 5) The armed forces are the guardians of these taboos, and the role of the armed forces within the state is a taboo subject" (24).

36. The names of Loti and Farrère often appear in the writings of the Menk group as influential contemporary writers who misrepresent the figure of the Armenian in their literature. Shahan Shahnur's article "Fransahay Doghants'k'" (French Armenian Parade), later published in a book compilation *T'ert'is Giragnōreay T'iwě* [The Sunday Issue] (Beirut: Hradaragut'iwn Krikor K'ēosēiani, 1958), chronicles various contemporary French Armenian literary exchanges. The article focuses particularly on the works of Maurice Barrès (1862–1923), a French novelist and politician, known for his right-wing, anti-Semitic, and nationalist politics. In his discussion of a Barrès travelogue, Shahnur references Loti in relation to an Armenian man in Syria. Overall, Shahnur's article provides a good overview of the racist representations of Armenian characters in French popular literature of the time. Additionally, Shahnur published an unfavorable book review of a Claude Farrère pamphlet dedicated to his senior Pierre Loti. The review of the pamphlet, titled *Loti*, appears in the second issue of *Menk'*. Reviews, *Menk: Revue littéraire armenienne*, no. 2 (1931): 121.

37. Sarafian, *Ishkhanuhin* [The Princess], 11.

38. Sarafian, *Ishkhanuhin* [The Princess], 28.

39. Here, we can assume that the fictional romance between an Armenian and a Turk would have been just as problematic for Sarafian's contemporary readers as the story of incest. In fact, Turkish Armenian romances seldom appear in Armenian texts. One other example is the postgenocide novel of a feminist, female writer Zaruhi Bahri. Originally from Istanbul, Bahri published *Dakrě* (The Brother-in-Law). Set in Constantinople of the 1870s, the novel tells the story of a love affair between its Armenian heroine and a Muslim Ottoman diplomat. Aside from being a tragic love story, the novel offers commentary on women's sexual rights, as it is the brother-in-law of a widowed Armenian woman who facilitates the arrangement of biweekly visits between her and the diplomat for personal financial gain.

40. In this passage, Sarafian refers to Aram's love as *egheragan*, for which I have used one of the word's technical translations, "tragic," meaning mournful or elegiac. My chosen translation's indirect evocation of the genre of Greek tragedy is intentional and befits Aram and Aïshé's story, which has striking resemblances to the story of Electra and Orestes of Aeschylus's trilogy *The Oresteia*.

41. Sarafian, *Ishkhanuhin* [The Princess], 50, 52, 63.

42. Sarafian, *Ishkhanuhin* [The Princess], 67.

43. "In fact, the murder of the father introduces in the relationship of the survivors an incestuous love by suppressing the foundational law of difference. From that point on, how can loving not become an incestuous affair?" Beledian, *Cinquante ans*, 227.

44. Krikor Chahinian writes that a few members of Menk opposed the story's publication, finding its content "immoral and defamatory toward Armenians." *Gensakrut'iwn ew Madenakidut'iwn Shahan Shahnuri* [Biography and Bibliography of Shahan Shahnur], 33. He attributes the group's breakup partly to this disagreement. He also comments on the postpublication criticism that Shahnur received in the Armenian-language press of the diaspora.

45. The French-Armenian Agreement of 1916 established an Armenian legion unit within the French Army, with the aim of securing the liberation of the Cilicia region in the Ottoman Empire. Although close to forty-eight hundred Armenian volunteers fought against the Turks and Germans in Adana and Palestine on its behalf, France disbanded the legion and recognized Turkey's sovereignty over the area in 1920.

46. Shahan Shahnur, "'Buynuzlě'nerě [The Cuckolds]," 148.

47. Shahnur, "'Buynuzlě'nerě [The Cuckolds]," 148, 149.

48. Shahnur, "'Buynuzlě'nerě [The Cuckolds]," 150.

49. The "banality of evil" is a phrase that Hannah Arendt introduces in her 1963 work *Eichmann in Jerusalem: A Report on the Banality of Evil* to propose that great evils in history are not executed by fanatics but rather by ordinary people who accept the premises of the state and regard their actions as normal. In "Theaters of Justice: Arendt in Jerusalem, the Eichmann Trial, and the Redefinition of Legal Meaning in the Wake of the Holocaust," Shoshana Felman argues that the point of Arendt's book is not to define evil, but to reflect on the significance of legal meaning after the Holocaust: "If evil is linguistically and legally banal (devoid of human motivations and occurring through clichés that screen human reality and actuality), in what ways, Arendt asks, can the law become an anchor and a guarantee, a guardian of humanity? How can the law *fight over language* with this radical banality (the total identification with borrowed language)? When language itself becomes subsumed by the banality of evil, *how can the law keep meaning to the word humanity?*" (206). Here, too, Shahnur's story of revenge evokes the legal and political implications of Arendt's phrase.

50. Shahnur, "'Buynuzlě'nerě [The Cuckolds]," 150.

51. Shahnur, "'Buynuzlě'nerě [The Cuckolds]," 153.

52. At the bottom of the story when it was published in *Menk'*, Shahnur adds a note that presents the above writing as the preface of an upcoming novel titled *Ortik' Orodman* [Sons of Thunder]. *Menk: Revue littéraire armenienne*, no. 3 (1932): 159. Although the novel was never published, Krikor Chahinian claims that its manuscript was written and then destroyed by the author himself. Chahinian claims that manuscripts of two other novels, *Mahě ew ir Aruarts'annerě* (Death and Its Suburbs) and *Menakhōsut'iwn* (Monologue), were also destroyed. They were to contribute to a series subtitled *Badgerazart Badmut'iwn Hayots'* (An Illustrative History of Armenians), of which *Nahanchě Aŕants' Erki* (The Retreat without Song) is the first. Chahinian, *Gensakrut'iwn ew Madenakidut'iwn Shahan Shahnuri* [Biography and Bibliography of Shahan Shahnur], 50.

4. Tradition Resurrected

1. These lines are from an introductory piece, which accompanied the 1960 publication of Meloyan's play *Anaŕag Ortin* (The Prodigal Son), published with its twin, a novel called *Mayrĕ* (The Mother). The set was published under the title *Asduadzareal K'aghak'i Erguoreagnerĕ* (The Twins of the Divine City), and it brought together two pieces written by Meloyan in 1910. Ghevont Meloyan, *Verhishumner* [Remembrances], 128.

2. For example, Michael Arlen, *Passage to Ararat*; and Peter Balakian, *Black Dog of Fate*. For an extended discussion, see Shirinian, *Armenian-North American Literature*.

3. The play's third edition includes paratextual information about the play's 1920 and 1948 performances, as well as notes on its public acclaim and prizes. Léon G. Méloyian, *Arménouche: Drame en cinq actes*.

4. Henceforth, I will refer to this title as *Nahanchĕ Aŕants' Erki*, or simply as *Nahanchĕ*.

5. Announcement, *Haŕach*, May 12, 1929, 3.

6. Krikor Chahinian identifies N. D. as Desdegiwl. Chahinian, *Gensakrut'iwn ew Madenakidut'iwn Shahan Shahnuri* [Biography and Bibliography of Shahan Shahnur], 43.

7. N. D., "Krakhōsaganner [Reviews]," 158.

8. Fenerjian, "Nor Kirk'er [New Books]," 301.

9. N. D., "Krakhōsaganner," 159.

10. Although the colloquial and uncensored speech and register of *Nahanchĕ* distinguish it from previous Western Armenian novels, N. D.'s commentary on the novel's innovative tone refers also to its sharply abrupt and detached style. He calls it the novel's "staccato" tone and claims that it is what "all the new writers are using in almost every country," thus making a case for his previous comment regarding Armenian literature's entry into European literature. N. D., "Krakhōsaganner," 160.

11. Fenerjian, "Nor Kirk'er," 303.

12. Here, Chobanian uses the word *kaghut'ahayut'iwn*, "exiled community of Armenians," for what I have translated as "diaspora."

13. Chobanian, "Agnarg mĕ," 105–6.

14. Shahnur, *Nahanchĕ Aŕants' Erki*, 21.

15. Chobanian, "Agnarg mĕ," 111.

16. See Khayadjian, *Chobanian et le mouvement armenophile*.

17. For an elaborate discussion of France's assimilationist approach to the incorporation and the subsequent discrimination of Armenian genocide survivors during the 1920s and 1930s, see M. Mandel, *In the Aftermath of Genocide*, 19–51.

18. Chobanian goes as far as to compare Shahnur's and his generation's representation of the French to the Orientalist writings of Pierre Loti and Claude Farrère, without marking any distinction between their unequal positions of power: "And our young

writers should not commit, against any nation, the crime that the Lotis and the Farrères committed against us, after coming across only a handful of Armenians or Greeks." Chobanian, "Agnarg mě," 112.

19. Fenerjian, "Nor Kirk'er," 303.

20. Shahnur, *Nahanchě*, 23.

21. See note 18.

22. I would like to complicate my criticism of Chobanian's inverse Orientalism, which I understand as the East's internalization of the West's Orientalist gaze, by noting that the writers of Menk were also prone to forms of Orientalism, not in inverse fashion but in reverse. In their refusal of the West and publicly pledged affinity to the "Orient," they exoticized the East in the language of French Orientalism. For an illustrative example, see Shavarsh Nartuni's "Menk', Menk', Menk'," which begins with the following French epigraph from Pierre Louys: "La poésie est une fleur d'Orient, qui ne vit pas dans nos serres chaudes. La Grèce elle-même l'a reçue d'Ionie" (Poetry is a flower of the Orient that cannot live in our hot conservatories. Even the Greeks got it from Ionia). *Menk: Revue littéraire armenienne*, no. 1 (1931): 42.

23. Chobanian, "Agnarg mě," 113.

24. Chobanian, "Agnarg mě," 113.

25. Shahnur, *Nahanchě*, 9.

26. Mgrdich Barsamian, "Kirk'er ew Tēmk'er [Books and Figures]," 229.

27. Shahnur, *Nahanchě*, 124.

28. Krikor Beledian, whose critical works offer great insight regarding the presence of the Other in Shahnur's novel as well as in the other novels of the Paris boys, claims that the symbol of the Armenian Church stands in opposition to not simply sexuality, but rather a sexuality that follows the model of prostitution, or pornography. Further, he separates the Armenian and French domains that constitute Bedros/Pierre's identity through the following oppositions: "Pour Pierre, la différence fondamentale qui sépare l'Arménien de l'Autre se distribue suivant l'opposition du moral/immoral, pur/impur, Dieu/prostituée, Arméniens/Françaises" (For Pierre, the fundamental difference that separates the Armenian from the Other is distributed according to the opposition of moral/immoral, pure/impure, God/prostitute). Beledian, *Cinquante ans*, 140.

29. Criticizing Vorpuni's depiction of a "failed" character, Chobanian asks, "Why has Vorpuni not preferred to select a protagonist, the likes of whom, praise the Lord, our race has offered many of and offers still today, in large numbers, within our diaspora communities? If there are those who wander, crumble, mourn, and perish, well, in reality, in our contemporary community, young men who have created a new life through hard work, who have established themselves and secured a future are greater in numbers. In my opinion, it is precisely this image that one needs to reveal in a novel, where it could still be possible to depict the filth of poverty, yet oppose that with the victorious character of a noble and brave man." Chobanian, "Agnarg mě," 107.

30. Chobanian, "Agnarg mě," 114.

31. Quoted from the article's reprint in *Sp'iwŕk'*: Shahnur, "Azadn Gomidas [Gomidas the Free]," 3.

32. Arpik Misakian, the daughter of Shavarsh Misakian, the founder of *Haŕach*, took over the newspaper's editorship following her father's death. On the occasion of the controversy surrounding "Azadn Gomidas" (Gomidas the Free), she chimed in on the side of Shahnur in an article titled "Inch'u ays tam-tamě [Why All This Tumtum?]." Arpik Misakian, "Inch'u ays tam-tamě," *Haŕach*, Feb. 13, 1970, 2.

33. Shahan Shahnur died on August 20, 1974. The "Azadn Gomidas" (Gomidas the Free) controversy was the last heavily publicized debate that he participated in.

34. For a more elaborate discussion of the political divide among French Armenians, see M. Mandel, *In the Aftermath of Genocide*, 119–34.

35. See R. Hrair Dekmejian, "The Armenian Diaspora."

36. Chahinian, *Gensakrut'iwn*, 37. It is possible that the Zartarian brothers' animosity was fueled by the publication of an unfavorable article Shahnur wrote about the short story "Kampŕě" (The Mastiff) by the brothers' father, Rupen Zartarian. Rupen Zartarian was a popular literary figure and a teacher of Armenian language in Constantinople. He was murdered in 1915 along with other intellectuals. Shahnur's article "Kragan Ēch Mě" (A Literary Page) was published in the 1958 collection of essays in *T'ert'is Giragnōreay T'iwě* (The Sunday Issue). The essays of the collection were articles published in Parisian journals and newspapers between the years 1931 and 1939. The Zartarian brothers' physical confrontation with Shahnur took place in 1936, making it likely that Shahnur's article contributed to it.

37. Shahnur suffered from Pott's disease and a more general tuberculosis of the bones.

38. Armen Lubin's French-language literary production includes *Fouiller avec rien* (Paris: René Debresse, 1942), *Le passager clandestin* (Paris: Gallimard, 1946), *Sainte Patience* (Paris: Gallimard, 1951), *Transfert nocturne* (Paris: Gallimard, 1955), *Les hautes terrasses* (Paris: Gallimard, 1957), *Feux contre feux* (Paris: Tirage à Part des *Cahiers des saisons*, 1964), and *Feux contre feux* (Paris: Grasset, 1968).

39. Chahinian, *Gensakrut'iwn*, 95.

40. It is interesting to note that a little over a decade before his transition into Lubin, Shahnur created a character that would serve as his real-life precursor. *Nahanchě*'s Suren is an Armenian intellectual in Paris who has decided to immerse himself in French traditions and write only in French. As literary personas, Shahan Shahnur and Armen Lubin are opposite in nature (prose/poetry, Armenian/French) and ignore each other.

41. Shahan Shahnur, "Azadn Gomidas [Gomidas the Free]," *Sp'iwŕk'*, 2.

42. Quoted from the letter's reprint: Vahagn Davtian, "Pats' Namag Shahan Shanurin [Open Letter to Shahan Shanur]," 70.

43. Davtian, "Pats' Namag Shahan Shanurin," 70.

44. Although Shahnur does not make a reference to Soviet Armenia, he does make a brief reference to Eastern Armenians as "our backward cousins." Shahnur, "Azadn Gomidas [Gomidas the Free]," *Sp'iwṙk'*, 3.

45. Shahnur, "Azadn Gomidas [Gomidas the Free]," *Sp'iwṙk'*, 2.

46. Shahnur, "Azadn Gomidas [Gomidas the Free]," *Haṙach*, Jan. 25, 1970, 2.

47. Shahnur, "Azadn Gomidas [Gomidas the Free]," *Sp'iwṙk'*, 2.

48. Here is a comparison of the original sentence and its revised version: "After all, what are we today, if not a group of wretched and miserable pariahs, persecuted slaves, and a target for ultimate scorn." Shahnur, "Azadn Gomidas [Gomidas the Free]," *Sp'iwṙk'*, 2. "What are we today after all, in this year 1935 of our dispersion, if not a vagabond of wretched and wounded pariahs, a target for political pity, not to say scorn." Shahnur, "Azadn Gomidas [Gomidas the Free]," *Haṙach*, 2.

49. In fact, even the commemorative press that Shahnur received upon his death could not escape controversy. Arpik Misakian published an article titled "Shahnuri Mahuan Aṙt'iw Jshtumner yev Khorhrtadzut'iwnner [On the Occasion of Shahan Shahnur's Death: Corrections and Reflections]," *Haṙach*, Sept. 15, 1974, 1–2, in response to a *Sp'iwṙk'* article written by Simon Simonian. Misakian took issue with Simonian's representation of Shahnur's death, thus providing detailed descriptions of his last days in the hospital. Furthermore, Misakian corrected many biographical facts regarding Shahnur's income, for the *Sp'iwṙk'* article had referred to a list of Armenian donors, claiming that they had secretly provided the author's livelihood from 1939 to 1974. Noubar Agishan, a Shahnur scholar, in his book dedicated to the life and work of the author, takes a less confrontational approach, opting instead to not merit the controversy any discussion. Commenting on the public debate that ensued owing to what he calls a "misunderstanding," he writes, "We do not wish to address the mayhem that erupted around that article." Agishian, *Shahan Shahnur: Geank'n u Kordzě* [Shahan Shahnur: His Life and Work], 46.

50. "Mah Shahan Shahnuri [Death of Shahan Shahnur]," 47.

51. Krikor Keoseian, "1929-Haṙachi T'ert'ōně-1979, *Nahanchě Aṙants' Erki* [1929–1979, *Haṙach*'s Serial Novel: *The Retreat without Song*]," *Haṙach*, Mar. 29, 1979, 2.

52. Keoseian, "1929-Haṙachi T'ert'ōně-1979," 2.

53. For a discussion of the connection between photography and pornography and the subsequent symbolic implications of the connection between retouching and the destruction of paternal law, see Marc Nichanian, "Shahan Shahnurě ew Hariwrameagneru Zaweshdě [Shahan Shahnur and the Centuries-Old Farce]" and "The *Retreat* of Shahan Shahnur." Also, for a comparative study of *Nahanchě* in the context of the diaspora's initial novels, see Beledian, "Ergtimin Eṙangiwnin Měch [The Ambiguous in the Triangle]."

54. I discuss Sarafian's definition of *azkaynagan*, which I translate as "pan-national," in chapter 1 of this book.

55. Beledian, *Cinquante ans*, 138.

56. "'Nahanchĕ' Nerkʻin Sbaïrman Abrankʻ [*Nahanchĕ* as an Object of Internal Consumption]," 52.

57. Narekatsi's *Book of Lamentations* is often referred to as "Narek."

58. Shahnur, *Nahanchĕ*, 152.

59. Shahnur, *Nahanchĕ*, 153.

60. "'Nahanchĕ' Nerkʻin Sbaïrman Abrankʻ'," 49.

61. Shahan Shahnour, *The Retreat without Song*, 104.

62. Kudian's choice to omit rather than summarize the Narek passage, as well as other instances of inclusion/exclusion in his translation, make it apparent that he translated from the original publication and not the Soviet edition.

63. "Ampoghchagan Tsʻangĕ Vazkēn Shushaniani Kragan Ashkhadankʻneru [The Complete List of Vazken Shushanian's Literary Works]."

64. *Mtʻin Badanutʻiwn* (Youth in the Dark, 1956), *Siroy ew Argadzi Dghakʻĕ* (Boys in Love and Adventure, 1957), *Siroy ew Meghkʻi Bardēz* (Garden of Love and Sin, 1958), *Mahuan Aïakasdĕ* (Sail of Death, 1959) *Aïachin Sērĕ* (First Love, 1959), *Jermag Varsenig* (White Varsenig, 1960), and *Panasdeghdzin Ginĕ* (The Poet's Wife, 1982) are first publications, published in Beirut.

65. Shushanian, *Mart Mĕ Or Ararat Chʻuni*, 26, 40.

66. Skiwdar, now Üsküdar, was an Armenian-populated part of Constantinople throughout the nineteenth century. It is where Shahnur grew up and attended Berberian Armenian school prior to leaving for France in 1923.

67. Shushanian, *Mart Mĕ Or Ararat Chʻuni*, 22.

68. Shushanian's journalistic writings often revolve around his desire to combine his nationalist and socialist sentiments. Although first a member of the Armenian Revolutionary Federation, Shushanian, along with colleagues like Lewon Mozian and Mesrob Kuyumjian, created a split within the party and formed a separate European faction. In 1932, they published a periodical, *Mardgotsʻ* (Battery). For a more elaborate discussion of Shushanian's political ideology, his antidefeatist stance, and his involvement with *Mardgotsʻ*, see Beledian, *Cinquante ans*, 123–29.

69. Shushanian, *Mart Mĕ Or Ararat Chʻuni*, 37.

70. Shahnur, *Nahanchĕ*, 163–64. Also, the haunting questions "Who am I?" and "What am I?" that Lokhum poses in Shahnur's *Nahanchĕ* reverberate in Sarafian's book of prose poetry *Vēnsēni Andaïĕ*, written in 1947 and published in 1988. Sarafian writes a series of these questions in a similar formulation: "Who am I that I have not inherited a single drop of my fearful father's and mother's faith? . . . What am I that I condemn my nation, but judge the world according to its suffering, which I deem above all others?" Nigoghos Sarafian, *Vēnsēni Andaïĕ* [The Forest of Vincennes], 40.

71. Sarafian, "Azkayinn u Michazkayinĕ," 72.

72. Sarafian, "Azkayinn u Michazkayinĕ," 72. In calling for the joining of various Armenian communities within a main web, Sarafian writes, "What miracles we can

receive from their [the communities'] distinct and local conditions and through the parallel developments of various cultures." Sarafian, "Azkayinn u Michazkayině," 71.

73. Zarian, "Azkayinn u Michazkayině," 107.

74. "Exile is strangely compelling to think about but terrible to experience," writes Edward Said in his introduction to *Reflections on Exile*. Referencing this distinction between the intellectual reflection and empirical experience of displacement, Ali Behdad critiques the category of "minor" literature in postcolonial studies, arguing that there is "a fundamental split between a tendency to consider the state of being 'minor' an essential experience that is disempowering and a consideration of it as a matter of critical positionality that is intellectually empowering." Behdad in Lionnet and Shih, *Minor Transnationalism*, 225. Sarafian's and Zarian's discussion in *Zuart'nots'* calls attention to a similar split between the aesthetics of dislocation and the experience of deterritorialization.

5. Homogenous Time

1. For a more elaborate discussion of the history of the word *sp'iwřk'* in the post-1915 Armenian diaspora, see Khachig Tölölyan, "'Sp'iwřk'' Hghats'k'i Ants'ealn u Nergan [The Past and Present of the Concept of 'Diaspora']." He claims that the term gained widespread usage partly owing to Simon Simonian's establishment of the journal *Sp'iwř'k'* in Beirut, in 1958.

2. Razmik Panossian has later referred to this distinction as "internal diaspora" (Armenian communities inside the USSR) and "external diaspora" (predominantly Western Armenian communities outside the USSR). Panossian, "Between Ambivalence and Identity in Armenia-Diaspora Relations," 150.

3. "Hay Sp'iwřk'ě Arjěk' ě [The Armenian Diaspora Is Valuable]," 1.

4. Levon Sharoyan, *Simon Simonian: The Last Scion of the Mountaineers*, 72.

5. "Hay Spiwřk'ě [The Armenian Diaspora]," inside cover.

6. Today, most scholars refer to the exiled Western Armenian population of the years immediately following the genocide as "diaspora," unwillingly effacing the history of self-naming that came to distinguish the early years from the later years of dispersion. Khachig Tölölyan has offered a timeline of the concept's evolution in the Armenian language, dating *sp'iwřk'*'s (diaspora) popularization a decade later than my proposition. Tölölyan, "'Sp'iwřk'' Hghats'k'i Ants'ealn u Nergan." Kevork Bardakjian, in *A Reference Guide to Modern Armenian Literature*, abandons "diaspora" altogether and uses the capitalized form of "Dispersion" to refer to the postgenocide Armenian population across the many decades of the twentieth century. Bardakjian, *Reference Guide*.

7. The refugees' "homecoming" did not turn out to be the joyous occasion many had hoped for. The postwar economy of Soviet Armenia was not ready to receive and integrate the repatriates, who were soon discriminated against by their Eastern Armenian kin. Stalin's government, too, soon turned against them. Accused of having links to the

West or of being too nationalist, many of them ended up in prison camps. See Ronald Suny, "Soviet Armenia."

8. Tölölyan, "Rethinking Diaspora(s)."

9. Bardakjian, *Reference Guide*, 202.

10. Zareh Vorpuni, *Tēbi Ergir* [Toward Homeland], 24.

11. S. Aghapian, E. Topchian, and A. Hakhverdian, eds., *Sovetahay Grakanut'yan Patmut'yun* [The History of Soviet Armenian Literature], 512–13.

12. Bardakjian, *Reference Guide*, 204.

13. Sevan Deyirmenjian, "Kaghut'ahay Kroghneru Hamakumarĕ ew Dzarugian [Community Armenian Writers' Conference and Dzarugian]," *Karun*, 80.

14. Boston's *Hayrenik' Monthly*, for instance, regularly published reports about the process of the union's formation and the first Congress in its September, October, November, and December 1934 issues.

15. Aghapian, Topchian, and Hakhverdian, *Sovetahay Grakanut'yan Patmut'yun*, 526.

16. *Echmiadzin Monthly*, the official publication of the Catholicosate of Armenia, announced the Soviet Armenian Writers' Union's decision to include a discussion of contemporary diaspora (*ardasahmanean*) literature in its Second World Congress. The announcement refers to the invited diaspora writers as "celebrated representatives of Armenian literature outside of Armenia." *Echmiadzin Monthly* 3, nos. 4–5 (1946): 71.

17. See Yenovk Armen's "Hayasdani Kroghneru Miut'ean Hamakumarĕ ew Ardasahmani nergayats'ut'iwnĕ [The Soviet Armenian Writers' Union's Congress and Representation from Abroad]"; and Levon Mozian's "Kroghneru Yergrort Hamakumarĕ [The Second Writers' Congress]."

18. The framing of the congress, and more generally of Armenian literature, serving a role in Soviet Armenia's repatriation campaign was explicitly articulated by the congress organizers and picked up by diaspora periodicals sympathetic to the Soviet project. In his press-release type article published in Beirut's *Ani*, Hmayag Siras, the secretary of the Soviet Armenian Writers' Union, writes, "There's a strong desire among diaspora Armenians to return to the motherland and the Soviet government using all means to gather our exiled brothers. In these sacred times, our literature, through its truthful expression, has a lot of work to do in this regard." Hmayag Siras, "Sovedagan Kroghneri B. Hamakumarĕ [Soviet Armenian Union's Second Congress]," 351.

19. For example, see Hayg Ohanian, "Kragan Ughineri Vray [On Literary Paths]."

20. An editorial note refers to the invited writers as "pitiable and no-name scare crows." *Nayiri* 10–12 (June–Sept. 1946): 602.

21. While Arshag Chobanian was a literary giant known as the father of the French Armenian intellectual community, he was not among the invited, probably owing to his relationship with the purged former Armenian Communist Party leader Aghasi Khanjian, which made him persona non grata in Yerevan until the post-Stalin era.

22. While Chobanian argues that Soviet Armenia is a place where Armenians can live freely and urges diaspora Armenians to embrace it as their homeland, he criticizes the state's orthography reforms and the arrests of several artists on charges of nationalism. Arshag Chobanian, "Kronik [Chronicle]," *Anahid* 12, no. 1 (1946): 51–64.

23. Kurken Der Vartanian, "Kaght'ahay K'raganutean Shurch [On Migrant Armenian Literature]," 63.

24. Language preservation in the diaspora developed synonymously with identity preservation. As Razmik Panossian points out in *The Armenians: From Kings and Priests to Merchants and Commissars*, "The nationalist leaders of post-Genocide diaspora realized the importance of a key cultural marker around which modern Armenian identity could be cemented. Given their secular attitudes, religion and the Armenian church could not have been the means. Language was therefore used as the common denominator, as the unifying element—more specifically *western* Armenian, its literature and intellectual traditions" (299).

25. As early as 1935, *Hasg*, the mouthpiece of the Cilicia Catholicosate published in Antelias, Lebanon, reported of organized efforts to convert the Turkish-speaking sectors of the Armenian refugee population into Armenian speakers. "Bayk'ar T'rk'akhosut'ean Tēm [Movement against Turkish Speaking]." Vahé Tachjian has traced how many Beirut-based newspapers like *P'iwnig, Nor P'iwnig*, and *Yep'rad* published similar articles against the usage of the Turkish language a full decade earlier, in the 1920s. Tachjian, "L'usage du turc et le renouveau identitaire chez les Arméniens du Liban et de Syrie dans les années 1920–1930."

26. In *(Re)constructing Armenia in Lebanon and Syria: Ethno-cultural Diversity and the State in the Aftermath of a Refugee Crisis*, Nicola Migliorino argues that the postgenocide Armenian refugees in Lebanon and Syria consisted of at least two linguistic groups. Natives of Cilicia used Turkish as their day-to-day language, whereas those who came from Armenian *vilayets* in eastern Anatolia were predominantly Armenian speaking (74).

27. In "Bayk'arě Soved Kroghneru Yergrort Hamakumarin Tēm [The Controversy around Soviet Armenian Writers' Second Congress]," A. Eljanian summarizes the ARF's criticism of the congress within a political framework and calls out newspapers like *Arewelk', Aztag, Aztarar*, and *Husaper* for publishing the criticism. In a series of articles devoted to highlighting the lasting value of the congress, A. Eljanian provides a counterperspective to the congress's criticism. "Inch' Shahets'ank' Hay Kroghneru Hamakumarēn [What Did We Gain from the Armenian Writers' Congress?]," pts. 1–3, *Ararat*, Nov. 2, 4, 6, 1946.

28. Note that a more extensive version of Isahakian's quotation is as follows: "One literature is one people. A people's literature is the aesthetic history of that group's tendencies and desires, its suffering and its faith, its triumphs and its downfalls." Avetik Isahakian, "Patsman Khōsk [Opening Remarks]," 342.

29. Isahakian, "Patsman Khōsk," 345.

30. Andrei Zhdanov, "Sovedagan Kraganutʻean Masin [On Soviet Literature]."

31. Hrachia Krikorian, "Sovedahay Kraganutʻiwnĕ ew Nra Hedakay Zarkatsʻman Ughinerĕ [Soviet Armenian Literature and Pathways for Its Future Development]."

32. Eduard Topchian, "Ardasahmanean Zhamanagagitsʻ Hay Kraganutiwnĕ [Contemporary Armenian Literature Abroad]," 477.

33. The authors specifically criticized in Topchian's report, Levon Shant, Hamasdegh, and Hagop Oshagan, were all affiliated with or close to the ARF.

34. Topchian, "Ardasahmanian Zhamanagagitsʻ Hay Kraganutʻiwnĕ," 484.

35. Hovhannes Aghbashian quoted in "Hayasdani Sovedagan Kroghneri Hamakumarĕ," 68.

36. Vahé Vahian, "Dbaworutʻiwnner Hayasdani Soved Kroghneru B. Hamakumarēn [Impressions from Soviet Armenian Writers' Union's Second Congress]."

37. Vahé Vahian, "Hayasdani Soved Kroghneru B. Hamakumarin Shurch [Concerning the Second Congress of Soviet Armenia's Writers]," 469.

38. Aralez are winged, doglike creatures in Armenian mythology believed to have the power to lick the wounds of heroes to bring them back from the dead. The title of Vahian's memoir may be a reference to or perhaps a rewriting of the French Armenian writer Shahan Shahnur's 1933 collection of short stories, published as *Haralēzneru Hashdutʻiwnĕ* (The Betrayal of the Aralez) in Paris. The collection presents the exilic life of survivors in a hopeless light, suggesting the symbolic failure of the Aralez to tend to their wounds in the aftermath of the genocide.

39. Vahé Vahian, *Haralēzneru Hashdutʻiwnĕ* [The Reconciliation of the Aralez].

40. In Aleppo, Teoleolian was the coeditor of the daily *Arewelkʻ* (1946–56) and the principal of the Karen Jeppe secondary school (1947–56). After moving to Egypt, then Lebanon in the late '50s, he settled in Boston in 1960 and edited the daily *Hayrenikʻ* from 1966 to 1978. Bardakjian, *Reference Guide*, 530–31. ʻMinas Teoleolian was the father of American literary scholar Khachig Tölölyan, the founding editor of *Diaspora: A Journal of Transnational Studies*. To help the reader distinguish between the two, both mentioned in this chapter, I have kept Minas Teoleolian's transliterated last name, since his publications are in the Armenian language.

41. A. Amadian, "Sovedahay Kroghneri Hamakumarĕ ew Menkʻ [The Soviet Armenian Writers' Union Congress and Us]," 68.

42. For more on Menk's development of a literary platform based on the concepts of "language as home" or "little Armenias," see Shahan Shahnur's "Menkʻ'" in *Haṙach* (January 24, 1932) and Nigoghos Sarafian's untitled piece in *Menkʻ*'s inaugural issue (41–44), both discussed in chapter 1 of this book.

43. Sevan Deyirmenjian has argued that Teoleolian and Dzarugian failed to understand the extreme circumstances of the oppressive regime that Topchian lived under. For Deyirmenjian, Topchian could not have written the report in any other fashion.

Deyirmenjian, "Kaghut'ahay Kroghneru Hamakumarě ew Dzarugian [Community Armenian Writers' Conference and Dzarugian]," 81.

44. Minas Teoleolian, "Hasdadumner Kroghneru Hamakumarin Shurch [Clarifications Regarding the Writers' Congress]," 597.

45. The critique of Eastern Armenian's fate under Soviet rule is not particular to this post–World War II moment. In a 1932 article, the Eastern Armenian intellectual Simon Vratsian refers to Armenian spoken in Soviet Armenia as "monkey language," citing the emergent literary standard's borrowings from Russian. Vratsian, "'Menk' ew 'Duk'' ['We' and 'You']," 149.

46. Arshag Chobanian, "Arewmdahay Lezvi u Kraganut'ean Abak'an [The Future of Western Armenian Language and Literature]," 2.

47. In "Aram Vdaranti Inchbes Meřaw" (How did Aram Vdaranti Really Die?), Nayiri's editorial raises question about why Charek was singled out in being granted permission to stay in the Soviet Union, why the description of his illness was left ambiguous, and why the announcement of his death came accompanied by so many signatures. It also calls attention to the fact that Aram Charek was a former member of the ARF. Nayiri 3, no. 5 (1947): 301–2.

48. While ideological tensions between Soviet and diaspora writers predated the 1946 Congress, the congress's backlash in the press certainly amplified the strained relations. As a result, in 1948, Soviet authorities ordered the executive body of the Soviet Armenian Writers' Union to evaluate, reprimand, and reeducate writers who had sent their work to diaspora periodicals for publication. Amaduni Virabian, Hayasdaně Stalinits' Minchew Khrushchov [Armenia from Stalin to Khrushchev], 147.

49. "Hay Mamulin Aradě [The Stain of the Armenian Press]," 509. In this editorial piece, the journal reproduces excerpts from various publications, including Ararat, Zart'onk', Ep'rad, and Miyut'iwn, written against Hagop Oshagan. The quotation was originally published in Zhoghovurti Tsayn on March 14, 1946.

50. Eduard Boyajian, "U Sgsink' Mdadzel [Let's Start Thinking]."

51. Editorial, "Hamakumarēn Gagngalenk' [What We Expect from the Conference]," 376. A few months later, Eduard Boyajian offers a more elaborate list of the conference's aim, including as one of its goals "the development and steady preservation of our language." Boyajian, "Kroghneru Hamakumarin Anhrajeshdut'iwně [The Necessity of the Writers' Conference]," 625.

52. Antranig Dzarugian, "Imatsagan Sharjum: Kroghneru Hamakumarě [The Writers' Conference]," 293.

53. Dzarugian, "Imatsagan Sharjum: Kroghneru Hamakumarě," 290.

54. The word more commonly used in periodicals to refer to this project was kaghut'ahay (exiled community of Armenians) rather than sp'iwřk'ahay (diaspora Armenian). See its first announcement by Nayiri's editorial team, "Bēdk e Khosi Krakēdě [The Critic Must Speak]," 230.

55. In 1938, Armenians established a neighborhood called Sisuan in Shtora, Lebanon. Several years later, the village gained popularity when renowned intellectual Nigol Aghpalian took up residence there and initiated community-building efforts. Shtora was often selected as the meeting place for political conferences with neighboring countries. Sisag H. Varjabedian, *Hayerě Lipanani Mēch* [Armenians in Lebanon], 3:484.

56. See Vazken Vanantian, "Michin Arewelk'i Hay Kroghneru Hamakumarě, Anor Anhrajeshdut'iwně ew Patsumě [The Middle Eastern Armenian Writers' Conference, Its Necessity, and Its Opening]" and five articles all titled "Michin Arewelk'i Hay Kroghneru Hamakumarě [The Middle Eastern Armenian Writers' Conference]."

57. The projected conference agenda announced in advance by the executives of the Armenian Writer's Association of Syria and Lebanon included two other items that were left out of the conference: the issue of a diaspora publishing house and the Diaspora Armenian (Kaghut'ahay) Writers' Congress. *Nayiri* 4, no. 6 (1948): 504.

58. Garo Sasuni, "Pats'man Khōsk' [Opening Remarks]," 610.

59. Minas Teoleolian, "Mamulě Sp'iwřk'i Mēch [The Press in Diaspora]," 639.

60. Following a 1921 policy to obliterate illiteracy, Soviet Armenian orthography was reformed in 1922, while Western Armenian in the diaspora maintained classical orthography. Bardakjian, *Reference Guide*, 202.

61. Vanantian, "Michin Arewelk'i Hay Kroghneru Hamakumarě, Anor Anhrajeshdut'iwně ew Patsumě [The Middle Eastern Armenian Writers' Conference, Its Necessity, and Its Opening]," 99.

62. Puzant Yeghiayan, "Sp'iwřk'i Hay Kraganut'iwně [Armenian Diaspora Literature]," 15.

63. See Sasuni "Pats'man Khōsk'"; and Eduard Boyajian's "Artsagě Sp'iwřk'i Mēch [Prose in the Diaspora]."

64. Teoleolian, "Mamulě Sp'iwřk'i Mēch," 641.

65. The debate around language did not display the clear institutional divisions of political debates. For instance, Soviet Armenia's reformed orthography was not widely welcomed by diaspora's pro-Soviet publications, which continued to publish in classical orthography. But not everyone shared Teoleolian's view that Eastern Armenian was in decline. In "Mer Arewelahayerēně" (Our Eastern Armenian), Ardag Tarpinian offers a defense of Eastern Armenian and celebrates the existence of state institutions that can cultivate it and protect its legacy. In contrast, he describes the anarchic state of Western Armenian, wherein each writer is left to amend or create grammatical and orthographic rules, which strips Western Armenian writers of the right to criticize the properly standardized form of Soviet Armenian.

66. Vahé Oshagan, "Tadroně Sp'iwřk'i Mēch [Theater in the Diaspora]."

67. Boyajian, "Artsagě Sp'iwřk'i Mēch."

68. Teoleolian, "Mamulě Sp'iwřk'i Mēch," 641.

69. Vanantian, "Michin Arewelkʻi Hay Kroghneru Hamakumarĕ [The Middle Eastern Armenian Writers' Conference]" (April 1949).

70. Mushegh Ishkhan, "Panasdeghdzutiwnĕ Spʻiwṙkʻi Mēch," 618.

71. While other centers in the Middle East, mainly Jerusalem and Cairo, participated in these efforts of institutionalization, they did so in the capacity of interlocutors and supporters. My argument for "centering" diaspora in Lebanon, as I will discuss in the next chapter, takes into account language standardization efforts facilitated by the establishment of publishing houses, day schools, and textbooks. Jerusalem's *Husaper*, for instance, openly vowed support for the Middle Eastern Writers' conference and, in the midst of the public discussion in its wake, published a series of surveys that could be seen as contributing to the conference's forthcoming agenda. The survey, both the questionnaire and the compiled responses, appeared in serial form throughout 1947. The questionnaire posed the following four questions:

1) Can Western Armenian's regional dialects survive the newly formed conditions?

2) Does the reformed orthography correspond to the spirit and standards of the Armenian language? What spelling-related changes do you recommend?

3) Do you find the use of foreign words necessary? If not, what means do you recommend to limit this atrocity?

4) What should be the state language of our homeland: Eastern, Western, or hybrid? In the case of Eastern Armenian being officially adopted as a state language, what do you think will be the fate of Western Armenian? Editorial, "Hay Lezui Khntirĕ [The Question of the Armenian Language]," *Husaper*, Apr. 7, 1947, 31.

72. The editorial of *Pakin*'s second issue explicitly identifies the journal's aim as centralizing diaspora's discourse: "*Pakin* was called to life to serve as a central and enthusiastic stage." *Pakin* 1, no. 1 (1962): 2.

73. Levon Sharoyan, *Simon Simonian: The Last Scion of the Mountaineers*, 60.

74. Nicola Migliorino, *(Re)Constructing Armenia in Lebanon and Syria*, 114.

75. For a more in-depth discussion of the Armenian day-school movement in the United States, see Anny Bakalian, *Armenian-Americans: From Being to Feeling Armenian*.

76. In his biography of Simon Simonian, Levon Sharoyan claims that Sevan Publishing, in its twenty-eight years of existence, printed the literary works of 190 authors in more than 475 titles. Sharoyan, *Simon Simonian*, 62. Sisag Varjabedian estimates that from 1945 to 1975, Armenian presses of Beirut altogether published about 50 books a year. Varjabedian, *Hayerĕ Lipanani Mēch* [Armenians in Lebanon], 4:76. Even during the first ten years of the Lebanese Civil War, from 1975 to 1985, more than 700 Armenian-language books were published in Beirut. Marc Nichanian, *Ages et usages de la langue Armenienne*, 379.

77. Hagop Oshagan, "Spʻiwṙkʻi Kʻraganutʻean Abakʻan [The Future of Diaspora Literature]," 81.

78. In a 1948 article, Eduard Topchian argues that following World War II, Western Armenian literature became increasingly imperialist in its ideology. He grants no

productive value to the category of "diaspora" when it comes to literary production. Rather, when referring to diaspora's output, he prefers the political designation of "Tashnag-nationalist literature," framing it as ARF propaganda literature. Eduard Topchian, "Tashnagts'agan Kraganut'iwnē ew Michazkayin R̆eagts'ian [Tashnag Literature and the International Reaction]." While framed within the language of autonomy by the WASL, the "diasporization" of Western Armenian literature was seen by Soviet Armenian writers as the indoctrination of literature within the political ideology of the ARF.

6. Symbolic Territory

1. Nigoghos Sarafian, "Nor Nuiryalner Bēdk' en Mezi [What We Need Are New Devotees]," 10–11.

2. Joanne R. Nucho, *Everyday Sectarianism in Urban Lebanon: Infrastructures, Public Services, and Power*, 51–72. Nucho argues that sectarian belonging in Lebanon is negotiated through property claims and that the Armenian case, as demonstrated by the example of Arakadz (an Armenian refugee settlement in the municipality of Bourj Hammoud), entailed a process of forging a dwelling she calls "permanently temporary," referring to the temporary property rights the neighborhood's inhabitants had received from the municipality. She writes, "Arakadz . . . while not necessarily protected from the possibility of eventual destruction, circulates as an image of nostalgia, an important locus of collective memory for Lebanese Armenians" (52). In contrast, popular Lebanese Armenian histories deemed Sanjak, a refugee camp with similarly temporary property rights, a backward space, not worthy of being lived in permanently.

3. S. Stepanyan, "Sp'iwr̆k'ahay Keank'i Ejer̆ě [The Pages of Diasporan Armenian Life]," 133.

4. Nicola B. Schahgaldian, "Ethnicity and Politics in Lebanon," 55.

5. Shahali, "T'rk'erēn Mi Khosir [Don't Speak Turkish!]," *Ararat*, Feb. 16, 1946, 1.

6. Migliorino, *(Re)constructing Armenia in Lebanon and Syria*, 123, 124. For Migliorino, the centralization of intellectual life in Beirut was not unique to the Armenian case but was rather reflective of a larger trend in the Middle East wherein intellectuals from Syria, Egypt, and Palestine escaped persecution and oppressive regimes and found refuge in Lebanon, where they could write more freely. Indeed, in *The Book in the Islamic World: The Written Word and Communication in the Middle East*, George Atiyeh claims Lebanon of the 1960s as the "Mecca" of publishing in the Arab world, precisely for the freedom it afforded writers in contrast to other Middle Eastern countries with nationalized book industries (242).

7. Hagop Gulludjian makes a case for literacy as the most decisive feature of language vitality by arguing that "even a smallest possible market of producers may impact far and wide, ensure continuity over time, and inspire new consumers in unexpected places." Gulludjian, "Language Vitality through 'Creative Literacy,'" 107.

8. Garo Sasuni, *Badmutʿiwn Arewmdahay Arti Kraganutʿean* [The History of Modern Western Armenian Literature], 6–7.

9. Sarah Corse, *Nationalism and Literature: The Politics of Culture in Canada and the United States*, 7; Nel Van Dijk, "Research into Canon Formation: Nationalism, Literature, and an Institutional Point of View," 122; Pierre Bourdieu, "The Market of Symbolic Goods."

10. Both Sasuni and Teoleolian specify middle and high school students as their target audience. Sasuni also acknowledges the many potential readers who have left the Armenian school network early to enter the workforce. In his introduction, he addresses them directly as "the Armenian youth, who want to familiarize themselves with Armenian literary history by individual effort [inkʿnashkhadutʿyamp]." Sasuni, *Badmutʿiwn Arewmdahay Arti Kraganutʿean*, 5.

11. Sasuni, *Badmutʿiwn Arewmdahay Arti Kraganutʿean*, 387.

12. For example, Mushegh Ishkhan's *Arti Hay Kraganutʿiwn* [Modern Armenian Literature], published in three consecutive volumes by Hamazkayin of Lebanon from 1973 to 1975, groups Western Armenian literary production into three distinct periods, ending with the genocide: Awakening (1850–85), Realism (1885–1900), and Aestheticism (1900–1915).

13. Sasuni, *Badmutʿiwn Arewmdahay Arti Kraganutʿean*, 393.

14. Minas Teoleolian, *Tar Mě Kraganutʿiwn*, 1:5.

15. Teoleolian, *Tar Mě Kraganutʿiwn*, 2:2.

16. Teoleolian, *Tar Mě Kraganutʿiwn*, 2:4.

17. Teoleolian, *Tar Mě Kraganutʿiwn*, 2:9.

18. Teoleolian, *Tar Mě Kraganutʿiwn*, 2:28, 3.

19. Simon Simonian, "Khmpakri Oradedrēn [From the Editor's Diary]," 1.

20. Vazken Kaprielian, *Spʿiwřkʿahay Kraganutʿiwn* [Armenian Diaspora Literature], 92–93.

21. Teoleolian, *Tar Mě Kraganutʿiwn*, 2:9.

22. Varjabedian, *Hayerě Lipanani Měch*, 2:29–79.

23. Teoleolian, *Tar Mě Kraganutʿiwn*, 2:30.

24. Suvir Kaul, *Poems of Nation, Anthems of Empire*, 10.

25. The majority of Mushegh Ishkhan's poems can be categorized as *hayetsʿi*. In other words, they address the experience of being Armenian in the world. His 1968 collection *Dařabankʿ* (Suffering) stands as an exception. The collection consists of existential reflections on the modern human condition. While the poems are informed by politics of war and migration, they seldom evoke the Armenian experience particularly. Rather, they are songs that lament injustice and suffering in broad strokes. The collection was the recipient of the Kevork Melidinetsi Literary Prize, established by the Armenian American writer Melidinetsi and facilitated by the Holy See of Cilicia in Antelias, Lebanon. Varjabedian, *Hayerě Lipanani Měch*, 3:23–26. Many poems from this collection have been used

as lyrics to songs composed and performed by Arthur Meschian, Harout Pamboukjian, and Viken Yacoubian.

26. Mushegh Ishkhan, *Osgi Ashun* [Golden Autumn], 277. This book contains multiple collections of poems written over several decades, beginning in the 1930s.

27. Ishkhan, *Osgi Ashun*, 276, 277.

28. Hamasdegh, *Hayu Okin* [The Armenian Spirit], 3, 4.

29. Ishkhan, *Gyank' ew Eraz*, 6.

30. This poem was written later in the author's life, on April 4, 1982. While the words addressed to his migrating compatriots could apply to the experience of postgenocide dispersion, they were written amid the Lebanese Civil War, then in its seventh year. Therefore, they more immediately refer to Armenians' exodus from Lebanon as a result of the violence. An estimated one hundred thousand Armenians left Lebanon during the war years, 1975–90. According to Nicola Migliorino, while precise data is unavailable, the Lebanese community anecdotally refers to losing half its population during the war. Migliorino, *(Re)constructing Armenia in Lebanon and Syria*, 165.

31. Ishkhan, *Osgi Ashun*, 245.

32. Mushegh Ishkhan, *Arewmar* [Dusk], 13.

33. Mushegh Ishkhan, "Mushegh Ishkhani Panasdeghdzut'iwnnerēn [From Mushegh Ishkhan's Poetry]."

34. Ishkhan, *Osgi Ashun*, 7.

35. Vahé Vahian, *Osgi Gamurch* [Golden Bridge], 35, 33, 23, 27, 24.

36. Ishkhan, *Osgi Ashun*, 240.

37. Ishkhan, *Osgi Ashun*, 258.

38. Vahian, *Osgi Gamurch*, 20.

39. Vahian, *Osgi Gamurch*, 21.

40. Varjabedian, *Hayerě Lipanani mēch*, 4:35.

41. Edward Said, "On Mahmoud Darwish," 113.

42. Salam Mir, "Palestinian Literature: Occupation and Exile," 110.

43. Mahmoud Darwish, "Who Am I, without Exile?," in *The Butterfly's Burden*, 89–90.

44. In an interview with Helit Yeshurun, Darwish endows a poem with the capacity to reconcile loss: "In my situation, there are no essential differences between the story of my childhood and the story of my homeland. The rupture that occurred in my personal life also befell my homeland. Childhood was taken from me at the same time as my home. There is a parallelism and a unity in the tragic aspect of the matter. In 1948, when this great rupture of ours took place, I jumped from the bed of childhood onto the path of exile. I was six. My entire world turned upside down and childhood froze in place, it didn't go with me. The question is whether it's possible to restore the childhood that was taken by restoring the land that was taken, and that's a poetic quest that gives rhythm to the poem itself. Finding the child Mahmoud Darwish who once was is possible only in the

poem. Not in life." Helit Yeshurun, "Exile Is So Strong within Me, I May Bring It to the Land: A Landmark 1996 Interview with Mahmoud Darwish," 48.

45. Liam Brown, "Samih al-Qasim and the Language of Revolution."

46. Taniel Varujan, "Hay Lezui Khntirĕ [The Issue of the Armenian Language]," *Azadamard*, May 24, 1911, 710.

47. Ishkhan, *Osgi Ashun*, 11.

48. Ishkhan, *Osgi Ashun*, 11.

49. Jacques Hagopian, "Menk' [We]," 272–73.

50. Armen Anush, "Makaghat'ner [Ancient Parchments]," 223.

51. Interview with Maha Arida of the weekly *Magazine*, reprinted in Varjabedian, *Hayerĕ Lipanani mēch*, 4:442, 443.

52. In examining Armenian experience in Lebanon during an earlier period, the 1940s and 1950s, Tsolin Nalbantian similarly argues, "For Armenians in Lebanon, the centre of Armenian life was in Lebanon, and not some distant or imagined homeland, although the Armenian press and the associate political parties upheld these representations." *Armenians beyond Diaspora: Making Lebanon Their Own*, 198.

53. H. Oshagan, "Sp'iwṙk'i K'raganut'ean Abak'an [The Future of Diaspora Literature]," 81.

54. Bakalian, *Armenian Americans*, 307.

55. Shushan Karapetian, "Eastern Armenian Speakers as Potential Western Armenian Learners: Reflections on Second Dialect Acquisition," 65.

56. Vazken Aleksanian et al., "Pazmats'ayn Zruyts' Sp'iwṙk'ĕ ew Ir K'raganut'iwnĕ' Niwt'in Shurch [A Polyphonic Debate about Diaspora and Its Literature]," 48. The participants of the debate were Hatoutiun Kurkjian, Vazken Dedeyan, Krikor Chahinian, Kourken Kasabian, Haroutiun Armenian, Hasmig Seropian, Vazken Aleksanian, and Sahag Toutjian.

57. Many years later, *Ahegan*'s editor Krikor Chahinian proposes yet another distinguishing rubric to refer to the diaspora's literary output. He makes a distinction between literature produced in the diaspora, particularly in the early years of dispersion, that reflects on the provincial life of Armenian communities in the Ottoman Empire and Armenian literature that speaks to the diasporic experience. He calls the former *sp'iwṙk'i hay k'raganut'iwn* (diaspora's Armenian literature) and the latter *sp'iwṙk'ahay k'raganut'iwn* (diaspora-Armenian literature). Krikor Chahinian, "Sp'iwṙk'ahay K'raganut'ean Sgzpnaworut'iwnĕ [The Origins of Diaspora Armenian Literature]," 74.

58. Spivak, *Death of a Discipline*, 15–16.

Bibliography

Adorno, Theodor. *Prisms.* Translated by Samuel Weber and Shierry Weber. Cambridge, MA: MIT Press, 1983.

Agamben, Giorgio. *Remnants of Auschwitz: The Witness and the Archive.* Translated by Daniel Heller-Roazen. New York: Zone Books, 2002.

Aghapian, S., E. Topchian, and A. Hakhverdian, eds. *Sovetahay Grakanut'yan Patmut'yun* [The History of Soviet Armenian Literature]. Vol. 1. Yerevan: SSR Armenian Studies Academia, 1967.

Agishian, Nubar. *Shahan Shahnur: Geank'n u Kordzĕ* [Shahan Shahnur: His Life and Work]. Los Angeles: Abril, 1982.

Ajarian, Hrachia. *Hayots' Lezvi Patmut'yun.* Vol. 2. Yerevan: Haypet Press, 1951.

Akçam, Taner. *From Empire to Republic: Turkish Nationalism & the Armenian Genocide.* London: Zen Books, 2004.

———. *A Shameful Act: The Armenian Genocide and the Question of Turkish Responsibility.* New York: Henry Holt, 2006.

Aleksanian, Vazken, Haroutiun Armenian, Krikor Chahinian, Vazken Dedeyan, Kourken Kasabian, Hatoutiun Kurkjian, Hasmig Seropian, and Sahag Toutjian. "Pazmats'ayn Zruyts' 'Sp'iwřk'ĕ ew Ir K'raganut'iwnĕ' Niwt'in Shurch [A Polyphonic Debate about Diaspora and Its Literature]." *Ahegan* 4, no. 1 (1969): 43–63.

Alishan, Leonardo P. "Crucifixation without 'the Cross': The Impact of the Genocide on Armenian Literature." *Armenian Review* 38, no. 1–149 (1985): 27–50.

Altınay, Ayşe Gül, and Fethiye Çetin. *The Grandchildren: The Hidden Legacy of "Lost" Armenians in Turkey.* Translated by Maureen Freely. Piscataway: Routledge, 2014.

Amadian, A. "Sovedahay Kroghneri Hamakumarĕ ew Menk' [The Soviet Armenian Writers' Union Congress and Us]." *Hayrenik' Monthly* 15, no. 5 (1947): 68–74.

"Ampoghchagan Tsʻangě Vazkēn Shushaniani Kragan Ashkhadankʻneru [The Complete List of Vazken Shushanian's Literary Works]." *Hayrenikʻ Monthly* (Mar. 1943): 111–12.

Anderson, Benedict. *Imagined Communities: Reflection on the Origin and Spread of Nationalism.* London: Verso, 1983.

Anush, Armen. "Makaghatʻner [Ancient Parchments]." In vol. 2 of *Tar mě kraganutʻiwn* [A Century of Literature], edited by Minas Teoleolian, 223–24. Cairo: Husaper Press, 1956.

Apter, Emily. *Against World Literature: On the Politics of Untranslatability.* London and New York: Verso, 2013.

———. "Global Translation: The 'Invention' of Comparative Literature, Istanbul, 1933." *Critical Inquiry* 29, no. 2 (2003).

———. *The Translation Zone: A New Comparative Literature.* Princeton, NJ: Princeton Univ. Press, 2006.

"Aram Vdaranti Inchʻbēs Meřaw [How Did Aram Vdaranti Die?]." *Nayiri* 3, no. 5 (1947): 301–2.

Arendt, Hannah. *Eichmann in Jerusalem: A Report on the Banality of Evil.* New York: Penguin Books, 2006.

Arlen, Michael J. *Passage to Ararat.* Minnesota: Hungry Mind Press, 1975.

Armen, Yenovk. "Hayasdani Kroghneru Miutʻean Hamakumarě ew Ardasahmani Nergayatsʻutʻiwně [The Soviet Armenian Writers' Union's Congress and Representation from Abroad]." *Arewmudkʻ,* Sept. 15, 1946.

Asdvadzadrian, A. "Sovedagan Hayasdan." *Hayrenikʻ Monthly* 15, no. 1 (1947).

Aslanian, Sebouh. "Reader Response and the Circulation of Mkhitʻarist Books across the Armenian Communities of the Early Modern Indian Ocean." *Journal of the Society for Armenian Studies.* Vol. 22 (2013): 31–70.

Atiyeh, George. *The Book in the Islamic World: The Written Word and Communication in the Middle East.* Albany: State Univ. of New York Press, 1995.

Bahri, Zaruhi. *Dakrě* [The Brother-in-Law]. Paris: Der Hagopian Press, 1941.

Bakalian, Anny. *Armenian-Americans: From Being to Feeling Armenian.* New Brunswick, NJ: Transaction, 1993.

Balakian, Peter. *Black Dog of Fate.* New York: Broadway Books, 1997.

Bardakjian, Kevork. *A Reference Guide to Modern Armenian Literature, 1500–1920.* Detroit: Wayne State Univ. Press, 2000.

Barsamian, Mgrdich. *Arti Hay Kraganutʻiwn: Ardasahmani Kroghner* [Contemporary Armenian Literature: Writers of the Diaspora]. Paris: Araxes Press, 1941.

————. "Kirk'er ew Tēmk'er." *Geank' ew Aruesd Darekirk'* (1931): 228–29.

————. "Kirk'er ew Tēmk'er." *Geank' ew Aruesd Darekirk'* (1934): 106–14.

Barthes, Roland. *Camera Lucida: Reflections on Photography.* Translated by Richard Howard. New York: Hill and Wang, 1981.

"Bayk'ar T'rk'akhosutean Tēm [Movement against Turkish Speaking]." *Hasg Monthly* 4, no. 3 (1935): 33–34.

Bchakjian, Movses. "Interview with Zareh Vorpuni, Part A." *Pakin* 19, no. 10 (1980): 50–59.

————. "Interview with Zareh Vorpuni, Part B." *Pakin* 19, no. 11 (1980): 50–64.

"Bēdk e Khosi Krakēdě [The Critic Must Speak]." *Nayiri* 3, no. 4 (1947): 229–31.

Behdad, Ali. "Global Disjunctures, Diasporic Differences, and the New World (Dis-)Order." In *A Companion to Postcolonial Studies,* edited by Henry Schwarz and Sangeeta Ray, 396–409. London: Blackwell, 2000.

Beledian, Krikor. *Cinquante ans de littérature arménienne en France.* Paris: CNRS Editions, 2001.

————. "Ergtimin Erangiwnin Mēch [The Ambiguous in the Triangle]." *Dram* (1980): 317–56.

————. "L'expérience de la catastrophe dans la literature arménienne [The Experience of Catastrophe in Armenian Literature]." *Revue d'histoire arménienne contemporaine* 1 (1995): 127–97.

————. "Hart'koghēn Zuart'nots' [From Hart'kogh to Zuart'nots']." *Harach: Midk' ew Aruesd,* May 9, 2004.

————. "In the Language of Catastrophe." Translated by Talar Chahinian. *Absinthe: World Literature in Translation* 23 (Winter 2017): 39–50.

————. "Menk'-i art'iw [On Menk]." *Asbarēz/Horizon: Kragan Haweluadz* 1, no. 9 (1986).

————. "Nshum." *Gayk'* 3 (1993): 42–44.

Benjamin, Walter. *The Arcades Project.* Translated by Howard Eiland and Kevin McLaughlin. Cambridge, MA: Belknap Press of Harvard Univ. Press, 2002.

Berberian, Houri. *Roving Revolutionaries: Armenians and the Connected Revolutions in the Russian, Iranian, and Ottoman Worlds.* Oakland: Univ. of California Press, 2019.

Beshigtashlian, Nshan. *Sitonna* [Sedona]. Paris: Nerses Press, 1928.

Beukian, Sevan. "'National Anxiety' and Homosexuality in Post-Soviet Armenia: National Identity through Trauma and the Memory of Genocide and War." In *Soviet and Post-Soviet Sexualities,* edited by Richard C. M. Mole, 150–70. Abingdon: Routledge, 2019.

Bhabha, Homi K. *The Location of Culture*. London: Routledge, 1994.

Boudjikanian-Keuroghlian, Aida. *Les Arméniens dans le région Rhone-Alpes: Essai géographique sur les rapports d'une minorité ethnique avec son milie d'accueil.* Audin-Lyon: Associations des Amis de la Revue de Géographie de Lyon, 1978.

Bourdieu, Pierre. "The Market of Symbolic Goods." *Poetics* 14 (1985): 13–44.

Bournoutian, George. "Eastern Armenia from the Seventeenth Century to the Russian Annexation." In *The Armenian People: From Ancient to Modern Times*, edited by Richard G. Hovannisian, 2:81–108. New York: St. Martin's Press, 1997.

Boyajian, Eduard. "Artsagĕ Sp'iwṙk'i Mēch [Prose in the Diaspora]." *Nayiri* 4, nos. 7–8 (1948): 612–17.

———. "Imats'agan Sharjum: U Hima Mdadzenk' [Intellectual Movement: And Now Let Us Think]." *Nayiri* 3, no. 1 (1947): 45–47.

———. "Kroghneru Hamakumarin Anhrajeshdut'iwnĕ [The Necessity of the Writers' Conference]." *Nayiri* 3, no. 11 (1947–48): 624–26.

———. "U Sgsink' Mdadzel [Let's Start Thinking]." *Nayiri* 3, no. 1 (1947): 45–47.

Brah, Avtar. *Cartographies of Diaspora: Contesting Identities*. London: Routledge, 1996.

Braziel, Jana Avans, and Anita Mannur, eds. *Theorizing Diaspora*. Oxford: Blackwell, 2003.

Brown, Liam. "Samih al-Qasim and the Language of Revolution." *Middle East Eye*, Feb. 12, 2015. https://www.middleeasteye.net/big-story/samih-al-qasim-and-language-revolution.

Brubaker, Roger. "The 'Diaspora' Diaspora." *Ethnic and Racial Studies* 28, no. 1 (2005): 1–19.

Caruth, Cathy, ed. *Trauma: Explorations in Memory*. Baltimore: John Hopkins Univ. Press, 1995.

———. *Unclaimed Experience: Trauma, Narrative and History*. Baltimore: Johns Hopkins Univ. Press, 1996.

Chahinian, Krikor. *Gensakrut'iwn ew Madenakidut'iwn Shahan Shahnuri* [Biography and Bibliography of Shahan Shahnur]. Antelias: Armenian Catholicosate of Cilicia, 1981.

———. *Shahan Shahnur: Ak'sor ew Aruesd* [Shahan Shahnur: Exile and Art]. Antelias: Armenian Catholicosate of Cilicia, 1985.

———. "Sp'iwṙk'ahay Kraganut'ean Sgzpnaworut'iwnĕ [The Origins of Diaspora Armenian Literature]." *Pazmavēb* 1–4 (1996): 70–88.

Chahinian, Talar. "The Paris Attempt: Rearticulation of (National) Belonging and the Inscription of Aftermath Experience in French Armenian Literature between the Wars." PhD diss., Univ. of California at Los Angeles, 2008.

Chobanian, Arshag. "Agnarg mě Ayzhmean Hay Mdawor Geank'in Vray: Ardasahmani Mēch [A Look at Contemporary Armenian Intellectual Life: Abroad]." *Anahid* (Mar.–Apr. 1930): 100–115.

———. "Arewmdahay Lezui u Kraganut'ean Abak'an [The Future of Western Armenian Language and Literature]." *Anahid* (July–Dec. 1946).

———. "Aṙoghchn u Vadaṙoghchě Shahan Shahnuri Kraganut'ean Mēch [The Strengths and Weaknesses of Shahan Shahnur's Literature]." *Anahid* 10 (1939): 79–93.

———. "Azkayinn u Michazkayině Kraganut'ean Mēch [The National and International in Literature]." *Zuart'nots'* 1, no. 1 (1929): 12–15.

———. "Erek' Hay Herosagan Nahadagner [Three Armenian Heroic Martyrs]." *Anahid* 12, no. 1 (1946): 1–9.

———. "Hay Azkin Paregamneṙ [Friends of the Armenian Nation]." In *Annuaire Franco-Armenien*, 120–35. Paris: Masis Press, 1927.

———. "Kronik [Chronicle]." *Anahid* 12, no. 1 (1946): 51–64.

———. "Kronik [Chronicle]." *Anahid* (July–Dec. 1946).

———. "Kronik [Chronicle]." *Anahid* (Jan.–June 1947).

Chormisian, Levon. *Hamabadger Arewmdahay Mēg Taru Badmut'ean: Hay Sp'iwṙk'ě, Fransahayeru Badmut'iwně* [Overview of Western Armenian Centennial History: Armenian Diaspora; French Armenian History]. Beirut: Doniguian & Sons Press, 1975.

Cohen, Robin. "Diasporas and the Nation-State: From Victims to Challengers." *International Affairs* 72, no. 3 (1996): 507–20.

Corse, Sarah. *Nationalism and Literature: The Politics of Culture in Canada and the United States.* Cambridge: Cambridge Univ. Press, 1997.

Dadrian, Vahakn N. *The History of the Armenian Genocide.* New York: Berghahn Books, 1995.

Dalke, Anne. "Original Vice: The Political Implications of Incest in the Early American Novel." *Early American Literature* 23, no. 2 (1988): 188–201.

Danielian, Suren. *Sp'iwṙk'ahay Vēbě* [The Diasporan Armenian Novel]. Antilias: Holy See of Cilicia, 1992.

Darwish, Mahmoud. *The Butterfly's Burden.* Translated by Fady Joudah. Port Townsend: Copper Canyon Press, 2007.

Davtian, Vahagn. "Pats' Namag Shahan Shahnuri [Open Letter to Shahan Shahnur]." *Pakin* 9, no. 2 (1970).

Dekmejian, Hrair R. "The Armenian Diaspora." In *The Armenian People: From Ancient to Modern Times*, edited by Richard G. Hovannisian, 2:413–45. New York: St. Martin's Press, 1997.

Der Matossian, Bedross. *Shattered Dreams of Revolution: From Liberty to Violence in the Late Ottoman Empire*. Stanford, CA: Stanford Univ. Press, 2014.

Der Matossian, Bedross, and Barlow Der Mugrdechian, eds. *Western Armenian in the 21st Century: Challenges and New Approaches*. Fresno: Press at California State Univ., 2018.

Der Vartanian, Kurken. "Kaght'ahay K'raganut'ean Shurch [On Immigrant Armenian Literature]." *Hayrenik' Monthly* 16, no. 6 (1948): 62–64.

Deyirmenjian, Sevan. "Kaghut'ahay Kroghneru Hamakumarě ew Dzarugian [Community Armenian Writers' Conference and Dzarugian]." *Karun* 36, no. 10 (2002): 78–86.

Donabédian, Anahid. "La politique linguistique en Arménie: De l'Union Soviétique à la République indépendante." In *Langues et pouvoir, de l'Afrique du Nord à l'extrême Orient*, edited by S. Chaker, 171–85. Paris: Edisud, 1998.

Dzarugian, Antranig. "Imatsagan Sharjum: Kroghneru Hamakumarě [The Writers' Conference]." *Nayiri* 3, no. 5 (1947): 290–97.

———. "Khosk Kraganut'ean Arvesdi ew Kragan Golkhozi Masin [A Word on the Literary Arts and Literary Economy]." *Nayiri* (June–Sept. 1946): 604–15.

———. *T'ught' ar̀ Erevan* [Letter to Yerevan]. Aleppo: Ani Press, 1945.

Eaglestone, Robert. "Knowledge, 'Afterwardness,' and the Future of Trauma Theory." In *The Future of Trauma Theory: Contemporary Literary and Cultural Criticism*, edited by Gert Buelens, Sam Durrant, and Robert Eaglestone. London: Routledge, 2014.

Editorial announcement. *Echmiadzin Monthly* 3, nos. 4–5 (1946): 71.

———. *Hayrenik' Monthly* 1, no. 1 (1922): 2.

———. *Menk: Revue littéraire armenienne*, no. 1 (1931): 3.

Editorial note. *Menk: Revue littéraire armenienne*, no. 1 (1931): 4.

Edwards, Brent Hayes. *The Practice of Diaspora: Literature, Translation, and the Rise of Black Internationalism*. Cambridge, MA: Harvard Univ. Press, 2003.

Ekmekcioglu, Lerna. *Recovering Armenia: The Limits of Belonging in Postgenocide Turkey*. Stanford, CA: Stanford Univ. Press, 2016.

Eng, David L., and David Kazanjian, eds. *Loss: The Politics of Mourning*. Berkeley: Univ. of California Press, 2003.

Englund, Axel, and Anders Olsson, eds. *Languages of Exile: Migration and Multilingualism in Twentieth-Century Literature*. Bern: Peter Lang, 1994.

"Erekʿ Ēngernerě [The Three Friends]." Review. *Geankʿ ew Aruesd Darekirkʿ* (1932): 161–62.

Felman, Shoshana. "Theaters of Justice: Arendt in Jerusalem, the Eichmann Trial, and the Redefinition of Legal Meaning in the Wake of the Holocaust." *Critical Inquiry* 27, no. 2 (2001): 201–38.

Felman, Shoshana, and Dori Laub, MD. *Testimony: Crisis of Witnessing in Literature, Psychoanalysis, and History*. New York and London: Routledge, 1992.

Fenerjian, K. "Nor Kirkʿer [New Books]." *Zuartʿnots* 1, nos. 6–7 (1929–30): 301–4.

Freud, Sigmund. "Mourning and Melancholia." In *The Freud Reader*. New York: W. W. Norton, 1989.

———. *Totem and Taboo*. Translated by James Strachey. London: Routledge & Kegan Paul, 1960.

Ganguly, Debjani. *This Thing Called the World: The Contemporary Novel as Global Form*. Durham, NC: Duke Univ. Press, 2016.

Gilmore, Leigh. *The Limits of Autobiography: Trauma and Testimony*. Ithaca, NY: Cornell Univ. Press, 2001.

Goekjian, Gregory F. "Diaspora and Denial: The Holocaust and the 'Question' of the Armenian Genocide." *Diaspora: A Journal of Transnational Studies* 7, no. 1 (1998).

Gulludjian, Hagop. "Language Vitality through 'Creative Literacy.'" In *Western Armenian in the 21st Century: Challenges and New Approaches*, edited by Bedross Der Matossian and Barlow Der Mugrdechian, 103–32. Fresno: Press at California State Univ., 2018.

Hadjian, Avedis. *The Secret Nation: The Hidden Armenians of Turkey*. London: I. B. Tauris, 2018.

Hagopian, A. "Nor Kirkʿer [New Books]." *Zuartʿnotsʿ: Revue Arménienne d'Art et de Litterérature* 2, no. 3 (1931): 65–67.

———. Reviews. *Zuartʿnotsʿ: Revue Arménienne d'Art et de Litterérature* 2, nos. 4–5 (1931): 101–4.

Hagopian, Jacques. "Menkʿ [We]." In *Tar mě kraganutʿiwn [A Century of Literature]*, edited by Minas Teoleolian, 2:272–73. Cairo: Husaper Press, 1956.

Hall, Stuart. "Cultural Identity and Diaspora." In *Theorizing Diaspora*, edited by Jana Evans Braziel and Anita Mannur. London: Blackwell, 2003.

"Hamakumarě [The Conference]." *Nayiri* 3, no. 6 (1947): 368–70.

"Hamakumarēn Gagngalenk' [What We Expect from the Conference]." *Nayiri* 3, no. 6 (1947): 376.

"Hamakumar Michin Arewelk'i Hay Kroghneru Hamakumarĕ [The Conference of Middle East's Armenian Writers]." *Nayiri* 4, no. 6 (1948): 504.

Hamasdegh. *Hayu Okin* [The Armenian Spirit]. *Pakin* 1, no. 1 (1962): 3–5.

"Havasdikĕ [Assurance]." *Pakin* 1, no. 2 (1962): 1–2.

"Hayasdani Sovedagan Kroghneri Hamakumarĕ [The Congress of Soviet Armenian Writers]." *Echmiadzin Monthly* 3, nos. 8–10 (1946): 65–69.

"Hay Mamulin Aradĕ [The Stain of the Armenian Press]." *Nayiri* 8–9 (Apr.–May 1946): 508–10.

"Hay Spiwṙk'ĕ [The Armenian Diaspora]." *Ergunk'* 4, no. 3 (1932): inside cover.

"Hay Sp'iwṙk'ĕ Arjēk' ē [The Armenian Diaspora Is Valuable]." *Sp'iwṙk'* 1, no. 2 (1958).

Hirsch, Marianne. *The Generation of Postmemory: Writing and Visual Culture after the Holocaust.* New York: Columbia Univ. Press, 2012.

Hovannisian, Richard G., ed. *The Armenian Image in History and Literature.* Malibu: Undena, 1981.

———. "The Armenian Question in the Ottoman Empire, 1876–1914." In *The Armenian People: From Ancient to Modern Times,* edited by Richard G. Hovannisian, 2:203–38. New York: St. Martin's Press, 1997.

———. "Denial of the Armenian Genocide in Comparison with Holocaust Denial." In *Remembrance and Denial: The Case of the Armenian Genocide,* edited by Richard G. Hovannisian, 207–21. Detroit: Wayne State Univ., 1998.

Isahakian, Avetik. "Patsman Khōsk [Opening Remarks]." *Ani* 1, no. 7 (1946): 342–45.

Ishkhan, Mushegh. *Arewmar* [Dusk]. Beirut: Hamazkayin Vahe Setian, 1986.

———. *Arti Hay Kraganut'iwn* [Modern Armenian Literature]. Vol. 1. Beirut: Hamazkayin, 1973.

———. *Arti Hay Kraganut'iwn* [Modern Armenian Literature]. Vol. 2. Beirut: Hamazkayin, 1974.

———. *Arti Hay Kraganut'iwn* [Modern Armenian Literature]. Vol. 3. Beirut: Hamazkayin, 1975.

———. *Daṙabank'* [Suffering]. Antelias: Armenian Catholicosate of Cilicia, 1968.

———. *Gyank' ew Eraz* [Life and Dream]. Beirut: Onibar Press, 1949.

———. "Mushegh Ishkhani Panasdeghdzut'iwnnerēn [From Mushegh Ishkhan's Poetry]." Oct. 3, 2013. www.asbarez.com.

————. *Osgi Ashun* [Golden Autumn]. Beirut: Sevan Press, 1963.

————. "Panasdeghdzutiwně Sp'iwřk'i Měch." *Nayiri* 4. nos. 7–8 (1948): 617–23.

"Jagadin Vray [On the Front]." *Zuart'nots': Revue Arménienne d'Art et de Litterérature* 1, no. 1 (1929): 1.

Jinbashian, Ishkhan. "Keriragan Hayerēn: Lezun Hamaynagerdumi Sharzhěnt'ats'k'in Měch [Surreal Armenian: Language amid the Process of Community Construction]." *Pazmavēb* 154, nos. 1–4 (1996): 89–98.

Just, Daniel. "The Modern Novel from a Sociological Perspective: Towards a Strategic Use of the Notion of Genres." *Journal of Narrative Theory* 38, no. 3 (2008): 378–97.

Kaplan, Brett Ashley. *Unwanted Beauty: Aesthetic Pleasure in Holocaust Representation.* Urbana: Univ. of Illinois Press, 2007.

Kaprielian, Vazken. *Sp'iwřk'ahay Kraganut'iwn* [Armenian Diaspora Literature]. Yerevan: Yerevan State Univ. Press, 1987.

Karapetian, Shushan. "Eastern Armenian Speakers as Potential Western Armenian Learners: Reflections on Second Dialect Acquisition." In *Western Armenian in the 21st Century: Challenges and New Approaches,* edited by Bedross Der Matossian and Barlow Der Mugrdechian, 59–80. Fresno: Press at California State Univ., 2018.

Kasbarian, Sossie. "The Myth and Reality of 'Return': Diaspora in the Homeland." *Diaspora: A Journal of Transnational Studies* 18, no. 3 (2015): 358–81.

Kaul, Suvir. *Poems of Nation, Anthems of Empire.* Charlottesville: Univ. Press of Virginia, 2000.

Kazanjian, David. "Between Genocide and Catastrophe." In *Loss: The Politics of Mourning,* edited by David L. Eng and David Kazanjian, 125–47. Berkeley: Univ. of California Press, 2003.

Keoseian, Krikor. *Nahanchě Ařants' Erki* [The Retreat without Song]. *Hařach,* Mar. 29, 1979.

————. *Namagani.* Vol. 1, Shahan Shahnur's letters to Krikor K'ēosēian. Watertown, MA: Mayreni, 2001.

————. *Namagani.* Vol. 2, Shahan Shahnur's letters to Gurgēn Mahari and Antranik Andrēasian. Watertown, MA: Mayreni, 2004.

Kesteloot, Lilyan. *Black Writers in French: A Literary History of Negritude.* Translated by Ellen Conroy Kennedy. Philadelphia: Temple Univ. Press, 1974.

Kévorkian, Raymond. *The Armenian Genocide: A Complete History.* London and New York: I. B. Taurus, 2011.

Kh., A. "Haralēzneru Tawajanut'iwně / Shahan Shahnur [The Betrayal of the Aralez by Shahan Shahnur]." *Hayrenik' Monthly* 12, no. 8 (1933–34): 158–60.

Khayadjian, Edmond. *Archag Chobanian et le mouvement armenophile en France.* Marseilles: CRDP, 1986.

———. *P'orts Dara-Krut'ean Masin/ Essai sur l'exil* [An Essay on Exile]. Beirut: Collection "Diaspora Arménienne," 1978.

Krikorian, Hrachia. "Sovedahay Kraganut'iwně ew Nra Hedakay Zarkats'man Ughinerě [Soviet Armenian Literature and Pathways for Its Future Development]." *Ani* 1, nos. 8–9 (1946).

Kristal, Efraín. "The Incest Motif in Narratives of the United States and Spanish America." In *Internationalität nationaler literaturen*, edited by Udo Schöning. Göttingen: Wallestein Verlag, 2000.

Kurkjian, Harutiun. "Hay Kraganut'ean Michazkaynats'man Khntiré [The Issue of Armenian Literature's Internationalization]." *Harach: Midk' ew Aruesd*, July 2, 2006.

LaCapra, Dominick. *Writing History, Writing Trauma.* Baltimore: Johns Hopkins Univ. Press, 2001.

Leys, Ruth. *From Guilt to Shame: Auschwitz and After.* Princeton, NJ: Princeton Univ. Press, 2007.

Lionnet, Françoise, and Shu-mei Shish, eds. *Minor Transnationalism.* Durham, NC: Duke Univ. Press, 2005.

Lubin, Armen. *Feux contre feux.* Paris: B. Grasset, 1968.

———. *Les hautes terrasses.* Paris: Gallimard, 1957.

———. *Les logis provisoires.* Paris: Mortemart Rougerie, 1983.

———. *Sainte Patience.* Paris: Gallimard, 1951.

MacCannell, Juliet Flower. *The Regime of the Brother: After Patriarchy.* London: Routledge, 1991.

"Mah Shahan Shahnuri [Death of Shahnur Shahnur]." *Pakin* (Oct. 1974): 43–49.

Mandel, Maud S. *In the Aftermath of Genocide: Armenians and Jews in Twentieth-Century France.* Durham, NC: Duke Univ. Press, 2003.

Mandel, Naomi. *Against the Unspeakable: Complicity, the Holocaust, and Slavery in America.* Charlottesville: Univ. Press of Virginia, 2006.

Mann, Carol. *Paris between the Wars.* New York: Vendome Press, 1996.

Marashlian, Levon. "Finishing the Genocide: Cleansing Turkey of Armenian Survivors, 1920–1923." In *Remembrance and Denial: The Case of the Armenian Genocide*, edited by Richard G. Hovannisian, 113–46. Detroit: Wayne State Univ., 1998.

Matiossian, Vartan. "In Lieu of a Conclusion." In *Western Armenian in the 21st Century: Challenges and New Approaches*, edited by Bedross Der Matossian and Barlow Der Mugrdechian, 147–50. Fresno: Press at California State Univ., 2018.

———. *The Politics of Naming the Armenian Genocide: Language, History and "Medz Yeghern."* London: I. B. Tauris, 2022.

McMurran, Mary Helen. "Transnationalism and the Novel: A Call for Periodization." *Novel: A Forum on Fiction* 42, no. 3 (2009): 531–37.

"Mēg Janabarh Miayn [One Path Only]." *Hay Kir*, no. 5 (1929): 1.

Meloyan, Ghevont. *Asduadzareal Kʻaghakʻi Erguoreagnerě: Mayrě ew Anařag Ortin* [The Twins of the Divine City: The Mother and the Prodigal Son]. Paris: Barsamian Books, 1960.

———. *Erekʻ Ěngernerě* [The Three Friends]. Paris: Hrant Samuel, 1931.

———. *Verhishumner* [Remembrances]. Paris: Barsamian Books, 1960.

Méloyian, Léon G. *Arménouche: Drame en cinq actes*. Paris: Éditions "Le Soleil," 1952.

"Mer Hankanagě [Our Manifesto]." *Mehean*, no. 1 (1914): 1–3.

"Mer Tirkʻě [Our Position]." *Ergunkʻ* 1, no. 2 (1929): 1.

Mesrob, Levon. *Hashishin: Badmagan Vēb* [The Hashishi: A Historical Novel]. Paris: Araxes Press, 1939.

Migliorino, Nicola. *(Re)Constructing Armenia in Lebanon and Syria: Ethnocultural Diversity and the State in the Aftermath of a Refugee Crisis*. New York: Berghahn Books, 2008.

Mikaelian, Paylak. *Ewa, Artsagurti Patsʻigner* [Eve]. Beirut: Edvan Press, 1956.

Miller, Donald, and Lorna Touryan Miller. *Survivors: An Oral History of the Armenian Genocide*. Berkeley: Univ. of California Press, 1993.

Mir, Salam. "Palestinian Literature: Occupation and Exile." *Arab Studies Quarterly* 35, no. 2 (2013): 110–29.

Misakian, Shavarsh. "Haygagan Hbadagutʻean Khntirě [The Question of Nationality for Armenians]." *Hařach*, Aug. 5, 1925.

———. *Ōrer ew Zhamer* [Days and Hours]. Paris: Hařach, 1958.

Mozian, Levon. "Kroghneru Yergrort Hamakumarě [The Second Writers' Congress]." *Arewmudkʻ* (Paris), Sept. 29, 1946.

Mufti, Aamir R. *Forget English! Orientalisms and World Literatures*. Cambridge, MA: Harvard Univ. Press, 2016.

N. D. "Krakhōsaganner [Reviews]." *Hayrenikʻ Monthly* 8, no. 2 (1929): 158–62.

"'Nahanchě' Nerkʻin Sbařman Abrankʻ [*Nahanchě* as an Object of Internal Consumption]." *Pakin* (June 1974): 37–54.

Nalbantian, Tsolin. *Armenians beyond Diaspora: Making Lebanon Their Own.* Edinburgh: Edinburgh Univ. Press, 2020.

Nartuni, Shavarsh. *Erusaghēm, Erusaghēm* [Jerusalem, Jerusalem]. Paris: Der Agopian Press, 1938.

———. "Letter to Hrant Palouyan." *Harach: Midkʿ ew Aruesd*, May 9, 2004.

———. "Menkʿ, Menkʿ, Menkʿ." *Menk: Revue littéraire armenienne*, no. 1 (1931): 37–40.

———. Reviews. *Menk: Revue littéraire armenienne*, no. 1 (1931): 61.

Nichanian, Marc. *Ages et usages de la langue Armenienne.* Paris: Editions Entente, 1989.

———. *The Historiographic Perversion.* Translated by Gil Anidjar. New York: Columbia Univ. Press, 2009.

———. *La perversion historiographique: Une réflexion arménienne.* Paris: Éditions Lignes, 2006.

———. "The *Retreat* of Shahan Shahnur." *Journal of Society for Armenian Studies* 4 (1988–89): 53–75.

———. "Shahan Shahnurě ew Hariwrameagneru Zaweshdě [Shahan Shahnur and the Centuries-Old Farce]." *Ahegan* 3 (1970): 82–104.

———. "The Style of Violence." *Armenian Review* 38, no. 1-149 (1985): 1–26.

———. *Writers of Disaster: Armenian Literature in the Twentieth Century.* Vol. 1. Princeton, NJ: Gomidas Institute, 2002.

———. "Zareh Orpuni: Zhamanag ew Hayrutʿiwn [Zareh Orpuni: Time and Fatherhood]." *Pazmavēb* (Venice) (1996): 99–140.

"Nor Hawadkʿě [The New Faith]." *Nor Hawadkʿ*, no. 1 (June 1924): 1.

Nucho, Joanne Randa. *Everyday Sectarianism in Urban Lebanon: Infrastructures, Public Services, and Power.* Princeton, NJ: Princeton Univ. Press, 2016.

Ohan, Garo. *Khrjitʿnerēn Minchʿew Khorhrtaran* [From Huts to Parliament]. Paris: De Navarre Press, 1933.

Ohanian, Hayg. "Kragan Ughineri Vray [On Literary Paths]." *Nayiri* 10–12 (June–Sept. 1946): 600–602.

Oshagan, Hagop. *Mayrenineru Shukʿin Dag* [Under the Shade of Cedar Trees]. Beirut: Alta Press, 1983.

———. "Spʿiwrkʿi Kʿraganutʿean Abakʿan [The Future of Diaspora Literature]." *Nayiri* 4, no. 1 (1948).

———. *Vgayuʿiwn mě* [A Testimony]. Aleppo: Nayiri Press, 1946.

Oshagan, Vahé. "Hay Spʿiwrkʿě Ir Hartsʿagannerov [The Armenian Diaspora and Its Questions]." *Pazmavēb* 1-4 (1996): 65–70.

———. "Literature of the Armenian Diaspora." *World Literature Today* 60, no. 2 (1986): 224–28.

———. "Modern Armenian Literature and Intellectual History from 1700 to 1915." In *The Armenian People: From Ancient to Modern Times*, edited by Richard G. Hovannisian, 2:135–74. New York: St. Martin's Press, 1997.

———. "Modernization in Western Armenian Literature." *Armenian Review* (Spring 1983): 62–75.

———. "Tadronĕ Spʻiwr̄kʻi Mēch [Theater in the Diaspora]." *Nayiri* 4, nos. 7–8 (1948): 624–27.

———. "The Theme of the Armenian Genocide in Diaspora Prose." *Armenian Review* 38 (1985): 51–60.

"Pakinin ar̄chev [In Front of Pakin]." *Pakin* 1, no. 1 (1962): 2.

Panossian, Razmik. *The Armenians: From Kings and Priests to Merchants and Commissars.* New York: Columbia Univ. Press, 2006.

———. "Between Ambivalence and Identity in Armenia-Diaspora Relations." *Diaspora: A Journal of Transnational Studies* 7, no. 2 (1998).

Pattie, Susan P. "Armenians in Diaspora." In *The Armenians: Past and Present in the Making of National Identity*, edited by Edmund Herzig and Marina Kurkchiyan. London: Routledge Curzon, 2005.

Peroomian, Rubina. *And Those Who Continued Living in Turkey after 1915: The Metamorphosis of the Post-genocide Armenian Identity as Reflected in Artistic Literature.* Yerevan: Armenian Genocide Museum-Institute, 2008.

———. *Literary Responses to Catastrophe: A Comparison of the Armenian and the Jewish Experience.* Atlanta, GA: Scholars Press, 1993.

Poladian, Garo. *Zruytsʻ* [Conversation]. Vol. 1. Paris: Araxes Press, 1952.

Prager, Jeffrey. "Psychology of Collective Memory." In *International Encyclopedia of the Social and Behavioral Sciences*, edited by N. J. Smelser and Paul B. Baltes. Oxford: Pergamon, 2001.

Rabaka, Reiland. *The Negritude Movement.* Lanham, MD: Lexington Books, 2015.

Radhakrishnan, R. *Theory in an Uneven World.* Oxford: Blackwell, 2003.

Rank, Otto. *The Incest Theme in Literature and Legend: Fundamentals of a Psychology of Literary Creation.* Translated by Gregory C. Richter. Baltimore: Johns Hopkins Univ. Press, 1992.

Rose, Guillian. *Mourning Becomes the Law: Philosophy and Representation.* New York: Cambridge Univ. Press, 1996.

Rowland, Antony. "Re-thinking 'Impossibility' and 'Barbarism': Adorno and Post-Holocaust Poetics." *Critical Survey* 9, no. 1 (1997): 57–69.

Safran, William. "Diasporas in Modern Societies: Myths of Homeland and Return." *Diaspora: A Journal of Transnational Studies* 1, no. 1 (1991): 83–99.

Sahakyan, Vahe. "Spaces of Difference, Spaces of Belonging: Negotiating Armeniannes in Lebanon and France." In *An Armenian Mediterranean*, edited by K. Babayian and M. Pifer, 247–67. Cham, Switzerland: Palgrave Macmillan, 2018.

Said, Edward. "On Mahmoud Darwish." *Grand Street*, no. 48 (Winter 1994).

———. *Orientalism*. New York: Vintage Books, 1978.

———. *Reflections on Exile*. Cambridge, MA: Harvard Univ. Press, 2000.

Sanasar, Paylag. Reviews. *Hayrenik' Monthly* 13, no. 6 (1935): 150–51.

Sanjian, Ara. "Sp'iwřk'i Hay K'aghak'agan Gusagts'utiwnneř (1921–1988) [Diaspora's Armenian Political Parties (1921–1988)]." *Nor Hařach*, June 14, 2016.

Sarafian, Nigoghos. *14 K'ert'uadz* [14 Poems]. Paris: Araxes Press, 1933.

———. *Anchrbedi Mě Krawumě* [An Outer Space Conquest]. Paris: J. Nersēs ew B. Êlēgean Press, 1928.

———. "Azkayinn u Michazkayině Kraganut'ean Mēch [The National and International in Literature]." *Zuart'nots'* 1, no. 2 (1929): 70–72.

———. "Haigazian Pařaran [Haigazian Dictionary]." *Bromēt'ēagan* [Promethean]. https://digilib.aua.am/.

———. *Ishkhanuhin* [The Princess]. Paris: Araxes Press, 1934.

———. "K'ragan Lghrjumner [Literary Meanderings]." *Nayiri* 5, no. 7 (1949).

———. "Menk'." *Menk: Revue littéraire armenienne*, no. 2 (1931): 67–70.

———. "Nor Nuiryalner Bēdk' en Mezi [What We Need Are New Devotees]." *Pakin* 57, no. 3 (2018): 5–19.

———. Untitled. *Menk: Revue littéraire armenienne*, no. 1 (1931): 42–44.

———. *Vēnsēni Andařě* [The Forest of Vincennes]. Edited by Krikor Beledian. Paris: Art Series, 1988.

Sasuni, Garo. *Badmut'iwn Arewmdahay Arti Kraganut'ean* [The History of Modern Western Armenian Literature]. 2nd ed. Beirut: Atlas Press, 1963.

———. "Kroghneru Hamakumarě [The Writers' Conference]." *Nayiri* 3, no. 6 (1947): 370–71.

———. "Pats'man Khōsk' [Opening Remarks]." *Nayiri* 4, nos. 7–8 (1948): 608–11.

Schahgaldian, Nicola B. "Ethnicity and Politics in Lebanon." *Armenian Review* (Spring 1983): 46–61.

Sevan, Gegham. *Sp'iwřk'ahay Grakanut'ean Patmut'ean Urwagdzer (1920–1945)* [Outline of the History of Diasporan Armenian Literature (1920–1945)]. Yerevan: Armenian SSH GA, 1980.

Shahnour, Shahan. *Retreat without Song*. Translated by Mischa Kudian. London: Mashtots Press, 1982.

Shahnur, Shahan. "Azadn Gomidas [Gomidas the Free]." *Haṙach*, Jan. 25, 1970.

———. "Azadn Gomidas [Gomidas the Free]." *Sp'iwṙk'* [Diaspora], Nov. 23, 1969.

———. "'Buynuzlĕ'nerĕ [The Cuckolds]." *Menk: Revue littéraire armenienne*, no. 3 (1932): 146–59.

———. *Nahanchĕ Aṙants' Erki: Badgerazart' Badmut'iwn Hayots'* [The Retreat without Song: Illustrated History of Armenians]. Beirut: Zartonki Series, 1948.

———. *Pats' Domarĕ* [The Open Calendar]. Paris: Haṙach Press, 1971.

———. *T'ert'is Giragnōreay T'iwĕ* [The Sunday Issue]. Beirut: Hradaragut'iwn Krikor K'ēosēiani, 1958.

———. *Zuyk mĕ Garmir Dedragner* [A Pair of Red Notebooks]. Beirut: Shirag, 1967.

"Shahnur-Dawt'ian Vējin Verchin P'ulĕ [The Last Phase in the Shahnur-Dawt'ian Debate]." *Pakin* (May 1970).

Sharoyan, Levon. *Simon Simonian: The Last Scion of the Mountaineers*. Translated by Vahe H. Apelian. Dubai: Armenian Cultural, 2017.

Shirinian, Lorne. *Armenian–North American Literature, a Critical Introduction: Genocide, Diaspora, and Symbols*. Lewiston, NY: E. Mellen Press, 1990.

———. "Lost Fathers and Abandoned Sons: The Silence of Generations in Armenian Diaspora Literature." *Armenian Review* 43, no. 1-169 (1990): 1–17.

Shushanian, Vazken. *Amran Kisherner* [Summer Nights]. Cairo: Husaper Press, 1930.

———. *Mart Mĕ Or Ararat Ch'uni Ir Hokwoyn Khorĕ* [A Man Who Has No Ararat in the Depth of His Soul]. Edited by Boghos Snabian. Beirut: Hamazkayin, 1998.

Simonian, Bebo. *Ēcher ew Niwt'er Kraganut'ean*. Antelias: Armenian Catholicosate of Cllicia, 2007.

———. "P'arizi Menk'in Deghĕ Sp'iwṙk'ahay Kragan Mamuli Badmut'ean Mēch [The Place of Paris's *Menk* in the History of the Armenian Diaspora's Literary Press]." *Haigazian Armenological Review* (Beirut) 12 (1992): 209–26.

Simonian, Simon. "Khmpakri Oradedrēn [From the Editor's Diary]." *Sp'iwṙk'* 11, no. 2 (1969).

———. "Shahan Shahnuri Mahuan Aṙt'iw [On the Occasion of Shahan Shahnur's Death]." *Sp'iwṙk'*, Sept. 8, 1974.

Siras, Hmayag. "Sovedagan Kroghneri B. Hamakumarĕ [Soviet Armenian Union's Second Congress]." *Ani* 1, no. 7 (1946): 348–51.

Smith, Roger W. "State Power and Genocidal Intent: On the Uses of Genocide in the Twentieth Century." In *Studies in Comparative Genocide*, edited by Levon Chorbajian and George Shirinian. London and New York: St. Martin's Press, 1999.

Snabian, Boghos, ed. *Mehean: A Compilation*. Aleppo: Cilicia, n.d.

Spivak, Gayatri Ch. *Death of a Discipline*. New York: Columbia Univ. Press, 2003.

Stepanyan, S. "Sp'iwrk'ahay Keank'i Ejerě [The Pages of Diasporan Armenian Life]." *Sovetakan Grakanut'iwn* 10 (1966): 132–36.

Stovall, Tyler. *Paris Noir: African Americans in the City of Light*. Self-published, 2012.

Stubbs, Jeremy. "Surrealist Literature and Urban Crime." In *The Cambridge Companion to the Literature of Paris*, edited by Anna-Louise Milne. Cambridge: Cambridge Univ. Press, 2013.

Suny, Ronald Grigor. "Eastern Armenians under Tsarist Rule." In *The Armenian People: From Ancient to Modern Times*, edited by Richard G. Hovannisian, 2:109–34. New York: St. Martin's Press, 1997.

———. "Soviet Armenia." In *The Armenian People: From Ancient to Modern Times*, edited by Richard G. Hovannisian, 2:347–87. New York: St. Martin's Press, 1997.

Tachjian, Vahé. "L'usage du turc et le renouveau identitaire chez les Arméniens du Liban et de Syrie dans les années 1920–1930." In *Les Arméniens du Liban: Cent ans de presence*, edited by Christine Babikian Assaf, Carla Eddé, Lévon Nordisguian, and Vahé Tachjian, 59–83. Beirut: Saint Joseph Univ. Press, 2017.

Tarpinian, Ardag. "Mer Arewelahayerēnē [Our Western Armenian]." *Bayk'ar: Year End Special Issue* (1949): 13–24.

Tatul, Vahram. *Hin ur Nor Dagher* [Old and New Songs]. Paris: Hay Kroghneru Ěngeragts'ut'iwn, 1941.

Tekian, Vehanush. *Dohmadzaŕ* [Family Tree]. Paramus, NJ: Vehart, 1997.

Teoleolian, Minas. "Hasdadumner kroghneru hamakumarin shurch [Clarifications Regarding the Writers' Congress]." *Nayiri* (June–Sept. 1946): 593–600.

———. "Mamulě Sp'iwrk'i Mēch [The Press in Diaspora]." *Nayiri* 4, nos. 7–8 (1948): 628–41.

———. *Tar Mě Kraganut'iwn (1850–1950)* [A Century of Literature (1850–1950)]. 2 vols. Cairo: Husaper Press, 1956.

Thomsen, Mads Rosendahl. *Mapping World Literature: International Canonization and Transnational Literatures*. London and New York: Continuum, 2008.

Tölölyan, Khachig. "Elites and Institutions in the Armenian Transnation." *Diaspora: A Journal of Transnational Studies* 9, no. 1 (2000): 107–36.

———. "The Nation-State and Its Others: In Lieu of a Preface." *Diaspora: A Journal of Translational Studies* 1, no. 1 (1991).

———. "Rethinking Diaspora(s): Stateless Power in the Transnational Moment." *Diaspora: A Journal of Transnational Studies* 5, no. 1 (1996): 3–36.

———. "'Sp'iwṙk'' Hghats'k'i Ants'ealn u Nergan [The Past and Present of the Concept of 'Diaspora']." *Pazmavēb* 1–4 (1996): 35–45.

Topchian, Eduard. "Ardasahmanian Zhamanagagits' Hay Kraganutiwně [Contemporary Armenian Literature Abroad]." *Ani* 1, nos. 8–9 (1946): 476–84.

———. "Tashnagts'agan Kraganut'iwně ew Michazkayin Ṙeagts'ean [Tashnag Literature and International Reaction]." *Sovetakan Hayastan* 4, no. 34 (1948): 42–45.

Totten, Samuel, and William S. Parsons, eds. *Century of Genocide: Essays and Eyewitness Accounts.* 2nd ed. New York and London: Routledge, 2004.

Vahian, Vahé. "Dbavorutiwnner Hayasdani Soved Kroghneru B. Hamakumaren [Impressions from Soviet Armenian Writers' Union's Second Congress]." *Ani* 1, no. 7 (1946): 352–54.

———. "Harachabah Kraganut'iwn [Avant-Garde Literature]." *Ani* 1, no. 7 (1946).

———. *Haralēzneru Hashdut'iwně* [The Reconciliation of the Aralez]. Vol. 6. Beirut: Ani Series, 1953.

———. "Havadavor ew Anshegh [Faithful and Just]." *Ani* 2, no. 1 (1947).

———. "Hayasdani Soved Kroghneru B. Hamakumarin Shurch [Concerning the Second Congress of Soviet Armenia's Writers]." *Ani* 1, nos. 8–9 (1946): 467–69.

———. *Osgi Gamurch* [Golden Bridge]. Beirut: Rotos Press, 1946.

———. "Semin Vray [On the Threshold]." *Ani* 1, no. 1 (1946).

Vanantian, Vazken. "Michin Arewelk'i Hay Kroghneru Hamakumaṙě [The Middle Eastern Armenian Writers' Conference]." *Hayrenik' Monthly* 26, no. 12 (1948): 97–103.

———. "Michin Arewelk'i Hay Kroghneru Hamakumaṙě [The Middle Eastern Armenian Writers' Conference]." *Hayrenik' Monthly* 27, no. 1 (1949): 98–103.

———. "Michin Arewelk'i Hay Kroghneru Hamakumaṙě [The Middle Eastern Armenian Writers' Conference]." *Hayrenik' Monthly* 27, no. 2 (1949): 100–107.

———. "Michin Arewelk'i Hay Kroghneru Hamakumaṙě [The Middle Eastern Armenian Writers' Conference]." *Hayrenik' Monthly* 27, no. 4 (1949): 102–7.

———. "Michin Arewelkʻi Hay Kroghneru Hamakumarĕ [The Middle Eastern Armenian Writers' Conference]." *Hayrenikʻ Monthly* 27, no. 5 (1949): 88–102.

———. "Michin Arewelkʻi Hay Kroghneru Hamakumarĕ, anor anhrajeshdutʻiwnĕ ew patsumĕ [The Middle Eastern Armenian Writers' Conference, Its Necessity, and Its Opening]." *Hayrenikʻ Monthly* 26, no. 11 (1948): 96–106.

Van Dijk, Nel. "Research into Canon Formation: Nationalism, Literature, and an Institutional Point of View." *Poetics Today* 20, no. 1 (1999): 121–32.

Varjabedian, Sisag H. *Hayerĕ Lipanani Mēch* [Armenians in Lebanon]. Vols. 1–5. Beirut: Sevan, 1981.

Virabian, Amaduni. *Hayasdanĕ Stalinitsʻ Minchew Khrushchov* [Armenia from Stalin to Khrushchev]. Yerevan: National Academy of Sciences of the Republic of Armenia, 2001.

Von Braun, Christina. "Blutschande: From the Incest Taboo to the Nuremberg Racial Laws." In *Encountering the Other(s): Studies in Literature, History, and Culture*, edited by Gisela Brinker-Gabler, 127–48. Albany: State Univ. of New York Press, 1995.

Vorpuni, Zareh. *The Candidate*. Translated by Jennifer Manoukian and Ishkhan Jinbashian. Syracuse, NY: Syracuse Univ. Press, 2016.

———. *Ew Eghew Mart* [And There Was Man]. Paris, 1964.

———. "Husher [Recollections]." Interview by Marc Nichanian. *Asbarēz/Horizon Kragan Haweluadz* 1, no. 1 (1986): 6–7.

———. *Pʻortsĕ* [The Attempt]. Beirut: Ēdvan Press, 1958.

———. *Tēbi Ergir* [Toward Homeland]. Paris: Araxes Press, 1947.

———. *Tʻegnadzun* [The Candidate]. Beirut: Sewan Press, 1967.

———. *Vartsu Seneag* [Room for Rent]. Paris: Atʻmajian Hradaragutʻiwn, 1939.

Vosdanig. *Arewelkʻēn Arewmudkʻ* [From East to the West]. Paris, 1932.

Vratsian, Simon. "'Menk' ew 'Duk'' ['We' and 'You']." *Hayrenikʻ Monthly* 10, no. 5 (1932): 146–54.

Walker, Christopher J. "World War I and the Armenian Genocide." In *The Armenian People: From Ancient to Modern Times*, edited by Richard G. Hovannisian, 2:239–74. New York: St. Martin's Press, 1997.

Wiekiorka, Annette. *The Era of the Witness*. Ithaca, NY: Cornell Univ. Press, 2006.

Yeghiayan, Puzant. "Spʻiwrkʻi Hay Kraganutʻiwnĕ [Armenian Diaspora Literature]." *Baykʻar: Year End Special Issue* (1948): 9–23.

Yesayan, Zabel. *Aweragnerun Mēch* [Among the Ruins]. In vol. 1 of *Erger*. Antelias: Armenian Catholicosate of Cilicia, 1987.

————. *Silihdari Bardēznerě* [The Gardens of Silhidar]. In vol. 1 of *Erger*. Ante-lias: Armenian Catholicosate of Cilicia, 1987.

Yeshurun, Helit. "Exile Is So Strong within Me, I May Bring It to the Land: A Landmark 1996 Interview with Mahmoud Darwish." *Journal of Palestine Studies* 42, no. 1 (2012): 46–70.

Zarian, Costan. "Azkayinn u Michazkayině Kraganut'ean Mēch [The National and International in Literature]." *Zuart'nots'* 1, no. 3 (1929): 106–9.

Zartarian, Hrach. *Mer Geank'ě* [Our Life]. Yerevan: Sovetakan Grogh, 1982.

————. *Oghpats'ogh Martik* [Lamenting Folk]. Paris: Pascal Press, 1954.

Zekiyan, Boghos Levon. *The Armenian Way to Modernity*. Venice: Supernova, 1997.

Zender, Kal F. *Faulkner and the Politics of Reading*. Baton Rouge: Louisiana State Univ. Press, 2002.

Zhdanov, A. "Sovedagan Kraganut'ean Masin [On Soviet Literature]." *Ani* 1, no. 7 (1946): 388–91.

Index

Abakay (newspaper), 47
Abov, Gevork, 178–79
acculturation, 27
active witnesses, 103–5
Adorno, Theodor, 107, 224n33, 230n44
advertising, 142
aestheticization, 54–55, 61–62, 107, 111
Agamben, Giorgio, 16, 234n17, 236n42
Aghbashian, Hovhannes, 169, 171, 174–75
Aghpalian, Nigol, 180
Ajarian, Hrachia, 7
Akçam, Taner, 14, 222n20
alienation, 75, 87
Amran Kisherner (Summer Nights)
    (Shushanian), 94, 160
Anahid (journal), 43, 44
"Ancient Land" (Ishkhan), 203
"Ancient Parchments" (Anush), 210–11
Anderson, Benedict, 40, 74, 227n12
Andonian, Aram, 11, 140
And There Was Man (Ew Eghew Mart)
    (Vorpuni). See Ew Eghew Mart
anthologies, 192–99
anti-Armenian propaganda, 180
Anush, Armen, 180, 210–11
Apter, Emily, 24
Arabic, 208
Arabs, 190–91
Arendt, Hannah, 134, 242n49

ARF. See Armenian Revolutionary
    Federation
Armenian Educational and Cultural
    Society, 180, 185–86, 200, 215–16, 256n12
"Armenian Grandmother's Prayer"
    (Ishkhan), 203
"Armenian Language Is the Home of the
    Armenian" (Ishkhan), 209
Armenian Literary Club, 49
Armenian Question, 228n20
Armenian Republic. See Soviet Armenia
Armenian Revolutionary Federation
    (ARF): history of, 222n19; leader-
    ship of, 180; nationalism to, 45, 55;
    politics of, 152; Russia to, 170–71;
    Soviet Armenia and, 178–79, 250n27;
    Turkey to, 190–91; Young Turk
    regime and, 56–57
Armenians: activism for, 44; anti
    Armenian propaganda, 180; in Bei-
    rut, 155–56; culture of, 147, 161–62;
    in dispersion, 84–85, 165–69; in
    Europe, 59–60, 146; in exile, 135–36;
    in France, 45–46, 99, 145–48, 197;
    genocide of, 10–11, 56–57; in Holo-
    caust, 71; identity of, 19–20, 64–65,
    67–68, 153–54; intellectualism of,
    38–42, 171–72, 179–80; Iranian, 168,
    198–99; to League of Nations, 68;

279

Pan-African consciousness, 39–40
pan-national literature, 63–64
*Panorama of Western Armenian
Literature (Hamabadger Arewmdahay Kraganut'ean)* (Oshagan, H.).
See *Hamabadger Arewmdahay
Kraganut'ean*
Panossian, Razmik, 13, 248n2, 250n24
paratextual dedications, 79–82
Paris: Armenians in, 11–12, 38–46;
Beirut and, 4, 25–26, 71; culture of, 5,
19, 93; literature of, 108; Menk generation in, 150–51; Middle East and,
171–72; poverty in, 98–99; solidarity movement in, 51; transnational
literature in, 38–46, 50–52. *See also*
Menk generation
passive language, 88–89, 109–10
"Paternal Love" (Vahian), 204
patriarchy: absence of, 82–83, 113,
130–31; in dispersion, 204; duties of,
88–89; financial responsibility in,
89, 94–95; in France, 84–85, 87; in
genocide, 75–76, 115, 135–36; incest
and, 241n43; matricide and, 90–91;
memory of, 79–81, 85–86, 92–93,
106; to Menk generation, 233n10;
in *Mer Geank'ĕ*, 53–54, 98–103; in
Middle East, 78; orphanhood and,
84; paternal law, 119; in *P'ortsĕ*,
53–54; postpatriarchy configurations, 109–14; poverty and, 98–103;
relationships in, 122–23; sex and,
120–21; survivors and, 233n9; in
transnationalism, 53–54; women
in, 89–90
Pats' Domarĕ (The Open Calendar)
(Shahnur), 153
Paulhan, Frédéric, 59
performativity, 89

Peroomian, Rubina, 230n44, 240n29
Poems of Nation, Anthems of Empire
(Kaul), 199–211
poetry: of Armenians, 199–211, 232n5;
in Beirut, 191–92; in diaspora,
197–98; Menk generation in, 178–79;
mystical poems, 157; prose and, 73;
of resistance, 207–8; Soviet Armenia
in, 205–6
politics: of acculturation, 27; of ARF,
152; of art, 61–62; of assimilation,
68, 177–78; of censorship, 158–59;
culture and, 25, 45; of diaspora, 2,
13–14, 64–65, 131–32; of dispersion,
163–64; of displacement, 206–7; of
Eastern Armenian, 168; of exile,
248n6; gender, 110; genocide and,
26, 55–56, 223n24; identity, 39; of
identity cards, 66–67; internal, 71; of
language, 6–11, 16, 21, 25–29, 168–69;
literature and, 15, 162; of Middle
East, 4; of Ottoman Empire, 12, 43,
126; of refugees, 250n25; in Russia,
163, 172–73, 178–79; of Vorpuni,
47–48; of WASL, 169, 178–87; of
Western Armenian, 50–51. *See also
specific topics*
pornography, 71, 246n53
P'ortsĕ (The Attempt) (Vorpuni): crisis
of responsibility in, 82–93; criticism
of, 143–44; *Mer Geank'ĕ* and, 26, 75,
77–82, 94–95, 106; patriarchy in,
53–54
postgenocide sexual desire, 123–31
post-memory, 107–8
postpatriarchy configurations, 109–14
Post–World War I Paris. See Paris
Post–World War II Beirut. *See* Beirut
poverty: in Paris, 98–99; patriarchy and,
98–103; racism and, 74; shame from,

83; stealing in, 95, 99–104; witnessing in, 103–5

Princess, The (*Ishkhanuhin*) (Sarafian). *See Ishkhanuhin*

Promethean (*Bromēt'ēagan*) (Sarafian). *See Bromēt'ēagan*

proper names, 121

prose. *See* literature; novels

prostitution, 116–23, 143, 148–49

publishing, 28, 185–86, 239n15

al-Qasim, Samih, 208

Rabaka, Reiland, 41

race, 39–42, 113

racism, 74, 113, 147

Rank, Otto, 112–13, 131

Realist Writers, 194

Reconciliation of the Aralez, The (*Haralēzneru Hashdut'iwnĕ*) (Vahian). *See Haralēzneru Hashdut'iwnĕ*

Reflections on Exile (Said), 231n69

refugees: in Beirut, 198; in Europe, 46; in France, 65–66, 68–69; genocide of, 250n26; identity of, 48–49; politics of, 250n25; racism and, 147; in Soviet Armenia, 167, 248n7

relationships, 89–90, 97–98, 112, 116–17, 122–23

religion: biblical poems, 157; Christianity, 8–9; culture and, 157; in dispersion, 148–49, 152; identity and, 9–10; incest in, 113; Islam, 8–9, 240n25; language and, 62–63; pagan gods, 201

Renaissance Writers, 194

Republic of Armenia, 23, 29, 66

Republic of Turkey. *See* Turkey

responsibility, 83–84, 88–93, 96, 103, 106, 140–41

Retreat without Song, The (*Nahanchĕ Aŕants' Erki*) (Shahnur). *See Nahanchĕ Aŕants' Erki*

revenge, 112, 124, 129–36

Revolutionary Writers, 194

Riazanov, David, 59

romance novels, 241n39

Romantic literature, 113

"Room for Rent" ("Vartsu Seneag") (Vorpuni). *See* "Vartsu Seneag"

Rose, Guillian, 235n23

Russia: to ARF, 170–71; Armenians to, 13, 66–67, 154–55; colonialism by, 23; communism in, 170; culture in, 173–74, 177–78; Europe and, 228n20; literature to, 176; in modernity, 57–58; nationalism in, 209–10; H. Oshagan to, 179; Ottoman Empire and, 34; politics in, 163, 172–73, 178–79; Turkey and, 22, 66–67, 213; after World War II, 171. *See also* Soviet Armenia

Said, Edward, 207, 231n69, 248n74

Sarafian, Nigoghos: on exile, 63–64, 163; on identity, 188–89; on language, 157; for Menk generation, 49–50; readers of, 241n39; reputation of, 27, 123; Shahnur and, 106, 135–36; support from, 179; on unity, 247n72; Vorpuni and, 112, 131. *See also specific works*

Sarafian, Nigoghos (works): *Bromēt'ēagan*, 63; *Ishkhanuhin*, 27, 54, 112, 123–31; *Khariskhĕn Heŕu*, 94, 123

Sasuni, Garo, 28, 180–81, 183, 191–92

Schahgaldian, Nicola, 190

Zartarian, Hrach (*cont.*)
229n37; Shahnur and, 153; Vorpuni
and, 79–82, 106. *See also specific
works*
Zartarian, Hrach (works): *Mer Geank'ĕ*,
26, 53–54, 75, 77–82, 94–106;
Orpats'ogh Martig, 139
Zartarian, Rafael, 153, 245n36

Zartarian, Rupen, 81, 233n11, 236n33,
245n36
Zekiyan, Boghos Levon, 222n15
Zhdanov, Andrei, 173
Zohrab, Krikor, 9, 74
Zuart'nots' (journal), 49–50
Zuyk mĕ Garmir Dedragner (*A Couple of
Red Notebooks*) (Shahnur), 139, 153

TALAR CHAHINIAN holds a PhD in comparative literature from UCLA and lectures in the Program for Armenian Studies at UC Irvine, where she is also visiting faculty in the Department of Comparative Literature. Her research interests include world literature, transnationalism, the politics of Western Armenian literary history and language, and questions in trauma, aesthetics, and representation. She has served as assistant editor of the *Armenian Review* (2010–17) and is currently coeditor of *Diaspora: A Journal of Transnational Studies.* She contributes regularly to the literary magazine *Pakin.*

CPSIA information can be obtained
at www.ICGtesting.com
Printed in the USA
LVHW031923080323
741122LV00005B/233